D1596958

Indiana Quakers Confront the Civil War

# Indiana Quakers Confront the Civil War

JACQUELYN S. NELSON

Indiana Historical Society
*Indianapolis 1991*

Printed in the United States of America

The paper in this publication meets the minimum requirements of American National Standard for Information Sciences—Permanence of Paper for Printed Library Materials, ANSI Z39.48-1984.

Library of Congress Cataloging-in-Publication Data

Nelson, Jacquelyn S. (Jacquelyn Sue)
    Indiana Quakers confront the Civil War / Jacquelyn S. Nelson.
        p.    cm.
    Includes bibliographical references.
    ISBN 0-87195-064-2 (casebound : acid-free paper)
    1. United States—History—Civil War, 1861–1865—Participation,
Quaker.    2. Indiana—History—Civil War, 1861–1865—Participation,
Quaker.    3. Quakers—Indiana—History—19th century.    I. Title.
E540.F8N45    1991
973.7'15286—dc20                                                                91-8983
                                                                                      CIP

To My Parents

# Contents

|  |  |  |
|---|---|---|
|  | Preface | IX |
|  | Introduction | XIII |
| Chapter 1 | The Quaker Background | 1 |
| Chapter 2 | Quaker Military Service | 9 |
| Chapter 3 | Why Did They Fight? | 29 |
| Chapter 4 | Response to Military Life | 45 |
| Chapter 5 | The Home Front | 59 |
| Chapter 6 | Quaker Opposition to the War | 79 |
|  | Conclusion | 95 |
| Appendix A | Offering of Franklin Elliott | 99 |
| Appendix B | Summary of Military Service by Meeting | 101 |
| Appendix C | Indiana Friends in Military Service | 107 |
| Appendix D | Soldiers Buried in Quaker Cemeteries | 237 |
| Appendix E | Ages of Quaker Soldiers | 261 |
|  | Notes | 263 |
|  | Selected Bibliography | 285 |
|  | Index | 299 |

# Preface

WHY Quakers? This question was asked of me innumerable times while researching and writing this manuscript. After all, Quakers, also known as Friends, composed merely 2 percent of the Hoosier population at the time of the Civil War, albeit higher than the Indiana Quaker population today.[1] How could one justify researching such a small group with its obviously limited impact on life in Indiana during the 1860s? Aside from there being little in print on Quakers in the Civil War, what made this tiny religious sect so attractive as a research topic was the relative abundance of untapped primary resource material, such as monthly and yearly meeting records and birth and death records, and the close proximity of Earlham College with its massive Quaker collection. Admittedly, though, I was not sure what, if anything, I would find.

Initially, because of my own interest in conscientious objection and the popular notion that Quakers refused to support war, the emphasis centered around the Quaker antiwar testimony. Early on, however, as the data indicated that many Friends supported the war through military service as well as on the home front, the theme shifted. Nevertheless, the final product, while focusing on those Friends who abandoned, at least temporarily, Quaker dogma against war, does include one chapter devoted entirely to those individuals who remained true to the peace testimony. The revelation that many Quakers in Indiana supported the Union, therefore, as I suspect occurs in much historical discovery, was accomplished quite by accident. I did not set out to prove such a hypothesis. Indeed, the fortuitous realization that Indiana Quakers participated in the Civil War runs counter to the historiography of the Society of Friends. That finding alone made this intellectual pursuit a tremendously gratifying experience.

In hindsight, writing about Quakers was logical for me. My best friend and close neighbor as I grew up in rural Indiana came from a Quaker family. In the carefree days of summer, we occasionally played with her cousin (also a Quaker) on her parents' farm just a few miles down the road. In the 1860s a Quaker family by the name of Marshall inhabited the farmhouse. Such facts, however, seemed unimportant then, especially to young people. Unbeknownst to me or anyone else at the time, letters, untouched and unread for decades and written by three of the Marshall boys who served in the Civil War, lay in the attic of that old house. Much later these letters were discovered and given to the Indiana Historical Society. After talking to an elderly Quaker descendant of that family and reading those letters, I realized those precious primary sources were found in a childhood haunt. In addition, I also discovered that I, too, had Quaker ancestry.

I would also like to take this opportunity to thank the many people without whose guidance, suggestions, and support this project could not have been completed. Particularly helpful was my doctoral committee chairman, Dr. William Eidson, who initially enlivened my fascination in the Civil War thirteen years ago and recommended this topic for my dissertation. In addition to giving sound advice, Dr. Eidson continually encouraged me to keep working when the task seemed formidable. He also, along with Dr. Sharon Seager, critiqued my first article on Quakers published in the *Indiana*

*Magazine of History.* Their patient and thorough criticism proved immensely valuable. Deep appreciation must also be extended to Dr. Morton Rosenberg, who, genuinely interested in the subject, took time out from his busy schedule to read and review all chapters in my original dissertation. His analysis was indispensable to the success of this current project.

Besides the aforementioned professors, I want to thank Dr. Arthur Funston, archivist at Earlham College, John Selch, newspaper librarian at the Indiana State Library, and the staff members of the Indiana Commission on Public Records, State Archives Division, the Indiana Historical Society, and the various county libraries in which I researched.

Finally, I wish to thank my husband, Van, a research design consultant at Ball State University, who not only provided editorial comment and encouragement but kept the car running throughout my two-year, fifteen-thousand-mile search for the data collected for this manuscript. He also, along with Mrs. Marta McCoy, a programmer analyst at Ball State's University Computing Services, developed a computer program and data base file from which to analyze the military records of Quakers who served in the Civil War.

As in any research project, however, in the final analysis I am totally responsible for the outcome. Any shortcomings or errors that may be discovered cannot be blamed on the high quality of help I received from those listed above. They are mine alone.

# Introduction

ALTHOUGH the American Civil War ended well over a century ago, the era continues to fascinate students and scholars of history. Perhaps no event in the annals of the United States has captured more fully the imaginations and enthusiasm of historians, novelists, poets, composers, journalists, movie producers, and Americans in general. Out of the passionate ordeal emerged some of America's greatest heroes and villains, immortalized forever by word and deed. Abraham Lincoln, Robert E. Lee, Jefferson Davis, Ulysses S. Grant, Stonewall Jackson, and John Wilkes Booth are but a few of the well-known actors in the four-year drama which unfolded in 1861.

Battles and campaigns, too, have made a permanent imprint on Americans. Inexhaustibly studied and refought by military strategists and historians, engagements at Gettysburg, Antietam, Chancellorsville, Shiloh, Missionary Ridge, Chickamauga, Atlanta, and Appomattox Court House have eternally impressed upon our hearts and minds the gallantry, courage, and patriotism shown by the young men of the North and South.

The enduring captivation of the Civil War is no less the result of generations of professional historians who have written and rewritten about events leading up to the war but have failed to achieve concurrence in regard to causation. Noted scholar Howard K. Beale wrote in 1946 that "historians whatever their predispositions, assign to the Civil War causes ranging from one simple force or phenomenon to patterns so complex and manifold that they include, intricately interwoven, all the important movements, thoughts, and actions of the decades before 1861."[1] This statement is not only a fitting description today, but also certainly was true even before hostilities commenced at Fort Sumter.

This book, which developed from a doctoral dissertation, is not an attempt to form a new school of historiography. It is, however, in the light of previously neglected research and sources only recently becoming available, an effort to undo a myth that has persisted among many historians for over one hundred years. The myth concerns the activities of members of the religious body known as the Society of Friends, or Quakers, during the Civil War. Their adherence to the belief that all wars were unlawful in the eyes of God has caused many historians to take Quaker nonparticipation in the American Civil War for granted. Much historical writing has focused upon the Friends' refusal to perform military service and the suffering they endured as a result. The most notable work with this emphasis is Edward Needles Wright's *Conscientious Objectors in the Civil War* (1931). Also mentioned in the historical literature concerning the Society is the benevolent work of Friends for blacks and in caring for sick and wounded soldiers, both during and after the war. No major work, however, chronicles the nonpacifistic labors of this religious sect.

The present investigation of the Society of Friends was broached with one major purpose in mind: narration of the activities of the Quakers who lived in the state of Indiana during the Civil War. Chapter 1 provides background information on the growth and development of the Society of Friends. Topics include a discussion of the origin of the Society in England, emigration to North America, migration to Indiana, and summation of the characteristics and beliefs of this religious denomination. Chapters 2, 3, and 4 focus upon those Quakers who performed military service. The historical evolution of the peace testimony, a historiographical essay of Quaker military service, plus the military record of the Society of Friends dominate the second chapter. A discussion of the difficult question of motivation follows. Chapter 4 addresses how these men of peace responded to the rigors of military life and war. The fifth chapter concentrates on those Quakers who remained on the home front but were active in many ways that supported the war effort. Finally, Chapter 6 recounts the activities of Quakers who steadfastly refused to participate in the war.

Several appendixes which expand on Quaker military history also have been included. Most notable is Appendix C. This addition to Chapter 2 lists the names and gives short biographies of Friends in Indiana who enrolled in the armed forces during the Civil War. The introduction to Appendix C is a detailed discussion of what kind of information is included in the portraits, as well as how it was obtained.

As noted, this study is limited to the members of the Society of Friends who lived within the state of Indiana between 1861 and 1865. Furthermore, this investigation centers only in those counties where Quakers resided and for whom monthly meeting records were found.[2] Most of the records have been microfilmed by the Indiana Historical Society and can be viewed at its library in Indianapolis. The majority of the original records are housed either in the Indiana Yearly Meeting House at First Friends Church in Richmond, Indiana, or the Western Yearly Meeting House in Plainfield, Indiana. There are a few exceptions, however, and the potential researcher should consult the seven-volume work by Willard Heiss, *Records of the Abstracts of the Society of Friends in Indiana* (1962-77) to determine exactly where the records are located. Because some of the original records have been lost, damaged, or not made available to the Society for microfilming, the author relied upon Heiss' *Abstracts* to cull information otherwise unobtainable.[3]

Most of the information for this book, then, was derived from local church records. The author also consulted the records of both the Indiana Yearly Meeting and the Western Yearly Meeting. Supplementary material was gleaned from Friends' manuscript collections housed in the Lilly Library of Earlham College, the Indiana State Library in Indianapolis, and the Indiana Historical Society. In addition, I wrote letters to all the Quaker churches in Indiana (approximately ninety), requesting them to place an appeal in church newsletters and bulletins for letters and diaries, possibly held by their members, that were written by Friends who lived in Indiana during the war years.

Besides the Quaker materials thus far noted, cemetery records of the counties designated for this study were used in the search for Quakers who served in the Civil War. These records, which supplemented the incomplete birth and death records in Heiss' *Abstracts*, were found in local libraries, county recorders' offices, and the Indiana Commission on Public Records, State Archives Division, in Indianapolis.[4] I also scanned local histories and available newspapers from most of the twenty-seven specified counties. A large number of secondary sources likewise proved useful.

One final note is imperative. During the nineteenth century several schisms divided the Society of Friends. From the main body of Orthodox Friends the Society split into Hicksite meetings and antislavery meetings. The religious creed differed only slightly among the three assemblages, and the antislavery Friends rejoined the main body of Orthodox Friends just prior to the outbreak of the Civil War. One of the congruent tenets of the three groups was opposition to all wars. The peace testimony, around which this manuscript develops, was consistent then, at least theoretically, throughout the entire Society of Friends. For purposes of this work the term "Quaker" or "Friend" collectively refers to any one of the three groups noted above. When reference is made to a specific monthly meeting, however, the reader should assume that, unless otherwise identified, it is an Orthodox meeting of Friends.

# I

# The Quaker Background

THE origin of the growth and development of the religious sect known as the Society of Friends, or Quakers, begins with its founder, George Fox, born in 1624. An Englishman of humble descent, Fox, obviously distressed with Anglican theology, severed ties with the Church of England and inaugurated his peripatetic ministry during the midst of the religious and political turmoil of seventeenth-century Great Britain. His teachings, which emphasized an Inner Light and a return to a more simple religion than the austere, unemotional, and complicated Anglican doctrine, were met with stern opposition from the established church. Nevertheless, Fox, jailed on several occasions for many crimes, including blasphemy, continued preaching as the Quaker movement gradually, then more rapidly, gained a foothold in England and surrounding countries.[1]

As their numbers grew, Quakers left Europe and emigrated to the New World, arriving first in Boston in 1656. The intolerant Puritan environment forced Friends to seek a more favorable religious climate. They found one in Rhode Island. As more Quakers fled to this tiny colony, a monthly meeting began there in 1658, and within three years, in 1661, the first yearly meeting in America was established at Newport.

Within the next forty years, five more yearly meetings were organized in America: Baltimore (1672), Virginia (1673), Philadelphia (1681), New York (1695), and North Carolina (1698).[2]

Geographical factors, especially the formidable barrier of the Appalachian Mountains, shaped the Quaker migratory pattern within North America. Friends moved south from Pennsylvania into Virginia, the Carolinas, and Georgia. By the time of the American Revolution, a few Friends also had settled in what is now eastern Tennessee and western Pennsylvania. Friends, always ardent supporters of religious freedom, composed an important element in the southern states until 1800, when many of them migrated to the Northwest, particularly to Ohio and Indiana, as a protest against slavery. A few Quakers also came to the Northwest for health reasons, but, according to one historian, the most common reason for movement out of the South was the desire for economic amelioration. Realizing that free labor could not compete economically with slave labor, many Friends sought to escape the degradation caused by the presence of slaves by journeying to free territories and states.[3]

The settlement of Quakers in Indiana began in 1806 when several families of Friends took up residence along the Whitewater River at the site of present-day Richmond. These Friends were attached to the monthly meeting in West Branch, Ohio (West Milton, Ohio), but as more Friends came to the Indiana Territory and the remoteness of their colony required a much closer meeting, the Whitewater Monthly Meeting was established in 1809. Year after year hundreds of Quakers from the East and the South moved into Indiana until new monthly meetings had to be created.[4]

The Friends who came to the Indiana Territory from the South, particularly North Carolina, generally traversed one of three routes. Quakers left North Carolina by way of the Yadkin River and Wood's or Flower Gap. They changed streams after reaching the New River and followed it until it became the Kanawha, which eventually flowed into the Ohio River. Quakers then crossed the state of Ohio by way of Gallipolis and Chillicothe to the Indiana Territory. Sometimes referred to as the Quaker route, this path was the most direct but not the easiest. Quakers traveling with loaded wagons thought it was best to leave the New River and take Daniel Boone's Wilderness Road into Kentucky. Turning northward to Cincinnati they moved on to the upper Whitewater Valley. Others migrated north across Virginia, turned westward, and treaded over Braddock's Road.[5]

The War of 1812 and its related Indian troubles temporarily halted the migration to the upper Whitewater Valley, but with the onset of peace the exodus out of the South resumed. The Indiana Yearly Meeting, with its headquarters in Richmond, was established in 1821, and by the fourth decade of the nineteenth century North Carolina, the center of the Society of Friends in the South, was drained of much of its Quaker population. By the time the southern Quaker migration was essentially completed, Richmond may have become virtually the equal to Philadelphia, the longtime center of the Orthodox Friends in the United States. Also, as Friends moved westward into Illinois, Iowa, and Kansas, a much closer yearly meeting was needed. Consequently, in 1858 the Western Yearly Meeting was established with headquarters at Plainfield in Hendricks County.[6]

These Quaker immigrants to Indiana and the Northwest embodied the middle and lower classes of society, owned few or no slaves, and, as noted, could not compete economically with slavery. So great was movement northward, including non-Quakers for similar economic reasons, that by 1850 one-third of Indiana's population was composed of first- and second-generation North Carolinians. Timothy Nicholson, who left North Carolina in 1855 to go to Richmond, Indiana, estimated that if twelve hundred Friends went to Richmond

between 1809 and 1819, then at least six thousand came from
the Carolinas, Virginia, and Georgia between 1800 and 1860;
at least three-fourths came from North Carolina.[7]

Although the Whitewater Valley attracted large numbers
of the Society, smaller congregations of Quakers settled in
other parts of the state. The Friends did not grow in numbers
as did other denominations as they neither engaged in evan-
gelism nor used missionary activities to gain converts. One
Indiana historian has estimated that Quakers probably
reached their greatest strength in Indiana by the 1850s when
a slight decline occurred thereafter. In 1850 Indiana, ranked
fourth among the states in the number of Friends' meetings,
was the home of about fifteen thousand Quakers supporting
eighty-nine churches. By the eve of the Civil War, ninety-
four churches were located in twenty-six counties.[8]

The Quakers suffered a serious schism during the two decades prior to the Civil War. The disputed issue was precip-
itated by controversial and heated discussion on how to deal
with the problem of slavery. Historically, the Quakers stim-
ulated the inauguration of the abolitionist movement. Indeed,
members had led a crusade to free their own slaves in the
eighteenth century. The larger question regarding abolition,
however, arose over Quaker involvement in antislavery organizations outside the embrace of the Society. In 1838 several
interested Friends gathered in Newport (Wayne County) to
discuss what position should be taken toward the growing
antislavery movement. They agreed to appropriate twenty-
five dollars for the purchase of antislavery material to be disseminated throughout the community. Hence, the area near
Newport became the focal point for antislavery Friends and
their activities. The leaders of the Indiana Yearly Meeting,
however, not pleased by this situation, closed meetinghouses
to antislavery lectures in 1841.[9]

One year later the Indiana Yearly Meeting "disqualified"
eight leading antislavery men. Realizing that they would have

to work outside the Indiana Yearly Meeting, approximately one hundred antislavery men then withdrew and formed the Indiana Yearly Meeting of Anti-Slavery Friends in Newport on 7 February 1843. Membership in this splinter group totaled about two thousand as this minority was scattered among eleven monthly meetings in eight counties. These Friends, whose meetinghouses earned the fitting sobriquet "Liberty Halls," worked vigorously to denounce slavery and colonization. They also became the most active organization in Indiana in promoting the Free Produce Movement.[10]

A perusal of the records of the Indiana Yearly Meeting of Anti-Slavery Friends written in the decade of the 1850s reveals that even some of these Quakers did not maintain the testimony against the use of products made by slave labor. In 1850 the meeting reported that $472 worth of goods not made by free labor had been purchased by members during the preceding year.[11] As the tumultuous 1850s progressed, the language of this yearly meeting on the subject of purchasing slave-labor products, reflecting an enlargement of expenditures for such goods, increased in intensity and earnestness of condemnation. In 1853, for example, the Anti-Slavery Society strongly rebuked such practice: "Do we not know the consumption of such articles is the main support of that iniquitous system?—that those who purchase them are virtually the slaveholders." The next year antislavery Friends trenchantly urged all quarterly meetings to be more "vigilant in their labors in regard to this testimony, and to spare no pains to prevent such violations hereafter, either in purchasing for sale or consumption."[12]

Imperceptibly, however, this schism was healed when the seceding group influenced Quakers from the main body to join them in a more sympathetic attitude toward abolitionists. The term abolition was also gradually losing its stigma, and a change was made in church discipline making it easy for the "seceders," many of whom had been disowned by their original monthly meetings, to return to the main body. Gradually the antislavery meeting lost membership and by 1857, with too few members for monthly and quarterly meetings, it was abandoned.[13]

Not only did Quakers become involved in the antislavery movement, but they were also the most prominent religious group that worked for the betterment of blacks, especially the Friends who resided in eastern counties such as Wayne, Randolph, and Henry. As fugitive slaves and other blacks began moving to Indiana, they tended to migrate toward Quaker communities; Quaker neighborhoods often served as settlements for blacks.[14] The Friends also founded two schools for the training of blacks: Union Literary Institute in Randolph County and White's Indiana Manual Labor Institute near Wabash.[15]

The Society of Friends in Indiana was also active in the temperance movement, prison reform, and the founding of educational institutions. Included among the schools opened by Quakers were Spiceland Academy, the Friends' Academy at Carthage, Bloomingdale Academy in Parke County, Blue River Academy in Washington County, Farmers' Institute in Lafayette, Westfield Friends' Academy, and Earlham College in Richmond.[16]

From the death of George Fox in 1691 to the outbreak of the Civil War, the standards of behavior and religious beliefs of the Quaker founder were reformed to meet the changing needs of the Society. Subsequent Quaker leaders and writers such as Isaac Pennington, Robert Barclay, and William Penn added much to the original attitudes and religious philosophy espoused by Fox. Besides the Inner Light, Quakers also were governed by a rather strict code of behavior called the *Discipline*. Having evolved over many years, the *Discipline* prescribed basic Quaker beliefs, standards of conduct, and rules of everyday living. Virtually every life situation from birth to death was carefully regulated and printed by this guide. Furthermore, Friends were expected to follow all of the advice in the *Discipline*; failure to obey Quaker precepts subjected members to disciplinary action, and Friends could ultimately lose their membership within the Society.[17] Thus, the behavior of individual Quakers was not always left to the dictates of the conscience.

Each local, or monthly, Quaker meeting was responsible for maintaining the high standards of conduct. Every monthly meeting submitted an annual written report to the Yearly Meeting on this subject. These yearly reports consisted of reading and answering eight questions, or "queries," on the state of the Society. Quakers also met weekly for worship, and once each month a business meeting was held. Quaker monthly meetings in the early nineteenth century were unique in that separate meetings were held for men and women. After a worship service the men and women entered different rooms; the minutes of the preceding monthly meeting were read, and then new business and concerns were transacted.[18]

Whereas the monthly meeting concerned itself with the local congregation, the quarterly meeting of the Society supervised the concerns of several monthly meetings within a defined geographical area. Representatives were sent to these meetings who knew and understood the problems, concerns, and business of the individual congregations. Held four times per year, these meetings were conducted in a similar fashion as the monthly meetings. A like pattern was followed for the yearly meeting. The answers to the annual queries were read and a general statement drawn up and included in the yearly meeting minutes. There was, however, a variety of business transacted as committee reports were read and vital statistics compiled.[19]

In sum, during the eighteenth and early nineteenth centuries the Society of Friends in the United States survived several divisive issues and grew into a reasonably large and well-ordered religious organization.[20] In spite of the Quaker belief in the Inner Light, however, church discipline, implemented at the local level by each monthly meeting, strictly regulated the everyday lives of Friends. The concept of moral autonomy, then, gave the illusion of much more freedom for the individual than actually existed.

In retrospect, the ensuing years which began in 1861 proved to be a real test for the unity of Friends as the long-standing Quaker adherence to peace clashed with a sense of duty to country. As the Civil War appeared on the Hoosier horizon, many monthly meetings faced a serious dilemma: to what degree could an individual follow his conscience when his actions violated a standard of behavior?

The following pages will show how Indiana Quakers, both individually and as a group, responded to the crisis of the Civil War.

# 2

# Quaker Military Service

MEMBERS of the Society of Friends have always believed that engaging in war is incompatible with being a Christian. As early as 1650 George Fox expressed principles of pacifism when he staunchly refused to bear arms for the British Commonwealth against Charles Stuart and was jailed in England. Several years later Fox recorded the Quaker antiwar tenet in his *Journal*:

> Our principle is, and our practices have always been, to seek peace and ensue it and to follow after righteousness and the knowledge of God, seeking the good and welfare and doing that which tends to the peace of all. . . . All bloody principles and practices, we . . . do utterly deny. . . . Christ said to Peter, "Put up thy sword" for "He that takes the sword, shall perish with the sword." And all plots, insurrections, and riotious meetings we do deny . . . and all wars and fightings with carnal weapons we do deny.[1]

Called the "most important and most continuous of all their beliefs" by eminent historian Daniel J. Boorstin, this Quaker precept was consistently reaffirmed up to and throughout the Civil War era in statements such as the following: "Friends maintain a testimony against . . . oaths, bearing arms and all military services, trading in goods taken in war."[2] Although the official position of the Society of Friends was to assume a pacifist stance, a sizable number of Friends, significantly more than previously known, discarded two hundred-year-old Quaker tradition and enrolled for military duty.

The origin of the irreconcilability of military force with Christian ideals can be traced to selected passages in the Bible. The Old Testament states: "And he shall judge among the nations, and shall rebuke many people: and they shall beat their swords into plowshares, and their spears into pruning-hooks: nation shall not lift up sword against nation, neither shall they learn war any more." Opposition to war was also found in Matthew in the Sermon on the Mount: "Thou shalt not kill; and whosoever shall kill shall be in danger of the judgment." Christianity was to require a greater perfection of the human character than required under the law. Men were neither to kill nor "cherish the passion of revenge." Jesus also says, "An eye for an eye, and a tooth for a tooth: but I say unto you, That ye resist not evil: but whosoever shall smite thee on thy right cheek, turn to him the other also." Later, in the same chapter, Jesus continues, "Thou shalt love thy neighbour, and hate thine enemy. But I say unto you, Love your enemies, bless them that curse you, do good to them that hate you. . . . Be ye therefore perfect, even as your Father which is in heaven is perfect."[3]

Other passages which supported the Quaker tenet against war were taken from Paul and James. Paul's writings in 2 Cor. 10:3-5 allowed Quakers to argue that the warfare of Christianity is not carnal, but spiritual—involving the destruction of evil imaginations. With the help of James, Quakers contended that if wars originated from the lusts of men then those who have restrained their lusts can no longer engage in them. The verse is: "From whence come wars and fightings among you? come they not hence, even of your lusts that war in your members?" A final quotation comes exclusively from Paul: "Now if any man have not the Spirit of Christ, he is none of his." In other words, if men do not have the same disposition as Jesus—humility, forbearance, love, forgiveness—or if they do not follow him as a pattern, or act as he would, they are not Christians.[4]

The peace testimony, however, was not based solely on the Scriptures. The Quaker concept of the Inner Light breathed life into the antiwar Bible passages and made it possible for the deeper meaning of the phrases to be revealed to the soul. Furthermore, this inward spirit enabled Friends, hypothetically, to triumph over the urge to participate in war. Nevertheless, Quakers were taught that they must obey the preceding tenets uniformly and on every occasion. If, during the course of their lives, Friends were exposed to war these principles must continue to be their guide; they were forbidden to seek revenge and were commanded to pray for their persecutors. The book of *Discipline* stated that Friends should "adhere faithfully" to the ancient testimony against war and avoid both offensive and defensive entanglements. They were neither to approve nor show "the least connivance at war" and were to restrain from participation in any trade or business in promotion of war. Thus, ideally, there was no such character as that of a Quaker soldier: "I am a soldier of Christ; therefore I can not fight."[5]

The theoretical implications of the biblical antiwar teachings, however, proved difficult if not impossible to observe in practical matters of life. The Society learned from early experiences in England during the seventeenth century that a fine line existed between compliance and noncompliance of the peace testimony. What if a Quaker was asked to muster with the militia? Was paying taxes, knowing that the revenue was designated for military purposes, a violation of Quaker creed? If a Quaker sold horses to the government during wartime, was he guilty of antiwar transgressions? In an attempt to clarify the vexatious relationship between pacifism and civil government, Friends periodically circulated tracts and statements outlining their position relative to specific situations.[6]

In the United States from the time of the American Revolution, strict adherence to the peace testimony was intermittently challenged both from within and outside the embrace of the Society. During the decade following the conclusion of the French and Indian War, for example, as American resistance to new British policies matured, Friends' reactions shifted from restrictive support of colonial opposition to disavowal of the revolutionary movement. Quakers withdrew their commiseration when threats of violence replaced constitutional arguments against English attempts to tax the colonies and the relatively peaceful nonimportation agreements. The six yearly meetings in North America adopted a policy which called for noninterference in the political affairs of the colonial action and disapproval of Friends who remained zealous in its support. By 1775 the Society opposed the Revolutionary War on the fundamental ground of rejection of the use of arms to achieve independence. But a political element was also present. Quakerism had evolved over its one hundred-year existence to include loyalty to the government—in this case the British Crown—and peaceful conduct toward the ruler—George III. Thus, by the eve of open conflict the position of Friends vacillated from neutrality to what many Quakers perceived to be loyalism.[7]

During the war Friends' adherence to pacifism came under attack both from revolutionary elements that requested Quaker support for and participation in the movement for colonial liberation and from the Society that required allegiance to Quaker dogma. As Quakers committed violations of the peace testimony, hundreds were purged from the sect. Those who followed Quaker teachings and refused to obey local laws, however, suffered the consequences imposed by civilian authorities. For example, Friends who accepted military service or paid military taxes and refused to submit apologies were disowned by their local meetings. Conversely, pacifist Quakers who declined to take oaths of allegiance to the colonial cause and renounce the king or evaded the draft were fined and often imprisoned. Clearly, the ramifications of the peace testimony placed Quakers in a serious dilemma as they were subjected to a conscientious tug-of-war throughout the War for American Independence.[8] Pacifism, a lofty if not admirable ideal in the transparent abstract, became obfuscated in the real world as in the crisis of the Revolution.

When the Civil War began in the spring of 1861 the Meeting for Sufferings of both the Indiana Yearly Meeting and the Western Yearly Meeting drafted messages to be distributed and read to all their respective monthly meetings. The former deplored the "disloyalty and civil strife" that had swept the country and encouraged Friends to act the part of Christ's disciples, adhering to his laws and commandments and maintaining the testimony against taking human life. Quakers, warned against yielding to the excitement of "existing circumstances," were urged to be on guard against involving themselves in the strife of parties. Sympathy was extended to those individuals who succumbed to temptations in matters relating to the support of war. They were advised to remember the truth and root of Quaker testimonies and "then to act according to an enlightened conscience and sound judgment."[9]

The Western Yearly Meeting distributed a similar plea for abstinence from war activities. Friends were encouraged to follow the Gospel and do all things that made for peace: "Blessed are the peacemakers for they shall be called the children of God." The meeting also advised that "when the sound of armies is heard, let us betake ourselves to prayer that our everlasting Father, the Prince of peace may hasten the day when nation shall not lift up sword against nations neither shall they learn war any more."[10]

Messages of advice also came from the Yearly Meetings of Friends held in London and Dublin. London Friends cautioned those in America that in the crisis of the United States it was important that Quakers' testimony to Christ be maintained; they were warned not to carry on with carnal weapons as theirs was a spiritual war. London Friends spoke especially to younger Friends: "No motive of patriotism can absolve you from your allegiance to your Lord and Savior." They were admonished to stay away from the "excitement of popular commotion, the tumult of party agitation, the strife of tongues." Dublin Friends desired that American Quakers "abide in the fear of the Lord, . . . and be enabled faithfully and patiently to endure whatever sufferings may be permitted to attend them."[11] Thus, opposition to war on theological grounds could not be compromised.

The yearly meetings in Indiana never reconciled Quaker participation in military service with Christian ideals. Even before the onset of war, in 1860 the Indiana Yearly Meeting exhorted members "at all times and under all circumstances, carefully to avoid anything which may lead to a compromise of it [testimony against war]." The Society also entreated parents to teach their children to be "disciples of the Prince of Peace, and to obey God rather than man." The next year the Indiana meeting reminded parents to "watch over their children and see that their minds are not filled with false views of military glory and achievements." In 1862 this same meeting extended condolences to young men who were tempted to enlist in the army out of love of country:

> We love our country and highly appreciate the excellent government under which we have enjoyed so large a share of liberty and security to person and property, and look with heartfelt sorrow upon the efforts to destroy it, but we . . . cannot believe that any cause is sufficient to . . . warrant us in violating what we believe to be the law of our Lord.

Two years later the Indiana Yearly Meeting recorded its "emphatic disavowal of all such services, as contrary to the Gospel of Christ, and . . . our religious society." In 1865 the Western Yearly Meeting expressed "deep solicitude and Christian sympathy [for the many young men who] notwithstanding the plain and clear language, both of prophecy and of the New Testament . . . have felt impelled, in the ardor of patriotism to take up arms in their country's defense."[12] Unquestionably, the wording of these sharp and unequivocal reprimands shows that the Quaker hierarchy demanded absolute allegiance to the peace testimony.

Assertions of the traditional belief that war is un-Christian have led historians erroneously to assume that few Friends actively participated in the Civil War. Margaret H. Bacon, historian and author of *The Quiet Rebels*, stated that only two or three hundred Quakers enlisted in the entire Union army, but that the largest number of them enrolled from Indiana. Historian Margaret E. Hirst noted that the Indiana Yearly Meeting of 1862 received reports that one hundred of their members from five monthly meetings had volunteered for the army; a "considerable number" from ten additional meetings also served. Had there been even two hundred serving from the latter ten congregations, the author declared, the total would have remained at only three hundred soldiers.[13]

In a study of the attitude of the Northern clergy toward the South during the war years, historian Chester Dunham wrote that when actual fighting commenced, Quakers maintained their pacifistic principles just as they had since colonial days. Quite simply, Friends believed that war was irreconcilable with the teachings of Christ and refused to participate in the hostilities. Historian Emma Lou Thornbrough recorded that "some" Quakers volunteered for military duty, and Stephen Weeks wrote only that some young Friends in the North joined the federal army. Eminent Quaker historian Rufus Jones commented that while deviations from the peace testimony occurred more frequently than expected, the total number of Quaker soldiers "appears small." Possibly three hundred members of the Indiana Yearly Meeting, asserted Jones, took up arms in the Civil War. Moreover, more Quakers who joined the armed forces came from urban areas than rural meetings. Elbert Russell and Peter Brock, both of whom relied heavily on Jones's work, reached the same conclusion: only a small number of Friends enrolled for military duty.[14]

But the preceding historians, as with most historical scholars, did not undertake systematic studies to determine how many Quakers took up arms in the conflict. Heretofore, generalizations on the number of Quakers in uniform during the Civil War have been based on "probabilities and surmise rather than statistical fact." As a matter of fact, Jones wrote that it was impossible "to discover the total number of these Quaker volunteers." Furthermore, the emphasis in the historical writing of American wars, especially the Civil War, has centered upon the Friends as pacifists and conscientious objectors, not as combatants.[15]

The Society of Friends, however, has long known that many of its members served in the Civil War. But even Friends' estimates of Quaker participation in the armed forces have been low. The authors of a history of the Jericho Friends Meeting in Randolph County wrote that when the war began many Quakers found it difficult to distinguish between what was good in abolishing slavery and bad about using war to accomplish that goal. Inevitably, the slavery issue prompted a large number of young men from the Jericho Meeting to volunteer for military duty. The Quaker community at Carthage echoed similar sentiments. In spite of Quaker opposition to all wars, "quite a few" Friends enlisted in military service from this small Rush County town. In the "History of New Salem Church" (Howard County), the author noted that with the commencement of the Civil War "a few members" of the meeting joined the armed forces. Except for the writer of the account of the Randolph County meeting, who listed the names of sixteen Quaker volunteers, the authors of these and other histories of monthly meetings generally made no attempts to determine an accurate number of Friends who bore arms.[16]

George W. Julian, a prominent Indiana politician whose mother was a Quaker from Wayne County, wrote in 1895 that the Quakers of the Indiana Yearly Meeting not only had a good antislavery record but a record of patriotism: "I think it is conceded that in proportion to their number they had more soldiers in the war for the Union than any other religious denomination." Willard Heiss, Quaker and historian, wrote that "many" Quakers served in the Civil War. Finally, letters written by Friends during the war also disclosed that many Quakers marched off to the battlefield. One Quaker, for example, wrote: "23 of our Springboro Boys going to start away . . . for the Army." Another recorded that the Southern rebellion had become so serious that "thousands" of Quaker boys all over America were going into the army.[17]

Just how many Indiana Quakers joined the Northern armies between 1861 and 1865? The response of the individual monthly meetings to members' military service provides an initial estimate of the number of Friends in uniform as well as the inconsistency of opinion in regard to having borne arms. In the midst of the war virtually all monthly meetings, recognizing that some of their members had violated the peace testimony, attempted to extend care to those individuals. Once each year, in reply to the annual questions, or "queries," on the religious and moral health of the meetings, most congregations reported that some Friends had strayed from the principles of peace and were guilty of engaging in military services. Never was the name of an individual listed in such statements, but a few of the meetings did include the specific number of Quakers believed to have violated church discipline. In September 1862, for example, the Back Creek

Monthly Meeting of Men in Grant County recorded with some alarm that eighteen members had enrolled for military duty. The Hopewell Monthly Meeting in Henry County also penned its concern when it noted that fifteen members had volunteered for the army. These statements frequently concluded with the phrase "some care taken," the presumption being that the meetings attempted to counsel their errant soldiers.[18]

The *Discipline* of the Society of Friends clearly explained the potential penalty for serving in the military. Violators of the peace testimony faced possible disownment (loss of membership) if counseling and advice proved ineffectual in convincing them to seek absolution for their combative conduct.[19] The monthly meetings, however, generally waited until the war was over before confronting the individuals who had joined the army. Some cases of military service remained unreported until 1869, four years after the fighting had ceased.

Once the monthly meetings received information that a member had committed military transgressions, two Friends were appointed to visit the individual and report at an ensuing meeting. Any Quaker who desired to maintain his membership within the Society of Friends could produce an "offering" or "acknowledgment" admitting his wrongdoing and, if the meeting accepted it, remain a member in good standing. Also referred to as "condemning" one's behavior, these apologies were usually brief and simply stated in written notes signed by those beseeching forgiveness. The following offering from the minutes of the Raysville Monthly Meeting in Henry County is a representative example of expiation:

> I herein acknowledge that I have deviated from the principles of the society of friends by enlisting in the service of the U.S. and am convinced that war and the principles actuating it are wrong and inconsistant with the Christian religion. I wish friends to pass my deviation by and continue me as a member as my future conduct may deserve.[20]

Unusually long apologies were rare, but one troubled Quaker, Franklin Elliott of the Milford Monthly Meeting in Wayne County, wrote a lengthy and sincere, yet poignant, condemnation of his military service. Reminded that God had spared his life when wounded at Stone's River in 1862, Elliott was determined to serve the Lord to the best of his ability. He had not only seen but suffered the terrifying consequences of combat. Indeed, the experiences profoundly affected him: "My hands shall no more be raised in violence against my fellow man."[21]

Some Quakers, fearful of being disciplined by the monthly meetings, penned offerings in advance of receiving treatment from Friends. Such apologies, although few in number, were called "free will" acknowledgments. The mother of a young Quaker veteran, for example, who was worried that a complaint against her son, Jose, would be brought before the meeting, wanted someone to counsel her son for his infraction. She wanted Jose to acknowledge that his military course of action was "inconsistant with the principals of peace," to avoid any impending disciplinary action which might sour him on the Society.[22] Although Jose did not apologize to his meeting, eleven Friends produced nonrequested offerings.

Despite the fact that they were often solicited and were frequently a prerequisite for remaining a member of the Society of Friends, condemnations reveal that some Quakers admitted fault for having enrolled in military service. Moreover, there was no feeling of triumph for these men; many were truly sorry for their military actions. Early in the war a professor at Earlham College wrote that some of the Quakers who had returned home from the battlefield "look with sorrow on their past course and are striving to justify themselves." In all, approximately 220 Indiana Quaker veterans conceded guilt for this breach of faith.[23]

A large number of veterans from virtually all monthly meetings whose records were examined, however, refused to admit wrongdoing for their military involvement. If Quakers

denied fault for their military actions, the committee that dealt
with them reported the soldiers as "treated without satisfac-
tion." After a period of deliberation the meeting either extended additional care to those Quakers, in hopes of eliciting
acknowledgments, or disowned them. If the monthly meeting chose the latter course of action, "testifications" of disownment were written and read at a subsequent meeting. The
committees later informed the ex-soldiers of the decisions
against them. The following disownment was excerpted from
the Raysville Monthly Meeting minutes of July 1861:

> Robert Parker who has had a right of membership in
> the religious society of Friends, has so far deviated
> from the peaceable principles held by our society as to
> enlist in the Armies of the United States and do mil-
> itary service therein for which he has been treated
> with, without being brought to see the error of his
> course. We therefore disown him from being a mem-
> ber with us.[24]

One hundred forty-eight Quaker soldiers lost membership
within their respective local assemblages for involvement in
military operations.

Thus, close scrutiny of the Quaker minutes recorded between 1861 and 1869 reveals that 368 Indiana Friends bore
arms in the Civil War and either apologized or were disowned
for their martial conduct. But there were others. Besides the
aforementioned Friends, at least 238 Quakers died in the war.
An additional 608 Quakers took up arms in the conflict but
avoided all disciplinary action by the monthly meetings.
Hence, the number of documented cases of Quaker participation in military service is 1,212, well above any of the estimates of previous writings, Quaker or non-Quaker.[25]

Numbers alone, however, are misleading in a state in which
more than two hundred thousand men and boys took up
arms for their country's cause. Based on this sole statistic,

the number of Quaker military men appears insignificant. Sixty-two percent of all Indiana males between the ages of fifteen and forty-nine bore arms in the Civil War. In contrast, the percentage of Friends in service in the same age range lies between 21 and 27 percent. Although there is a wide gap between the number of Friends in uniform and the total for the state of Indiana, the proportion of Quaker males aged fifteen through forty-nine who joined a military company is much higher than previous estimates, which ranged from 6 to 7.5 percent.[26]

Another way to determine the significance of Quaker involvement in the war is to compare the number of military Friends with the number of those who claimed exemption from military service because of religious scruples. Under President Lincoln's call of August 1862, for 300,000 men to serve nine months, all able-bodied white male citizens between the age of eighteen and forty-five were required to enroll in the state militia. Those Friends who remained staunchly committed to the peace testimony and refused to volunteer for military service could append to their signatures the phrase "conscientiously opposed to bearing arms." Registration records show that 2,170 Friends, nearly 1,000 more than the total who bore arms, so identified themselves. But in at least eight Indiana counties the number of Quakers in uniform exceeded the number of "conscientious" Friends. Grant County, for example, sent 124 Friends off to war while 119 Friends expressed opposition to fighting. Jay County enrollment records list 6 as "conscientious," but 20 Quakers took the field. And Madison County Quaker records show that 32 men joined the armed forces, yet only 16 Friends remained faithful to their antiwar tenet. The largest disparity in convictions occurred in Orange County where 19 Friends voiced religious scruples against war while 63 took up arms.[27]

Conversely, militia enrollment records also show that in a few counties the proportion of Quaker soldiers to those

Friends who were "conscientious" was extremely small. At
the Sugar Plain Monthly Meeting in Boone County, for example, 60 Friends requested "conscientious" status while only
6 bore arms. The Pipe Creek Monthly Meeting in Miami
County sent 13 soldiers into the army while 118 were designated as "conscientious."[28] Apparently some Quaker communities contained more antiwar sentiment than others.

In addition to the low appraisal of Quaker participation in
the Civil War by most historians, one writer, Thomas E.
Drake, asserted that on the whole there was no mass enlistment of Friends into the armed forces. According to him,
those who did volunteer for active duty broke away from the
Quaker majority as individuals, not as a group. Drake's analysis of Quaker involvement in the war is supported only to
a limited extent by the current findings. Out of a total of 181
regiments raised within the state of Indiana, for example,
Friends enrolled and served in at least 135 units. In addition,
several companies were composed of large groups of Friends.
Company F of the Sixth Regiment, three months' service,
was dubbed the "Quaker Company." Raised in Knightstown
and surrounding areas in southwestern Henry County with
heavy concentrations of Quakers, this company, one of the
first to be organized, totaled seventy-four men. Mustered into
service at Indianapolis on 25 April 1861 with William C.
Moreau as captain, the entire regiment, under the command
of Colonel Thomas T. Crittenden of Madison, Indiana,
fought in the first battle of the war at Philippi, Virginia, on
3 June. Returning to Indianapolis in August, all men of Company F were mustered out at the expiration of their terms of
service.[29]

Several companies in three-year regiments also were represented by large numbers of Friends. Companies A and D
of the Thirty-sixth Regiment, raised in southern Henry
County from the Quaker communities of Lewisville and
Greensboro, respectively, are two such units. The former,

under the command of a Quaker captain, William Davis Wiles, was reported to have had fifty Quakers in its service, while Captain Isaac Kinley of Company D recruited forty fellow Quakers for active duty. The Thirty-sixth Regiment saw considerable action including the battle of Shiloh, siege of Corinth, and the battles of Stone's River, Chickamauga, Chattanooga, and Atlanta. Finally, the *Howard Tribune* (Kokomo) boasted that a regimental company was raised among the Quakers in southwestern Howard County. Mustered in as Company G of the Eighty-ninth Regiment, this unit, largely utilized for guard and picket duty, reportedly traveled in excess of ten thousand miles. These men also participated in a few skirmishes and were periodically stationed at Fort Pickering, Memphis, Nashville, Vicksburg, and New Orleans throughout the war.[30]

Other Indiana regiments contained sizable aggregates of Friends. Company E of the 12th Regiment, three years' service, included twenty-five Quakers primarily from Morgan County. Hamilton County sent twenty-two Quakers to war in Company G, 147th Regiment, one year service, and twenty-one Friends in Company A, 101st Regiment, three years' service. Orange County Quakers were well represented in Company D, 66th Regiment, as eighteen Friends mustered in for three years. And seventeen Quakers enrolled in Company C of the 89th Regiment from Grant County.

Further analysis of Quaker military service shows that anywhere from five to sixteen Friends were represented in each of 57 companies in 41 regiments and 3 batteries of light artillery. The composition of 329 companies in 122 regiments and 9 batteries of light artillery, however, included four or fewer Quakers. And at least 35 regiments contained no Quakers.[31] Thus, while the majority of military companies embodied only a few Friends, evidence exists that in many companies Quakers enrolled for military duty in large groups.

Figure 1
Companies with 10 or more Quakers

| Company | Regiment | Number |
| --- | --- | --- |
| E | 12th | 25 |
| G | 147th (1 yr.) | 22 |
| A | 101st | 21 |
| D | 66th | 18 |
| C | 89th | 17 |
| A | 36th | 15 |
| D | 36th | 15 |
| I | 69th | 14 |
| F | 39th | 13 |
| D | 70th | 13 |
| A | 85th | 13 |
| B | 117th (6 mos.) | 13 |
| G | 89th | 12 |
| H | 21st | 11 |
| B | 24th | 11 |
| E | 57th | 11 |
| C | 84th | 11 |
| A | 133rd (100 days) | 11 |
| D | 69th | 10 |
| B | 90th | 10 |
| F | 131st | 10 |

Unless otherwise indicated, the above regiments
were three-year units.

Obviously, the war posed a serious dilemma not only for
the young fighting Quaker wrestling with his conscience but
also for the monthly meetings as well. Largely due to events
beyond their control, the meetings faced an agonizing moral
quandary in deciding which one of the twin evils that had
swept the land, war or slavery, was the more important. In
short, the monthly meetings had to come to grips with the
question of disciplining those Friends who challenged two
centuries of Quaker thought on war. Why did nearly half of
all Quaker soldiers escape punishment by the monthly meetings? In the broader context of Quaker history in the Civil

War era, the fact that 1,212 Friends bore arms and that 608 remained undisciplined may be indicative of a loosening of the strict code of behavior to which Quakers had been bound. Church discipline had begun to weaken during the years of the Civil War, and deviations from the code were not uncommon. Throughout the decade of the 1860s many Friends encountered charges for a wide range of violations such as marrying a non-Friend, not attending meeting, using profane language, departing from plain speech and dress, and drinking. Some of these Quakers lost their memberships within the Society by disownment. It is conceivable that those Friends who joined the armed forces could no more live up to the strict Quaker standards than those who committed other types of infractions. As a matter of fact, a large number of Friends who were disowned for military service also had other offenses charged against them simultaneously.[32] In these instances adherence to Quaker principles was weak in general.

Figure 2
Regiments with 20 or more Quakers

| Regiment | Number |
|---|---|
| 69th | 47 |
| 36th | 45 |
| 84th | 40 |
| 101st | 37 |
| 57th | 36 |
| 147th (1 yr.) | 35 |
| 89th | 34 |
| 12th | 30 |
| 39th | 29 |
| 90th | 26 |
| 21st | 23 |
| 139th (100 days) | 23 |
| 66th | 21 |
| 34th | 20 |

Unless otherwise indicated, the above regiments were three-year units.

Historians of Quaker meetings have offered a variety of explanations for Friends' military service over the last half century. Indiana Quaker historian Willard C. Heiss wrote that after the conclusion of the war in 1865, "the application of the Discipline to the lives of Friends became increasingly relaxed." Not only was disownment for violations of the peace testimony gradually abandoned, but also punishment for non-adherence to other Quaker beliefs abated. By the end of the nineteenth century, "except for serious matters," few Friends lost membership within the Society by disownment. Historian Thomas Drake wrote that Quaker soldiers were not disowned automatically for volunteering, for Friends could not bring themselves to be too strict with their young men who compromised one Quaker principle (antiwar testimony) to fight for another (abolition of slavery). Freedom and the Union seemed to be worth fighting for. Carthage Friends in Rush County held "considerable discussion" concerning the course of action and the type of attitude they should take in regard to Quaker military service. Based upon the long-recognized ideal among Friends that one should obey one's conscience, they decided that if a man believed it was his duty to go to war, then the meeting should respect his decision and allow him to retain his membership. Consequently, those Friends who joined the armed forces were continued as members of the Society. Jericho Friends also refrained from disapprobation of soldiers. They worried about their men and welcomed them back when they returned home safely. In all, fourteen of the meetings that the author researched refused to disown ex-soldiers.[33]

Historian Daniel Boorstin wrote that the greatest failure of the Society of Friends in America was its rigidity of beliefs and unwillingness to compromise. Writing specifically about the period before the American Revolution, Boorstin noted that "Quakerism had many qualities which would have suited it to become the dominant American religion." But Friends' increasingly uncompromising dogmas throughout the first

half of the eighteenth century laid the foundation for a wall
that was built around the Society by the mid-1750s. As Quakers gradually withdrew from society, their chances for growth
waned, too. The Quaker story in America, then, according
to Boorstin, was "one of the greatest lost opportunities in all
American history."[34]

The reactions of Quaker monthly meetings after the Civil
War perhaps show that Friends tried to compromise to avoid
further loss of membership. Since Friends had been reluctant
to proselytize before and during the Civil War, membership
lists were shrinking. Needing to stave off this decline, the
Society imperceptibly reduced the penalties for violations of
the Quaker discipline. Indeed, historian John William Buys's
assessment that the "Civil War proved a watershed . . . [for]
the Society of Friends" may be correct. Elbert Russell would
have agreed with Buys. Russell asserted that the Civil War
"made a definite break in the history of American Quakerism." The war forced the Society out of its "official isolation,"
which was brought on by adherence to the peace testimony,
and compelled many Quakers to reexamine the pacifist
tradition.[35]

Rufus Jones viewed the enlistment of Quaker soldiers as
part of the weakening of the peace testimony rather than as
part of the overall loosening of the code of behavior. Jones
noted that at the time of the Civil War the rank and file membership possessed little more than a "traditional adherence"
to the antiwar stand. Quakers gave little serious thought to
war, and for most Friends it was an "unexamined inheri-
tance." Although the formal position of the Society was one
of opposition to all wars, in the "lives of individual members, however, . . . [the incompatibility of war with Christian
ideals] had not become a settled, dominant, first-hand
conviction."[36]

In any event, those meetings that disowned Friends for
military service chose the unwavering position, in spite of the
Inner Light, that no circumstance was grave enough, even the

possible abolition of slavery, to justify taking up arms and subjecting young men to the ordeal of battle. Hindsight confirms that the war successfully terminated the rebellion and brought about the demise of slavery. In the eyes of some it was defensible to allow Quakers to rely upon this inward spirit, permitting Friends to do what they, as individuals, believed was right and welcome them as heroes upon their successful return from the field of combat; others disagreed.

# 3
# Why Did They Fight?

ONE of the questions that arises in relation to Quaker military service is why did these men violate their antiwar teachings and testimony and volunteer to bear arms? How can one reconcile the Quaker belief in the unlawfulness of war with killing another human being? At this juncture it is relevant to discuss the timely, if not baffling, question of motives. Among the sources utilized to unravel this enigma are letters written by Friends in uniform. Although Quaker writings on the subject of military service are sparse, these letters offer at least a partial explanation for what appears to have been contradictory, inconsistent, and anomalous behavior. Several themes emerge from these introspective personal accounts in regard to what factors prompted many Friends to defend the Union.

Some Friends joined the army for patriotic reasons. Quakers repeatedly asserted that they loved their country and were willing to obey the laws of the United States government under which they had been guaranteed religious freedom. Many Quakers ardently believed that by enlisting in military service they were not only loyally following their country but also serving God as well. These Christian soldiers, convinced that the federal government was justified in taking offensive measures against the Confederacy, expressed confidence that God would exonerate Abraham Lincoln's administration for its endeavor to restore the Union. Thus, while the elders of the Society of Friends argued that all wars were unlawful in the eyes of the Lord, some of the Quaker soldiers contended that there was a "right" war and just cause for fighting that would ultimately receive divine sanction.

Solomon Meredith, a Union general with a Quaker background who came from Centerville, Indiana, was an exemplary patriotic warrior. He, as well as some Friends who joined the military, invoked the deity not only to justify or perhaps rationalize his own and the government's militaristic actions, but also to give guidance to those in command of the United States. He prayed to God to direct the leaders of the Union to act from "pure motives," unite the country, and extinguish the "unholy rebellion." To him there was no course of action except to stand by President Lincoln's administration—anything less would most certainly lead to failure. He insisted that he had acted from pure and patriotic motives since the inception of the war and had not "one selfish thought."[1]

Another Friend, Daniel Wooton, echoed a similar patriotic view for joining the military in several letters in which he carefully explained how a Quaker could take up arms in the rebellion. He insisted that the cheapest way for the nation to obtain "justice" in the war was to hang every seceder and stated that "God will also justify us in doing so." Private Wooton conceded that the Bible says *"thou shalt not kill,"* but at the same time he believed that God gave to the United States the power to quell the rebellion in the quickest way possible. He was convinced, too, that by choosing the martial life "I would be serving my God."[2]

Some Quaker soldiers expressed a more nationalistic view of patriotism void of any spiritual direction. They saw the seceders as traitors and aggressors and said that the rebellion had to be crushed. A young private wrote that, although it was hard to leave his sister and mother, "they [the Confederates] are the agressers and must bear the concequ[ences]." Several months later, obviously in response to news from home that men were getting married to avoid military duty, he wrote: "So the people still continue to get married in stead of enlisting do they. I think there ought to be a law pased to prevent it." A Quaker from Economy repeated similar feelings of loyalty when he wrote in January 1863 that he was willing to serve out his time rather "than to acknowledge the independence of the South." In August of the same year, after participating in the fall of Vicksburg, he repeated his stance: "Am willing to go anywhere that will help to end the war." This man's brother, a soldier in another regiment, likewise wrote upon the reception of orders to march to Vicksburg: "You need not be uneasy about me, for I am going willingly." One Quaker soldier, however, tersely stated that he and his brother volunteered to "goo Fight for our Country."[3]

Eight Quaker soldiers from Morgan County also expressed the patriotic motive in their apologies to the monthly meeting. Although they asserted that, as a general principle, war was contrary to Christ's teachings, "in this particular instance . . . by the sternest necessity, we feel that we were following the path of duty to our government."[4]

In sum, love of country impelled many Friends to take an active role in the Civil War. Furthermore, this devotion to the United States apparently was of two types. One was a kind of Christian patriotism, a strong belief that God was on the side of the Union and would confirm the actions of the federal government in quelling the insurrection. The other rationale could be called national patriotism, also a strong feeling of loyalty to the Union but devoid of holy approbation.

At least one Quaker admitted in writing, however, that it was not true patriotism that motivated him to enroll in the army. This young man, Franklin Elliott, as previously noted, wrote a lengthy and revealing letter of condemnation for his actions in volunteering for military duty. In part he wrote: "I confess that it was not true Patriotic motives that led me to take up arms in the War . . . I did it ma[i]nly to gratify a stuborn and rebellious spirit within me."[5]

Another Quaker was disappointed and even ashamed that he was unable to join the army and fight for the Union. Anna Starr of Richmond wrote to her husband William, a Quaker volunteer, that she and brother Clinton had discussed the issue of Clinton joining the service. Only his sick and totally helpless wife prevented him from enlisting. Clinton *"extremely"* regretted his absence from military service and said that he would "always feel *ashamed* to *have to own* that he was not in this war."[6]

Although many Quakers believed that fighting could be justified for patriotic reasons, some expressed reluctance, if not outright rejection, to see their brothers join the affray, especially if they were younger or, in some cases, too young to fight. These men, convinced that it was their duty to defend and restore the Union, seemed to feel that one military man in the family was sufficient. A younger, less mature sibling might not be able to withstand the rigors of army life and could be influenced to participate in its seamy aspects: drinking, gambling, womanizing, and using foul language, all of which were frowned upon by the monthly meetings. Finally, of course, the gnawing fear of an agonizing death by disease or bullet plagued the elder brothers. Thus, Friends in uniform played the part of wise, experienced, and protective kinsmen.

Alonzo Marshall, one of three boys from the Marshall family in the war, wrote home that he would like to see his brothers but "would rather go in . . . battle without them than with them." When Swain Marshall received word that one of his younger brothers had talked of enlisting, he promptly scolded him for such ranting. Marshall told his parents to report Bub "to me and I think I will get him out of the notion. I think that before he gets old enough that the war will be over."[7]

Daniel Wooton mirrored similar familial feelings. Alarmed that one of his brothers expected to be drafted, he wrote: "I think that Dan is enough for our family. . . . But I dont want any more of them to be shot at thats all, for I fully aware that the sound of rifle balls is not as desirable music as some I have heard. But if it is necessary let them come too and all others that wish a free country." Later, a brother, James, enlisted much to Wooton's dismay: "I know he cannot stand a soldiers labor." Wooton urged all men, not just those bound by blood, to "see the error of fighting" before it was too late and they found themselves in an army uniform. Wooton, who had seen much suffering, death, and destruction, did not want any of his brothers "to pass through what I have already done." He acknowledged, however, that if men did choose to fight then they would know better how to sympathize with those who had already gone.[8]

The conviction that the war had to be taken to its conclusion and the rebellion quelled induced some Quakers to reenlist before their terms of service expired. Nourished by a feeling of pride that the army had accomplished much in the war, a comradery had developed which prompted these soldiers to reenroll. Although the number of Quaker combatants who registered twice for military duty is small—sixty-one—it represents approximately 5 percent of the total Quaker enrollment, only slightly less than the 5.4 percent computed for all of Indiana's troops. In addition, five of those veterans enlisted three times for service in Indiana regiments.[9]

A few surviving soldiers' letters contain convincing arguments for sustaining the military life. Swain Marshall, imbued with this patriotic fervor, at first thought that he would not reenlist until his old term of service was completed. He changed his mind, however, when confronted with the choice of either staying with his old regiment or being transferred to a new one: "I could not think of leiving the old eighth and going in some other regt." He was willing to serve three more years "faithfully and willingly, trying to do my duty to my country." Several months later he wrote home again noting that the government was paying a big bounty for recruits. He strongly urged that the draft be completed quickly to get the men in the field and was insistent that if Ulysess S. Grant and William T. Sherman each had a hundred thousand more men the war would conclude in less than a year.[10]

With only eleven months of service remaining, Daniel Wooton struggled with the same dilemma. Ultimately, he decided that since he had withstood the hardships thus far and bore the responsibility for the safety of his friends back home, he could harbor no thought of leaving his regiment. During his two-year tenure as a private, Wooton had become proud, almost chauvinistic, of the accomplishments of the Union army: "I never was much for pride but I am *too* proud of the victories achieved by the army of the Cumberland to even give *one* thought to leaving hir at this late day."[11]

Some Friends also volunteered, no doubt, because they were very young and could not comprehend the gravity and consequences of their decisions. While statistics indicate that the ages of Friends in uniform ranged from twelve through sixty-one, the largest group of Friends (and non-Friends) who served in the Civil War were the eighteen-year-olds. But at least one hundred Quaker boys, seventeen years of age or younger, enrolled for military duty.[12] As reports filtered back from army camps about the fun of military life, the youthful and impressionable boys at home, although legally bound by the constraints of age as well as morally restricted by the Quaker discipline, found it difficult to refrain from enlisting. As a further stimulus to recruitment, public rallies, parades, and picnics—replete with brass bands and speeches filled with patriotic jargon—were held in cities and towns across Indiana in and near Quaker communities. The festival-like atmosphere typical of these grand occasions likewise may have swayed even the most devout Friend to join the struggle to save the Union. Newspaper advertisements of such gatherings were often printed in bold-faced type to catch the eyes of virtually every reader.

Some of these youthful Friends also may have been influenced to bear arms by acquaintances or a brother or brothers already in the service. While some Quaker soldiers ardently opposed any more of their family members taking up arms, as earlier indicated, others may have actively recruited able-bodied siblings. Examination of Quaker birth and death records shows that at least seventy-four families saw two sons go to war, twenty families were represented by three sons, and four brothers joined the army in each of nine families. Seven father-son combinations also enlisted in Hoosier regiments.[13] One Quaker woman wrote that "Brother gone—As he enrolled amongst the thousands who have gone—Is he but a Lad of 17—so young & thoughtless—oh how truely lamentable!" The father of a young Quaker enrolled at Earlham College penned a letter to the school's superintendent, Walter Carpenter, pleading with him to influence his son, Lavinus, not to enlist in the army. Anxious that Lavinus would be induced to "take part in the Bloody strife," he wrote: "I wish thou would use thy Influence . . . to induce him either to stay with you in the school . . . or come home and stay with us." No evidence was found to determine whether or not Mr. Carpenter failed to communicate with Lavinus or if the young man simply did not heed the advice; he enlisted anyway. Lavinus King died only four days after mustering into the army.[14]

Economic conditions in the United States certainly prompted some Quakers to volunteer for active duty. Unemployment coupled with the use of bounties in recruitment were powerful incentives to financially distraught Friends in Indiana. Although the pay was low, thirteen dollars per month

for infantry privates throughout most of the war, the first few
months of the hostilities were beset by depression. Intermit-
tent joblessness faced many men until 1863; furthermore,
farm and factory wages remained low. Army life offered the
assurance of an income, although small and dependent upon
the continuation of the war, that the civilian employment
scene lacked.[15] Reflecting this concern for a steady income,
one Quaker wrote before his enlistment: "I dont think I shall
go yet a while at least . . . as long as I have work to do I shall
not go but if I run out of work and they want more men I
think Dan shall go."[16]

A few Quakers entered the armed forces to fill sorely
needed noncombat positions. Eli Patterson, for example, a
Quaker from Spiceland, volunteered for service on the expressed condition that he not be required to bear arms but
instead be assigned to hospital duty. When confronted by the
monthly meeting after the war, Patterson asserted that his
request was strictly adhered to by military authorities.[17] Examination of the war records of Quakers reveals that, although most Friends in uniform entered the service as combat
soldiers, approximately twenty of them dutifully worked in
the following essential, nonfighting roles: surgeon, assistant
surgeon, hospital steward, nurse, orderly, ambulance driver,
baggage-master on a hospital train, medical cadet, sanitary
agent, cook, chaplain, and medical examiner. A few Friends
also served their companies and regiments in the following capacities: bugler, wagoner, scout, guard, carpenter,
blacksmith, teamster, musician, artificer, quartermaster, and
paymaster.[18]

Several Quakers also enrolled for military duty for defensive purposes when Confederate General John Hunt Morgan
invaded the state of Indiana in the summer of 1863. Morgan's
penetration into southern Indiana late in the evening of 8 July
created much excitement, fear, and conflicting and exagger-
ated rumors prompting Governor Oliver P. Morton to issue

a call for citizens to organize for defense. In less than forty-eight hours sixty-five thousand men volunteered to repulse Morgan's daring raid. These Minute Men were organized into thirteen regiments and numerically designated from the 102nd to the 114th inclusive. Companies in which Quakers volunteered, frequently titled by colorful names such as Buck Tails and Liberty Tigers, were found in ten of these units. Although only the southern counties were imminently threatened, Quakers from central Indiana also responded to Morton's call. Quakers from the counties of Hamilton, Wayne, Hendricks, Randolph, Henry, Hancock, Madison, and Marion joined Friends from Orange and Washington counties in southern Indiana in repelling the rebel encroachment. When Morgan finally crossed the Indiana border into Ohio five days later, the crisis subsided, and the Minute Men were mustered out of service.[19] He left behind, however, a trail of destruction from Corydon to Versailles and brought the war frightfully close to many peaceful Indiana communities.

Only a few Quakers entered military service as draftees and substitutes—and for good reason. Like most of the Union soldiers who answered the call to arms and enrolled in the armed forces through voluntary enlistment, Quakers also sought to avoid the stigma of forced service and to receive the bounty money given only to volunteers. Clearly, Quakers viewed the likelihood of being drafted as an incentive to enlist. One Friend, for example, wrote that he and his brother "will goe befor we ar drafted." Of the 1,212 Friends in uniform from Indiana only 22, or 1.9 percent of them, waited to be conscripted into service, well below the 8.6 percent calculated for the entire state of Indiana. Furthermore, any person drafted could be excused from military service either by furnishing a substitute or, until the draft law of 1864, paying a commutation fee of $300. Research shows that 6 Quakers from Indiana entered the service as substitutes.[20]

Quakers who remained on the home front cited antislavery
sentiments as a motivator for military service. As noted earlier, a few letters and some of the histories of monthly meetings indicated that some Friends saw nothing wrong with
utilizing war to help free the slaves; by taking up arms they
compromised one Quaker principle to fight for another. William Stubbs Elliott, a Friend from Hamilton County, wrote
early in the war that Quakers were entering the army inspired
with abolitionist enthusiasm. Convinced that the war would
terminate the institution of slavery, Elliott, who later volunteered for military service, declared that "it is my duty to
abolish this curse from the nation." Similarly, James O. Bond,
author of an unpublished biography of a Quaker Civil War
veteran, implied that fear of the spread of slavery to the whole
nation prompted Quakers to bear arms. John W. Griffin, a
Friend from Spiceland, Indiana, also believed that there was
a "righteous war" to end slavery. To him the Quaker theory
of nonresistance was radical and, if implemented, would lead
to the destruction of the federal government. Thus, Griffin
asserted that neither the New Testament nor the early writings
of the church fathers required rigid adherence to the doctrine
of pacifism. Finally, historian Thomas Drake declared that
Friends saw the Civil War as God's way of punishing a nation
of slaveholders. He also wrote that abolitionist Levi Coffin
believed that the war would continue until slavery was
abolished.[21]

Interestingly enough, the idea that freeing the slaves
prompted Quakers to enroll in the armed forces was conspicuously absent from the letters written by the soldiers
themselves. Some Quaker correspondence, nevertheless, indicates that these combatants were curious about the blacks,
and at least one soldier was convinced that slavery had brought
on the war. Early in the conflict one Quaker, in response to
his parents' inquisitiveness about the "darkies," wrote home
that he had not yet seen any blacks; they had all been "run

farther south." Several weeks later he wrote that in passing a plantation the slave quarters "looked like a good sized town." This same soldier also saw the urgency of the bondsmen's liberation "so as to never get into another such fix as we are in now."[22]

Some Quaker soldiers, while expressing the need for the black man's emancipation, opposed the movement of blacks to the North. One Quaker, Swain Marshall, wrote that most of the men in his company favored abolition with the condition that the blacks "stay where they are." Another Friend in uniform not only echoed approval for the slaves' freedom but also wanted to "get the country clear of them; for my part I think we are getting a little more than our share of them here [Camp Wickliffe, Kentucky]." Swain Marshall's brother, Alonzo, only mentioned the blacks on one occasion, however, writing laconically that "there are any amount of slaves around here."[23]

Whatever the motives which prompted the Quakers to volunteer, many of them could not wait to serve their time and go home. One Friend, John E. Morgan, wrote home that his commanding officer thought he was "fooling away" his time by not reenlisting. Morgan asserted, however, that he "could not see it in that light." Another Quaker, who obviously detested military life, assured his mother that he would not reenlist:

> Mother the[e] need not be a fraid of me reinlisting the country may sink deper than the bottomless pit and 10 times deper than that for what I care with out the head managers will chang there mode of settling this rebellion from what it is at presant dear mother there is only 28 days after to nite that I haft too serve then if I am living I will come home sure they are tring too get me oll the time too goe fore one year but ten thousand times ten thousand dolars will not tempt me to goe.

He must have rejoined, however, for he wrote a letter dated 16 March 1865 from Camp Carrington, seven months after he promised his mother that his army career was over.[24] Unfortunately, he did not preserve for the historian the reason or reasons for making what appears to have been an abrupt change of attitude.

In spite of the fact that the majority of Quakers did not reenlist, most completed their terms of service. Only thirteen Quaker soldiers deserted their regiments, and only two were absent without leave, a mere 1.3 percent of the whole number of documented cases of Quaker military service. This figure compares very favorably with the 4.3 percent of the total Hoosier fighting force who abandoned their units. In addition, while most of the Quaker fighting men remained either recruits or privates, many of them earned and accepted appointments to higher rank. The categorical breakdown of Friends' military status is as follows: 115 corporals, 83 sergeants, 41 lieutenants, 16 captains, 2 majors, 2 colonels, 2 adjutants, 2 generals, and 2 provost marshals.[25]

Having been reared in a religious environment that taught the unlawfulness of war, an interesting question is whether or not these Quaker soldiers expressed doubts or regrets in regard to violating an important cornerstone of Quaker dogma. Those who produced apologies to the monthly meetings after the conclusion of the war certainly must have reflected on their martial past. While many expressed true sorrow for their actions, others, however, may have condemned their behavior merely to stay within the religious environment of friends and family. They embraced Quaker ideology in general but perhaps not the antiwar testimony in particular, especially since some felt that this war was a righteous war. It appears that most of the Quaker soldiers whose writings are available had no regrets due to their military performance. One soldier wrote that he was "not at all disapointed" with being a soldier and, with a touch of whimsy, added, "I never has the blues, and I am just like a Cat on a hot Brick." The mother of a Quaker soldier, worried about whether or not the monthly meeting would discipline her son, wrote after the war that "he says he has not done any thing he would be ashamed for any old friend to know." Swain Marshall assured his parents that the army was the place for him, and he could not come home when every available man was needed on the battlefield: "I get in better spirits every day."[26]

Early in his brief military career Daniel Wooton, perhaps questioning the wisdom of his decision, ruefully admitted that the army had taken him away from his friends. He movingly recorded that he had disobeyed the teachings of God under his mother's tutelage, but that it was too late to change his mind. A tinge of remorse can be detected in the following sentence in which he stated that he could have been "proclaiming the glad tidings . . . had he have minded the workings of *God* in his heart as his mother has oftimes entreated him to do. and when it was not too late." About one year later, however, Wooton asserted that he had not regretted his enlistment. A few months hence he reflected on his enrollment and appeared to have crossed the bridge of uncertainty. Now proud that he was a military man, Wooton hoped that he would "never see the Day I shall have to regret it."[27]

The collective military record of the Society of Friends in the Civil War undoubtedly is linked to the question of motivation. Evidence suggests that the reasons for the initial enrollment are indeed similar to the incentives for reenlistment, acceptance of promotion to higher rank, and completion of terms of service. In all probability, however, a thorough analysis of the question of motivation can neither be fully determined nor clearly understood. Indeed, many of the soldiers themselves may not have comprehended the complex issues behind the commencement of the hostilities well enough to know why they were fighting. The abolition of slavery, preservation of the Union, and, of course, patriotism were exceedingly emotional, if not simplistic, concepts that overshadowed the points of dispute between the North and the South. The Quaker concept of the Inner Light, the inward spirit that granted each individual the freedom to follow his own conscience and that seemingly could have vindicated Friends' military actions, also fails to provide the historian with a satisfactory answer to the perplexing inquiry.

A cursory comparison of the motives for enlistment of a large number of non-Quaker soldiers and the Indiana Friends in uniform shows striking similarity. In his highly acclaimed book, *The Life of Billy Yank: The Common Soldier of the Union*, Bell Irvin Wiley studied thousands of letters and diaries written by Union soldiers. He found several reasons why many young men of the North joined the armed forces.

First of all, significant numbers of men, caught up in the "prevailing excitement," saw the "lure of far places" as a way to seek change in their lives. The war and military service, then, could broaden the horizons of those who had never had the opportunity to travel. Once the fighting began, friends and associates already in the service coaxed those at home to join the hostilities. In 1863 the federal governmment adopted the first conscription plan, providing an additional impetus to enlistment. In order "to avoid the stigma of forced service" and to obtain the bounties awarded to volunteers, thousands of men rushed to enroll for military duty. In particular, the expectation of economic rewards served as an incentive for financially distressed men. Furthermore, some veterans indicated that "love of country and hatred of those who seemed bent on destroying its institutions impelled" them to join the fight for the United States. Wiley also noted that a desire to emancipate the slaves spurred some men to enlist in the army, although very few soldiers actually expressed this motive. Finally, preservation both of the Union and the country's system of government prompted many men to participate in the war.[28]

Clearly, the writings of the Quaker soldiers evince much of the same feeling and flavor discovered by Wiley in other manuscripts. It appears that the motives of Quakers differed insignificantly from those of the soldiers of Wiley's massive study. Once the war was set in motion at Fort Sumter, the incentives for enlistment transcended the religious scruples of those Friends who were determined to fight. Quaker combatants could indeed be included among Wiley's "common soldiers."

# 4
# Response to Military Life

UNDOUBTEDLY, the life of a soldier in wartime constituted a dramatic change in the life-styles of these young Quaker men, many of whom had never been far away from the comfortable confines of home, family, and the watchful eyes of the religious community. Many experienced a "cultural shock" of sorts as they witnessed first-hand the horrors of bloody conflict as well as the immoral and appalling behavior rampant in camp life. Mere survival depended upon Quaker participation in actions incomprehensible in civilian life. How, then, did the Quakers respond to the rigors and temptations of military life?

During the initial weeks of enlistment before participation in battle, when the terror of combat was a distant, unfathomable reality, many Quakers thought camp life was fun and actually enjoyed themselves. Some were impressed with the comradery, uniforms, and other accoutrements characteristic of a wartime emergency. After one week in the army one Quaker wrote: "We have lots of fun music of all cinds." Another Friend wrote that he enjoyed "camp life vary well . . . the Boys are quite lively." In addition, one Quaker scribbled in his diary that "we are still in camp having our usual good times." One soldier boasted that his position was that of "high private." His uniform, a pair of blue pants and a coat with brass buttons adorned with a light blue cord, was likewise reported with dignity: "I feel as proud as any juvenile in his first pair of boots. I have enjoyed the fun of camp, this far, as well as any."[1]

Another precombatant expressed similar sentiments. He wrote to his mother: "We haft to Drill fore times a day which is fun for me." After just three days in service one Quaker described a trip to Louisville, Kentucky. The men were forced to sleep on the open ground because tents had not yet arrived, but "I never slept better in my life. I awoke this morning before any of the regt. had got up, and looked all over the ground. it was considerable of a show to see a whole regt. lying on the ground at once." Two months later, now stationed at Camp Wayne, he entreated his parents to journey to Richmond and see them on dress parade: "It is a real nice sight." Another Quaker wrote of camp life: "I enjoy my self very well." And when the troops had to move south some of the men liked the weather there so much better than that in the North that they did not care if they returned home until spring. One soldier wrote: "Don't think the kind of weather you have had in the north this winter would suit me."[2]

Hence, strong feelings of excitement, self-esteem, and pride poured from soldiers' letters, not only as individuals but also as men who saw the company or regiment as one fighting unit. In some cases these emotions continued to mature as the war progressed; some did not want to come home to Indiana. Swain Marshall, more convinced with each passing day that the war must end in a Union victory, wrote: "I dont know how it would be with me, but think it would bore me to go home now when every man is needed." Daniel Wooton also was concerned about life outside the military. Late in 1863, with eight months of service to go, he stated that he was "about ready to retire from the life of a soldier and once more resume that of a citizen. How strange such a life will seem to me for a while at least."[3] But as noted earlier, Wooton, unable to abandon military life, did reenlist.

Of course, not all enlistees agreed that soldiering was fun, especially after the initial novelty of military life faded into the harsh, inescapable certainty of death, disease, exhaustion, hunger, filth, boredom, and homesickness. One young Quaker wrote that "soldiering is no fun to day sure . . . no Childs play." The loneliness of army life pervaded many of the soldiers' letters as they missed family and friends. One Friend, who admitted that he enjoyed the camp vitality, recorded, however, that "I can not get to see my friends as often as I would like." A few months later he poignantly expressed what so many soldiers experienced in the war: "I feel lonely out here with none of my friends to even cheer me with a kind word. *no* not hardly a letter to show me that they have not forgotten me neither forgotten those pleasant times which we have spent." One Friend, mirroring the same feeling, penned concisely, "I git lonesome."[4]

As a vital link with home and all the good things of life, Quakers anxiously awaited letters from friends and family. Daniel Wooton scolded one friend and said that she would probably write more often if she "appreciated the worth of letters as we do in the army: away from friends home and all that is dear to us." Virtually every piece of correspondence from these men also included a plea for more news from home. Swain Marshall often ended his letters with an appeal such as "write as soon as you can," and he frequently mentioned boats coming with a prayerful hope that a letter was on board for him. One Quaker soldier employed a scheme by which he felt assured of receiving dozens of letters. Swain Marshall's brother-in-law, John Macy, wrote forty letters in anticipation that he would receive replies in every mail call and be the envy of his comrades. Marshall wrote that Macy's tactic failed miserably—he "has not rec'd but two yet." Dejectedly, Macy read them over and over each time mail arrived so that the others would think he had been deluged with news from home.[5]

And like virtually all military men, the Quakers tired of the long war. One soldier laconically wrote, "I am tird of it [the war] and I think a man that says he ant is worse than a secesh." Martha Talbert White, a niece of abolitionist Levi Coffin, wrote in her diary that she had received a letter from her brother Isaac, a Quaker volunteer. He seemed to be discouraged about the war: "I think he is getting tired of it." Other enlistees, weary from the death and bloodshed surrounding them, reflected on the loss of friends: "How very meny of my old acquantancenecs have died since this war begun I could mention 20, and I am yet speard I trust for some good purpose."[6]

Many of the surviving letters written by Quaker volunteers recount the battles and skirmishes in which they were engaged. From these descriptions one can infer how these men and boys, who were taught to abhor killing, reacted to the bloody scenes of combat. The salient characteristic of the battlefield sketches, many of which were graphically recapitulated, was inurement to the shocking and ghastly sights, sounds, and smells of warfare. Quaker volunteers had lost their civilian sensitivity to the value of human life and the destruction of property. One Friend, for example, related matter-of-factly and without emotion one of his first battleground sights: "The dead had all been removed and buried but the ground was nearly covered with dead horses, some of them shot with buckshot and others with twelve-pound cannon balls, and the trees for half a mile around are all shot up. I saw where one cannon ball had struck a hard oak telegraph pole and cut it nearly down."[7]

Daniel Wooton wrote similarly. He confessed that he had become accustomed to the "increasing roar of artilery" which filled "the ear with its heavy sound" and permeated "the mind with dread" rather "than to enliven his spirit to mirth and jolity. But it has become so common a thing with us that we scarcely give time enough to think, of what is the result of such work." Approximately sixteen months later, he continued to write in the same vein. For him the fighting and killing had become so common "that soldiers never think of writing to their friends every time they get in a little *mix*." Aware of his insensitivity he cogently penned that he had been "isolated from all that is lovely; and placed in a position that knows naught but barbarity and the most gross sort of pleasures."[8]

At times some of the soldiers seemed to enjoy the warfare. The sights and sounds of battle evoked statements of grandeur from their pens, and they often noted how beautiful a battlefield scene could be to them. One Quaker soldier described the siege of Vicksburg with its constant barrage of shells as "one of the nicest sights in the world, to watch . . . of a night from here." How uncharacteristic of a Quaker to be enthralled by the destruction of life and property. Later, however, he wrote that the enemy "commenced whistling bullets too close to my head to be comfortable." Another soldier wrote that he saw the battle of Chattanooga from the top of the mountain (Lookout Mountain) and "it was a grand sight." Some Friends wrote with aggressive fervor. Swain Marshall wished that he could be in Richmond, the Southern capital, soon after its surrender: "I think I would try to fire the place."[9] Sometimes, too, Quaker soldiers expressed their feelings through the use of colorful but derisive words for the Confederate soldiers: rebs, secesh, grey backs, and cusses.

Did these Quaker soldiers admit to shooting back and killing the Confederates during the heat of battle? That Friends in uniform failed to adhere to Quaker tutelage in regard to taking human life under these extreme circumstances was probably not unexpected. Indeed, with no feeling of regret or remorse, some boasted that they had fired at and sometimes killed the rebels. Moreover, these men seemed more concerned about the possibility of missing their targets rather than accepting the responsibility for the death of the enemy. One Quaker, for example, described a skirmish in which his company gave the enemy "a few rounds and then they [Confederates] . . . went back." At Vicksburg, Swain Marshall and his colleagues worked for eleven days digging rifle pits and throwing up breastworks. In that time he shot over "two hundred cartridges at the cusses. Can't say whether I killed every shot or not." Several days later, while his company was in the trenches shooting at the Mississippi fort, Marshall noted that he "got some bully shots at the rebs heads when they would poke them up to shoot." One year later, in response to close enemy fire, Marshall recorded that he "gave them a *volley* and retreated." He took aim at the rebel entrenchment, "but as they all dodged down I could not tell whether I plugged one or not."[10]

John E. Morgan also recounted a skirmish with the Confederates in which "the whole of the rebs fired at our boys and I killed one of them. there was 9 balls hit him in the back and came out at his breast. poor fellow he never knew what hurt him." Earlier, this same soldier admitted to killing the enemy when he wrote that during a three-day scout "we kiled 3 rebs."[11]

Another interesting question that arises in relation to Quaker military service is whether or not these men maintained their religious beliefs during the war. Did they, for example, attend religious services in camp? Evidence is sparse in that most letters from these enlistees did not broach the subject. Although Friends did not usually send any preachers to military camps to minister to the spiritual needs of the soldiers, at least two Quakers did attend religious services of other denominations. Isaac Barker wrote that while on guard duty he heard the chaplain preach. Noting that only 150 men out of two regiments attended the worship service, he facetiously penned: "I think a few gallons of whisky and some cards will bring out a larger croud." Swain Marshall wrote home that he attended church services regularly, but that there were only two churches in the community near their encampment: Methodist and Baptist. Of the latter minister he wrote: "The Baptist Preacher has been a Union man all the time."[12]

While many soldiers enjoyed the looseness of moral conduct that accompanied military life, some Friends worried about the effect of the army environment on their own personalities. Some Quakers, no doubt, succumbed to temptation, but for those who did not, it was a struggle to maintain all of their moral traditions. Daniel Wooton was concerned about what effect camp life would have on his character when he wrote that "it is going to be verry hard for me to refrain from all the vices of camp life though hop I shall so far as I can." Two months later he echoed the same sentiments: "I am not as steady as I was when I left old Newport but this is a hard place for one to keep a good moral character."[13]

On the subject of temperance, Quakers were taught to avoid the unnecessary use of drink and not to import, sell, or make spirituous liquors. As the temptations of military life are well known, and previous writings have noted how difficult it was to maintain a good moral character in the army, several letters confirmed that at least some Quakers were successful in warding off this enticement. Long-fought battles and forced marches often necessitated protracted periods of abstention from alcohol. Many of the soldiers, however, drank heavily at the first opportunity. During these drinking bouts the Quaker boys were often asked to imbibe, and no doubt some of them did. One Quaker wrote home, however, that he would not use liquor except for medicine. Swain Marshall also promised his parents that he would not drink: "I have not tasted a drop since I [left?] home and dont intend too." A year later he reported that he attended temperance meetings three times per week. Marshall reassured his parents that he would remain "dry" as he and eight hundred men from his brigade signed a pledge promising not to consume any intoxicating liquor while in the service of the United States: "You need not be afraid of me braking it."[14]

Another comrade in arms, thankful for his Quaker background, mirrored the same feelings and was horrified by the behavior of his fellow soldiers. Obviously concerned about the effectiveness of the army due to immoderate drinking, he was distressed that so many men succumbed to such temptation but "thanks to our heavanly father and my early teachings and experiance I have proved to be proof against all perswasions and temtations, and I would to god I could say as much for my comrades. no one hase eny Idea how meny men are unfit for duty from the affetcs of these evels."[15]

Lest one becomes convinced that all Quakers persevered against allurements, research shows that some of them did not always adhere to their pious upbringing. These temptations were inevitably fostered by an environment not under surveillance by parents and church and dictated by the exigencies of war. Many soldiers missed the taste of good food, especially fresh fruit; some of them admitted to "confiscating" such items. Not only did Isaac Barker admit to eating cherries from nearby farms, he wrote that he went back to camp and sold them for fifteen cents a quart! One day Swain Marshall found a fellow busily selling watermelons and decided to help him a little. He sold three, pocketed the money, and took two for his trouble. Assuringly he wrote home, "You needn't think though, that I will steal or do any thing out of the way." More seriously, however, he described a two-day stay on a widow's plantation in Louisiana; her husband had been a captain in the Confederate army: "We eat about two hundred bu. of sweet potatoes and killed all the cattle and hogs on the place." In fact, one Quaker, William S. Elliott, admitted that he enjoyed such carnage: "We foraged a great many hogs and had a general good time."[16] Obviously these Quakers accepted this behavior as a necessary part of war.

That many of the Quaker soldiers experienced a transformation of character while in the army cannot be denied. Previous and additional excerpts from letters support this assertion and show that these Christian warriors participated in and boasted about the very activities they had been taught from childhood to abhor: killing, drinking, using foul language, and destroying property, for example. In coming to grips with this irregular behavior, perhaps it is well to understand that in the abstract the ascetic Quaker life could be achieved. The army, however, was not the "real" world, and many Friends had to compromise their principles in order to survive or at least be accepted in a rough, dangerous, crude, and sometimes feral environment. Placed in an aberrant situation, their responses, at worse, might be regarded as normal.

When several of the Quakers recited the beautiful and grand sights of battle, one must delve further into the mere narration of the events to grasp their meaning. Generally, these statements were written about situations in which the soldiers were in no immediate personal danger, as during the siege of Vicksburg, described earlier by Swain Marshall, or watching combat from afar. Perhaps seeing and hearing the shells smash through houses and explode in the midst of the enemy served to calm the anxiety and fear of having to meet their adversaries face to face. In this sense the soldiers knew that property and lives were being destroyed, but it was property and lives of featureless opponents, thus saving them from personal knowledge, contact, and responsibility. On the other hand, accounts written by Quakers of killing their foes occur when they were being fired upon, and nothing but survival was the guiding justification; such scenes were not reported in grandiose language.

Daniel Wooton is an excellent case of character metamorphosis. This young Quaker volunteer from Newport (now Fountain City in Wayne County) penned a series of fascinating letters from 1861 through 1863 to Miriam Green, a school friend also from Newport. The portrait that emerges from these letters was a boy battling, on the one hand, with his Quaker background relating to war and, on the other, seeing the need to defend the honor of the Union. This young man, initially uncertain of his destiny, changed over the course of two years from an unsure naive soldier to a proud fighting man.[17]

What makes Wooton so unique and important is that his letters reveal more of the inner conflict faced by Quakers during the Civil War than those written by most other Friends in uniform. Wooton, typical of many Quakers contemplating enlistment, was worried that his mother would oppose his decision. He wrote, however, that he could not "think that she will oppose my course as much as some others." Quakers who supported the war in this fashion knew that the consequences could be disownment by their monthly meetings; thus, many of them not only wrestled with their own consciences in deciding to violate the antiwar testimony, but also faced estrangement from family and the religious community alike.[18] This initial, lingering doubt soon vanished, however, after Wooton made his martial commitment.

Several months after his enrollment Wooton's letters contained statements of irresolution concerning his actions. He suffered misgivings about army life and seemed to have lost his self-worth when, in response to fear that he might be killed and not brought back home, he wrote: "But that would not amount to much any how." Wooton's psychological well-being improved greatly after an eight-month stint as secretary, then later, clerk, in hospitals in Mississippi and Tennessee. Returning to the field of battle, a renewed feeling of patriotism pervaded his pencraft as he scribbled that he had "returned to the field of strife to gain a *great* victory . . . for the sake of his country."[19]

By late summer of 1863 Wooton had crossed his Rubicon; he was absolutely convinced that serving his country in the war was the right course of action for him. He confidently wrote: "There was my duty to my country, to my God and my friends at home, and the object was which should I serve first. So I came to the conclusion by serving my country I would be serving my God and friends also, therefore I resolved to enlist and risk my chances with that of my fellow soldiers. And . . . I feel proud that I have enlisted."[20] For two years Private and, later, Lieutenant Wooton struggled with his conscience: the conflict between his strong Quaker background, having been taught that all wars were unlawful, and the need to serve God by supporting his country. At last, Wooton had no regrets about his military actions, and he seemed to have found his inner peace.

In comparing the reactions of Quakers to military life with those of Bell Wiley's study, it is interesting to note that similarities outweigh differences. Although some of the topics broached by Wiley's soldiers are absent from the limited number of Quaker missives, Friends' writings concerning their feelings about war and army life mirror his findings. Wiley concluded, for example, that reactions to camp life were generally favorable. Shortly after enlistment one of the New York recruits wrote, "I and the rest of the boys are in fine spirits . . . feeling like larks." And a young man from Illinois similarly boasted, "I never enjoyed anything in the world as I do this life." Boys from the country discovered, too, that military duties were no worse than those at home.[21] The Quaker recruits, overwhelmingly farm boys, may have felt the same.

In the early going, then, going to war, Wiley said, was a "tremendous picnic." All in all, Wiley concluded that even though many new soldiers detested the army and the regimented way of life, "a majority of soldiers were neither exuberant nor mournful in their initial reactions." When it came to the drill field, however, most recruits found life difficult, if not outright boring—unlike the Quaker quoted earlier. One Pennsylvanian wrote after nearly six months of service: "The first thing in the morning is drill, then drill, then drill again.

Then drill, drill, a little more drill. Then drill, and lastly drill. Between drills, we drill and sometimes stop to eat a little and have a roll-call."[22]

Other similarities abound. Virtually all soldiers craved letters from home, and the sound of mail call was likely to produce an outpouring of enthusiasm. So important was the receipt of letters that soldiers stopped all activity and rushed to the place of delivery. One Yank wrote that after mail call was announced, "every one of the boys jumped up to heare his name called out, it made the boys shout withe Joy to heare from home once more." One Northerner exclaimed after receiving letters from his wife and parents, "I can never remember of having been so glad before. I cried with joy and thankfulness." And one soldier wrote that he thought "more of a letter from home than I would a gold watch." The soldiers read and reread their cherished correspondence. Probably nothing else did more to boost morale than a steady stream of letters from home.[23]

Quakers also differed insignificantly on their descriptions of battles and skirmishes. Accounts of battles varied with the personalities and experiences of those who penned them. Most letters reflected a feeling of depression and gloom in the aftermath of a battle with heavy loss of comrades or a resounding defeat. But as soldiers gained more combat experience, according to Wiley, "the shock of both the fighting and the aftermath was considerably lessened." Many soldiers developed a degree of detachment from the horrifying consequences of warfare. One survivor of Antietam so stated: "We dont mind the sight of dead men no more than if they was dead Hogs. . . . The rebels was laying over the field bloated up as big as a horse and as black as a negro and the boys run over them and serch their pockets as unconcerned. . . . I was going through a Cornfield and I run acros a big graback as black as the ase of spade it startled me a little at first but I stopt to see what he had but he had bin tended too so I past on my way rejoicing."[24]

Some soldiers also boasted how many shots they fired in battle and the success of their marksmanship. One Yank proudly proclaimed that he gave the Rebels forty rounds in one advance, and another bragged he had expelled eighty rounds. An Ohio soldier told his wife that he had fired nearly two hundred rounds. Occasionally a soldier confessed proudly to killing. After the First Battle of Manassas one raw recruit wrote his father that "I had the pleasure of shooting three rebels dead and wounding another." Such bragging, however, was the exception rather than the rule. According to Wiley, some "preferred not to know the results of their fire."[25]

Undoubtedly, army life fostered an environment fraught with immoral influences. Preservation of moral traditions was a continuing struggle as swearing, gambling, stealing, womanizing, drinking, and other degenerating inducements tempted the soldiers at every turn. A soldier from Vermont wrote, "I will be a perfect Barbarian if I Should Stay hear 3 years." A Yank from Illinois similarly reported: "If there is any place on God's fair earth where wickedness 'stalketh abroad in daylight,' it is in the army. . . . Ninety-nine men out of every hundred are profane swearers . . . hundreds of young men . . . devote all their leisure time to [gambling]."[26]

Hundreds of other Yanks likewise testified. A Baltimore recruit wrote home that camp was "a hard school" and his comrades had been "ruined in morals and in health for they learning everything bad and nothing good." Later he reported that as for morals the army "is a graveyard for them." And one more soldier from Tennessee lamented to a brother about to join the ranks: "The army is the worst place in the world to learn bad habits of all kinds. there is several men in this Regt when they enlisted they were nice respectable men and belonged to the Church of God. but now where are they? they are ruined men." Wiley concluded, however, that men did not behave badly merely because they were soldiers. Many men came out of the military just as good as when they enlisted, some even better, but evil generally triumphed over good. Wiley claimed that loose morals resulted mainly from "the removal of accustomed restraints and associations, the urge to experiment with the forbidden, the desire to escape boredom," and the lack of adequate religious and recreational opportunities.[27]

The much maligned army diet also created opportunities for disciplinary problems within the ranks. Generally speaking, the men were well fed, but the fare was not always consistent and had little variety, especially during long marches and battles. The most common method of supplementing army rations was foraging—the confiscation of food and supplies from the Rebels. Although usually approved and organized by those in command, army officers were generally unsuccessful in controlling unauthorized foraging, and the men made great sport of it, often referring to their appropriations as "wild game." One Northerner bragged that when his compatriots "find a hog they down him & skin him & call it possum & it is very good eating for a hungry man." A Wisconsin surgeon wrote similarly: "Hogs run wild in the woods here. . . . Every hog seen is 'a wild hog' of course & in soldier parlance 'a slow deer' and very few escape alive." An Ohio soldier who uncontrollably chased chickens quipped upon their capture that "they are always sure to cackle at the Stars and Stripes and that would not do."[28]

In conclusion, it appears as though Quaker boys participated in many of the same activities as their comrades during the war. In addition, their reactions to military life, thoughts, fears, and hopes mirrored those with whom they commiserated. While religious training may have helped Quakers deter temptation, it is impossible to ascertain to what degree that was a factor. On the average, from the Quaker writings available, Friends' actions in wartime were indistinguishable from non-Friends.

# 5

# The Home Front

QUAKERS who remained on the home front during the Civil War faced a dilemma not unlike that which confronted the Quaker soldiers. Although the monthly meetings generally frowned upon overt support of the war, Friends quickly realized the needs of the government and of the soldiers and their families and, in the words of historian Margaret E. Hirst, showed a "loyal desire to serve the country and to relieve the sufferings of war." In June 1861 John Greenleaf Whittier, a particularly influential Quaker, issued a circular letter in which he called upon Friends to "mitigate the sufferings of our countrymen, to visit and aid the sick and the wounded, to relieve the necessities of the widow and the orphan."[1] Research supports Hirst's assertion and shows that a sizable number of Indiana Quakers, perhaps prompted by Whittier's humanitarian plea, answered the poet's call for duty. Furthermore, not only did Quakers volunteer to help ease the sufferings of war, but they also supported the war in a variety of activities neither envisioned nor sanctioned by Whittier.

When the Civil War began, the North was woefully unprepared to equip an army. That army, virtually nonexistent in the spring of 1861, swelled to almost three million men before the fighting ceased in 1865. Indiana, likewise, was deficient in army supplies and the necessary supply organization but was burdened, as were the remaining Union states, with the responsibility of equipping its volunteers for the first few months of the war. In order to correct the shortage of war matériel, the 1861 special session of the Indiana legislature appropriated $500,000 to procure arms for twenty thousand men. Robert Dale Owen, appointed by Governor Oliver P. Morton as agent of the state, was given the arduous task of purchasing such weapons. Owen, who remained in this important position until February 1864, bought a total of thirty thousand English Enfield rifles and other quantities of arms for the state. Governor Morton also established a state arsenal to manufacture ammunition. As no state funds had been allocated to finance the arsenal, arrangements were made to pay for buildings, materials, and wages on credit until the federal government reimbursed the state.[2]

Rifles and ammunition, however, comprised only a minute part of what was required for soldiers in wartime. During the initial hectic months of the war the state's quartermaster general was responsible for issuing these and other necessary items to Indiana troops. So many Hoosier men answered Lincoln's first call for troops in April 1861, however, that the state authorities could not furnish all of the needed supplies. After an appeal from Governor Morton, the citizens of Indiana responded by donating blankets, clothing, and other necessary articles. Quakers, too, contributed in this manner. In Wayne County, for example, Oran Perry, one of several persons designated to procure blankets for soldiers, stopped at the home of Charles F. Coffin, well respected Quaker philanthropist. Although Perry did not find the distinguished Friend at home, he explained his mission to Coffin's wife, Rhoda. In response to Perry's request, Mrs. Coffin replied, "Well, Oran, thee knows that we are opposed to war, but we keep our blankets in that cupboard at the head of the stairs, and if thee should help thyself thee knows I would not feel it my duty to resist thy action." Perry went upstairs to the cupboard. As he rummaged through the blankets trying to find those that were most worn, he was surprised to hear Mrs. Coffin, now standing on the landing a few feet away, state, "When I go to select blankets I always take the best."[3]

A few Quakers in Randolph County also responded to Morton's appeal. At least six Friends donated money to aid the volunteer companies in the Winchester area. Knowing that Quakers, too, volunteered for armed service, it seems likely that Friends on the home front in other counties, although opposed to war, also contributed.[4]

Thus, the state of Indiana through the quartermaster general, in conjunction with its loyal citizens, worked feverishly during the first few months of the war to furnish Hoosier soldiers with the needed army supplies. Indiana clothed and equipped the Sixth through the Twenty-eighth regiments as well as a few of the cavalry and artillery units. After August 1861 an assistant quartermaster of the United States, stationed in Indianapolis, took over this demanding job. Nevertheless, Governor Morton and other state officials continued to show interest in the welfare of Indiana soldiers. Efforts were continued to insure that troops who had left the state for active service were comfortably equipped.[5]

Although the manner in which the state of Indiana accoutred its volunteers is beyond the scope of this work, the urgency of supplying Hoosier troops became even more apparent with the approach of the winter of 1861. Governor Morton, now convinced that the federal government required more than the, heretofore, temporary help from the individual states, took measures to create a systematic and sustaining effort to assist Indiana's volunteers. Based upon the success of his first appeal for help from Hoosier citizens in April 1861, on 10 October 1861 Governor Morton issued a proclamation to the "Patriotic Women of Indiana." He asked the women of the state to manufacture articles "necessary to the comfort and health of soldiers in the camp and in the field." Specifically, Morton wanted blankets, socks, gloves, shirts, and underclothing sent to Indiana soldiers before the onset of winter. The response to the governor's proclamation was overwhelming. Not only did the citizens of Indiana furnish the items, but the residents also contributed money, sheets, pillows, pads, bandages, lint, and dressing gowns for hospital use. As a matter of fact, so liberal were these donations that the quartermaster general of the state issued a circular in late winter stating that the supply was sufficient.[6]

In the winter of 1861-62 the Indiana Sanitary Commission and those of other states and the larger organization known as the United States Sanitary Commission were organized. Created in February 1862 when Indiana troops suffered heavy casualties, the Indiana Sanitary Commission, under the guidance of Dr. William Hannaman, carried on the important work of not only equipping soldiers in the field but also caring for the sick and wounded. Although primarily orchestrated by private individuals, the Indiana Sanitary Commission was an excellent example of the citizenry, including hundreds of Friends, working together with the military. All of the goods and money collected by the Sanitary Commission were voluntary donations; the distribution of the supplies, however, was the responsibility of military agents whose salaries were paid by the state of Indiana. As the war continued, the Sanitary Commission expanded into a myriad of auxiliary societies and agents located in every county of Indiana. Newspapers published not only appeals for contributions but also lists of donors and the amount or articles given. Generally, local agents received the goods in the county seats and later forwarded them to Indianapolis for distribution.[7]

In spite of large amounts of money donated by the citizenry, as the war dragged on the Indiana Sanitary Commission required more funds. During the last two years of the war this agency organized "sanitary fairs" to raise the needed amounts. Tremendously successful, these social gatherings collected thousands of dollars for relief of the soldiers. In all, from 1862 through the first half of 1865, Indiana citizens donated in money and value of goods a total of $622,620.29 for the needs of volunteers.[8]

Not surprisingly, monthly meeting records are devoid of Quaker civilian support for the war. The Friends neither appointed committees to solicit donations nor reported any individuals for giving money or supplies to the Sanitary Commission. Nevertheless, on an individual and unorganized basis in many of the counties in which they resided, Quakers actively supported the men in uniform via the Indiana Sanitary Commission. From lists of voluntary contributors published in Indiana newspapers in and near Quaker communities names of Friends were included as donors.[9]

A few Quakers also served in responsible positions on committees established to procure items for the soldiers. Stephen R. Wiggins and John Roberts, Quakers of the Whitewater Monthly Meeting, for example, served on the Richmond Sanitary Committee. In Howard County two of the officers of the Ladies Union Aid Association formed to make clothing for the soldiers were Quakers. Two Parke County Quaker women were elected as president and secretary of the Bloomingdale Aid Society, and in Wayne County three Quakers accepted appointments to canvas the city of Richmond for supplies for the soldiers. Much later in the war two Quakers served on a committee at Richmond to organize a "Soldiers' Dinner," the proceeds of which were then donated to aid Hoosier volunteers.[10]

In addition to money, Friends donated the following items to the Indiana Sanitary Commission: linen, clothing, socks, shirts, underclothing, handkerchiefs, lint, pillowcases, bandages, dried fruit, beans, soap, salt, blankets, sheets, and towels. Interestingly enough, many of these Quaker contributors also signed the Militia Enrollment of 1862 as "conscientiously opposed to bearing arms." Thus, while many Friends evinced opposition to fighting, they freely gave money, food, clothing, and hospital supplies. At least one newspaper expressed its gratitude for the Quaker humanitarian effort. In a letter to the editor of the *New Castle Courier*, a traveling sanitary agent, John H. Lozier, wrote that the soldiers would be "thankful . . . to our good Quaker Friends around Spiceland for their contributions." Furthermore, the Quakers not only supplied Union soldiers, but they also sent clothing and food to sick Confederate prisoners. One Indiana newspaper praised this Quaker endeavor: "Can such an example of genuine charity be found in all secessiondom?"[11]

Letters written by Quaker soldiers demonstrate that the home folks, especially parents of the men in uniform, not only contributed to the soldiers' needs through the Sanitary Commission but also sent supplies directly to their military men. These letters often included solicitations for food and clothing and generous thanks upon their reception; likewise, the men suffered disappointment when nothing came. One Quaker, for example, gratefully thanked his wife for the recently received and badly needed socks. Another Friend wrote that he received "some cakes and other luxures." Soon after enrolling, one more Quaker, Alonzo Marshall, quickly missed the food and comforts of home. Writing from Camp Wayne in Richmond, Marshall requested a comforter, a jug of molasses, apples, and butter. Several months later, in response to living on corn bread for a "long time," Marshall was disheartened that the articles sent from home had not yet arrived: "I think it is a little doubtful about us ever getting them now." He assured his parents, however, that if the supplies arrived "they would not be thrown away." Alonzo's brother, Swain, also wrote home that he wanted to be near when the sanitary goods arrived and lay claim to a share: "I could do justice to some of them apples and taters."[12]

Not all Quakers in uniform, however, penned approval for the work of the Indiana Sanitary Commission. As a matter of fact, one Quaker soldier advised his stepmother never to give anything to the organization: "My advice to you is never to give another *bean* to it. I have seen as many sick and wounded soldiers as the most of fellows and I have the first one to hear say that he had ever received any thing from it. If you have anything to give just box it up and send it right to the one you want to have it."[13] Nevertheless, large numbers of soldiers did benefit from the benevolent work of Quakers and non-Quakers alike.

Quaker women were especially active in supporting Hoosier soldiers. They not only prepared food and made clothing to be sent to the men in the field but also wrote letters regularly to the soldiers offering encouragement and informing them of the events at home. As previously noted, Quaker soldiers begged for news from home. Swain Marshall was no exception when he wrote that he wanted news about the fighting "for we never hear the straight of anything here." Elvira Marshall, stepmother of the three Marshall boys in the war, eagerly aided the troops. In addition to her letter writing, Mrs. Marshall helped organize a chapter of the Daughters of Temperance (forerunner of the Woman's Christian Temperance Union) and encouraged other women to write to the men in uniform.[14]

The Quakers also contributed to the war effort in ways in which the monthly meetings did not always overlook. At least two Quakers from Grant County, for example, produced offerings for selling horses to government agents who were buying steeds for the army. Another Friend wrote the following account of his uncle, who lived in Randolph County during the war, "giving" a horse to the government. Supposedly, two prominent Winchester men approached "Uncle John" and made their request. "No," replied John, "you gentlemen know my sentiments. I cannot give Thee a horse. But

as Thee come back this afternoon, if Thee finds a filly tied to
a tree up near Horse shoe Bend, take her. She is Thine."[15]

Quakers also were reported to their meetings for other
violations of the antiwar testimony. Those actions included
accompanying war processions, administering oaths, enrolling the militia, encouraging volunteering, trading in military
land warrants, and paying money into township funds for
military purposes. In addition, one Friend produced an offering for manifesting the spirit of war by reading and talking
about the war. At the Mississinewa Monthly Meeting in
Grant County, Anderson Overman condemned his actions as
Enrolling and Examining Commissioner for the War Department. Another Quaker from Grant County wrote an acknowledgment for "taking a gun & going in search of
deserters." And the father of a Quaker combatant admitted
that in an "ungarded moment" he applied for money that his
son earned as a soldier.[16]

In regard to Quakers paying money into township funds
for military purposes, a comment is warranted. The men who
volunteered for the armed forces, obviously concerned about
how their families could provide for themselves in their absence, received economic support in the form of bounties. At
the beginning of the war some state authorities began to offer
these money bonuses to recruits as a condition of enlistment.
On 22 June 1861 the federal government added a bounty of
$100 in addition to the regular pay for three-year enrollees;
by 1864 the federal bounty had increased to $300 with an
additional $100 granted to veterans. In Indiana the counties
and townships shouldered the responsibility of financing the
bounty money. Local authorities saw these monetary bonuses
as a way to avoid the draft. They soon learned that a given
sum of money paid in advance filled the township and county
quotas much more rapidly than a larger amount of money
paid in installments, as was the pattern of the federal government. Thus, the local bounty system, however fraught with

inequality from county to county and an encouragement for desertion and "bounty-jumping," served as a stimulus to recruitment and was seen as the only alternative to elude forced service.[17]

Trapped in a seemingly inescapable dilemma, those Quakers who expressed conscientious scruples against war neither approved of the bounty system nor the draft. But by paying money into township funds Friends avoided the lesser of two evils and helped other men evade conscription. Monthly meeting records show that fifteen men from Hamilton, Grant, and Wayne counties produced satisfactory offerings for this offense. Also, two Quakers from Henry County gave money for the same purpose but, however, were not reported to their monthly meetings.[18]

One Quaker from Henry County, Caleb Johnson, received considerable criticism for accepting an appointment in 1862 as a tax collector for the federal government. When Johnson signed the Militia Enrollment of 1862 he asked the enrolling officer to append to his name the phrase "conscientiously opposed to bearing arms." An editorial in the *Richmond Jeffersonian* immediately called Mr. Johnson's attention to the inconsistency of his actions. In essence the editor wrote that those individuals who were opposed to fighting should also be opposed to accepting good-paying jobs made necessary by war. Another Wayne County newspaper, the *Broad Axe of Freedom*, however, rose to Johnson's defense in accepting the appointment. The editor of this publication asserted that Johnson was appointed to the government position long before the requirement to register for the draft was in force. Nevertheless, Johnson apparently received more disapproval than he could accept; soon after the vitriolic attack he declined the assignment.[19]

One Quaker, however, did work as an employee of the federal government as a tax collector. This Friend, disappointed that he was unable to enroll for military duty because

of his critically ill wife, found a way to serve his country when
he accepted an appointment as collector of the internal revenue for the eleventh congressional district of Indiana. In as-
senting to this position, this Quaker felt that "he was doing
*some* good to his government, in collecting and forwarding to
Washington the Revenue so much needed to carry on the
war."[20]

Although the Society of Friends understandably did not
contribute to the military establishment in any organized endeavor, Quakers did systematically try to mitigate the sufferings of war for both the soldiers and the civilian population.
Quakers in Lynn, Indiana, for instance, declined to give to
any war fund; they did, however, send supplies of warm underclothing to inmates of hospitals. The wife of Charles F.
Coffin, also concerned about the welfare of the soldiers, cared
for wounded and disabled soldiers and worked hard to find
employment for them.[21]

For the men in uniform Quaker church records and other
sources show that Friends distributed Bibles and thousands
of pages of religious tracts in hospitals, camps, and in the
field. Although Quakers acknowledged that in many ways
the Society could not participate in the war, they believed that
they should help the sick and wounded combatants in this
manner. The Friends' purpose was to make the soldiers'
"weary hours pass away pleasantly, and . . . to be instrumental
in turning their minds to serious reflection upon death and
eternity." Very early in the war Charles F. Coffin, for example, delivered a large basket of Bibles to Camp Morton.
In his first quarterly chaplain's report, O. V. Lemon of the
Thirty-sixth Regiment wrote that forty-five Bibles, nine
hundred New Testaments, and fifteen thousand religious
pamphlets had been distributed to the soldiers from donations
by the Society of Friends in Richmond. Quakers similarly
gave to hospitalized sick and wounded Confederate soldiers
and prisoners of war.[22]

The responsibility for raising the needed money for buying and distributing spiritual literature rested with the local book and tract committees formed in every monthly meeting. Under the auspices of the Indiana Yearly Meeting's Central Book and Tract Committee, these local committees reported annually to their monthly meetings. Although most of the local committees' yearly accounts simply stated that they had attended to their obligation with few particulars, some of them reported their activities in great detail. The Book and Tract Committee of the Milford Monthly Meeting in Wayne County, for example, reported early in 1865 that it had distributed 37,243 religious tracts to soldiers during the preceding year. The literature was dispensed in the following manner:

| | |
|---|---:|
| To soldiers in cars passing through the state | 1090 |
| To hospitals in Louisville, Ky. | 24500 |
| To hospitals in New Albany | 5000 |
| To hospitals in Jeffersonville | 3000 |
| To barracks | 500 |
| To soldiers on cars mostly in Indiana | 876 |
| To barracks in Louisville and Indianapolis | 320 |
| To rebel officers | 100 |
| To rebel prisoners | 757 |
| To soldiers in Ohio | 1000 |
| To soldiers in Memphis, Tennessee | 100 |

The Plainfield Monthly Meeting in Hendricks County recorded in 1864 that 4,400 pages of religious reading had been sent to Clarksville, Tennessee. The Bridgeport Monthly Meeting in Marion County distributed 11,310 pious tracts mostly among prisoners of war.[23]

Occasionally the book and tract committees forwarded other types of printed material and needed items to soldiers. The Fairfield Monthly Meeting in Hendricks County, for ex-

ample, collected and sent articles of clothing for the sick and
wounded combatants at Indianapolis. The Friends of the
White Lick Monthly Meeting in Morgan County raised
$26.15 to supply Confederate prisoners at Indianapolis not
only with Bibles and tracts but also with spelling books and
primary readers.[24]

The Central Book and Tract Committee of the Indiana
Yearly Meeting met quarterly throughout the war, recorded
the summation of the activities of the local committees, and
reported annually to the Yearly Meeting. In 1863 this committee distributed 313,470 pages of religious tracts. The
pamphlets were usually given directly to specific regiments,
hospitals, and prisoner-of-war camps; chaplains, individual
Quaker volunteers, and the Indiana Sanitary Commission as
well as the United States Christian Commission also received
the literature for dispersal. An excerpt from a meeting of the
Central Book and Tract Committee shows the wide geographical area in which it worked:

>  26,000 tracts to Prisoners of War at Chicago
>  14,000 tracts distributed by chaplains to soldiers at
>     Memphis
>  26,000 tracts to military hospitals at Evansville
>  25,000 tracts to military hospitals at Washington
>  11,500 tracts to the 69th Regiment at Richmond[25]

One of the hardest working Friends in this endeavor was
Elizabeth Comstock of the Rollin Monthly Meeting in Mich-
igan. Records of the Indiana Yearly Meeting's Central Book
and Tract Committee frequently commended her for distributing Bibles and religious literature to soldiers stationed all
over the western theater of war. According to her and others
who disseminated the Christian message, these religious
pamphlets were eagerly received and read, in part due to the
lack of any other type of reading material. Two chaplains

(neither names nor regiments listed), for example, reported that the tracts were "read with interest by many . . . and with especial profit by a few." O. V. Lemon stated that the tracts accomplished "positive good." And Chaplain Jones of the Eighty-fourth Regiment noted that the soldiers read the literature "with pleasure," and many men preserved them in cartridge boxes and scanned them later, sometimes while lying in line of battle.[26]

Other Quakers also volunteered to minister to the sick and wounded soldiers in hospitals and Confederates in prisoner-of-war camps. William Haughton of Henry County received money from his monthly meeting to cover the costs of such a trip; he conducted religious services in several prisons and one camp of soldiers. The Spiceland Monthly Meeting sent Mary H. Rogers to do similar duty. Sarah Smith, very active in distributing religious literature, also performed religious visitation for the soldiers on four different occasions. And Barnabas C. Hobbs of the Bloomfield Monthly Meeting in Parke County visited hospitals in Evansville and Terre Haute.[27] Thus, while the Friends did not usually send preachers to the battlefield, church records reveal that several Quakers volunteered to work in that capacity and comforted those afflicted by the ravages of war.

No doubt a few Quakers also worked in hospitals as civilian nurses. Historian Margaret E. Hirst wrote that many men and women of the Society of Friends helped in hospitals and in the medical service on the battlefield. Empirical evidence, however, is sparse at best; the author uncovered only two pieces of evidence to support this assertion. In an article entitled "Memories of a Quaker Meeting," writer Geneva V. Noland recalled that a Quaker woman, Lide Boston, had spoken in favor of buying a piano for a Friends' school as long as "Onward Christian Soldiers" was never played on it. Miss Boston had been a nurse during the Civil War and was a member of the Grand Army of the Republic. Having seen

more than her share of the miseries of war, Lide did not want
to hear any music which reminded her of the conflict. Martin
A. Reeder, who later served in the state legislature from Randolph County, was also a volunteer nurse through most of
the war.[28]

Quakers also worked during the war years to support the
families of Indiana volunteers. Although the government paid
the soldiers for their services, the low wages and the bounty
money received by enrollees could not feed and clothe a family
for three years. Therefore, on 11 November 1862 Governor
Morton, always concerned about the welfare of soldiers and
their families, issued an "Appeal to the People of the State of
Indiana" to offer assistance to soldiers' families. Just as contributions to the Indiana Sanitary Commission were voluntary, so were donations to the various societies that expanded
throughout the state of Indiana for this purpose. While it is
impossible to assess the degree to which the Quakers supported this venture, research shows that many Friends gave
to these organizations. At least one Friend, Isaac Wright from
Howard County, also served on a committee to solicit donations for the needy families of soldiers. Throughout the
war Friends periodically donated money, wood, flour, corn-
meal, potatoes, meat, fruit, beans, butter, molasses, and other
articles too numerous to list. At least one newspaper tersely
praised the Friends in Wayne County for supporting the families of volunteers: "Good for the Quakers."[29]

The Society of Friends also worked to alleviate the war-
induced suffering of white refugees from the South and West.
At the beginning of the war Quakers in Howard County sent
$300 and garden seeds to the suffering people of Kansas. A
few Randolph County Friends also offered monetary aid to
the needy citizens of that western state. In response to an
appeal from an Indianapolis organization, the Indiana Union
Refugee Relief Association, monthly meetings in Jackson,
Wayne, Randolph, Morgan, Rush, and Henry counties estab-

lished committees to help Southern whites, many of whom had fled northward. In addition to hundreds of dollars raised in Quaker communities, Friends also shipped clothing to these destitute people. The Quakers of the Walnut Ridge Meeting in Rush County sent over four boxes of clothing valued at $201.85 to needy Southerners. This type of relief activity engineered by Quakers, begun during the last months of the war, successfully accumulated money in amounts ranging from just under $12 from the West Union Monthly Meeting in Morgan County to approximately $300 from the Whitewater Monthly Meeting in Wayne County. Quakers of the latter meeting also assisted approximately one hundred white refugees who came to the Richmond area. Some of them remained in Indiana while others moved father west. In addition to money these indigent Southerners received food, wood, and furniture.[30]

Perhaps the most notable of all Quaker activities during the war years and those immediately afterward was their humanitarian work among the blacks, both slave and free. The Indiana Yearly Meeting, in conjunction with every monthly meeting, organized a Committee on the Concerns of the People of Color to aid enslaved blacks, and after emancipation, established freedmen's committees. Monthly meeting records are rife with reports of these two committees as Quakers toiled relentlessly to relieve the black man's impoverished existence. The Friends generously gave money, clothing, seeds, vegetables, and other provisions to needy blacks through their local committees and the Executive Committee for Freedmen of the Indiana Yearly Meeting. Quakers also offered spiritual guidance when, in response to a circular from the Indiana Bible Association, they donated money to purchase Bibles to be disseminated among blacks. Similarly, Quakers contributed money to the Central Book and Tract Committee; these funds procured religious pamphlets and distributed them among the Negroes.[31]

While most Friends who gave support to the blacks did so while remaining on the home front, several Quakers from the counties of Hendricks, Grant, Parke, Wayne, Randolph, and Morgan volunteered to go south and work among the freed people. Elkanah Beard of the Cherry Grove Monthly Meeting in Randolph County, for example, received permission to go south to work as a missionary among the freed blacks; upon returning home Beard stated that his religious trip was "truly satisfactory." A few Quaker men and women went south as teachers of the "contrabands." An excellent example of the efforts to educate blacks was the work of Job Hadley and his wife, Quakers from Hendricks County. They accompanied Levi Coffin, the famous abolitionist, to Cairo, Illinois, in December 1862, just prior to the effective date of Lincoln's Emancipation Proclamation. Finding the blacks, many of whom had recently fled from the South, in destitute condition, Coffin made mental notes of what they needed while the Hadleys opened a school for them. Furthermore, one Quaker letter shows that at least one Friend, while not reluctant to go south and teach the former bondsmen, was concerned about his ability to perform such crucial duties: "I feel that I am undertakeing no ordinary task and one which I often fear is more than I am competent to perform."[32]

A few Quakers also worked in the Indiana Freedmen's Aid Commission. This humanitarian organization, with auxiliaries in virtually every county, also distributed money, clothing, and provisions for the blacks. One Friend, Samuel C. Adams of the Bridgeport Monthly Meeting in Marion County, was appointed by this commission at Indianapolis to travel to the southern Mississippi valley and report on the condition of freedmen who had fallen behind the lines of the Union army. Another Quaker, a minister from Wayne County, received permission to travel as an agent of the Indiana Freedmen's Aid Commission to solicit funds and clothing for the freed blacks. Occasionally as a group the Society of Friends supported the Indiana Freedmen's Aid Commission through donations of money. One of the agents of this organization, a Dr. Clark of Indianapolis, visited the Bloomingdale Friends Quarterly Meeting in Parke County and made an appeal for aid. The response was overwhelming—over $200 was collected. The next day Dr. Clark was accompanied by Barnabas C. Hobbs, a Quaker minister from Bloomingdale, during his humanitarian sojourn to a Methodist church. One of the distributing agents of these sanitary goods was Walter Carpenter, former superintendent of Earlham College. A Wayne County newspaper lauded his selection and wrote glowingly of the work of the Quakers to help the suffering blacks: "The Friends have done much for this down-trodden race, and are . . . working faithfully for their comfort."[33]

Finally, the work of Levi Coffin cannot be neglected. Perhaps most famous for his role as an abolitionist, Coffin also worked to help the freed blacks. After his return from Cairo, Illinois, in December 1862, Coffin devoted all of his time and energy to help the former bondsmen. He wrote letters to Friends in Ohio and Indiana who collected supplies and forwarded them to him. No organization existed either for sending the articles to the freedmen or for distributing them once they arrived; hence, Coffin was instrumental in establishing the Western Freedmen's Aid Commission to implement this benevolent undertaking. Composed of members of different religious denominations, this organization was established in January 1863 with headquarters at Cincinnati, Ohio; Coffin became general agent of this operation.[34]

General Ulysses S. Grant, then commander of the southern division of the Union army, gave the Western Freedmen's Aid Commission free transportation to carry not only the supplies for the blacks but also to transfer the agents and teachers, many of whom were Quakers. Under Coffin's leadership these dedicated people worked in Tennessee, Kentucky, Illinois, Mississippi, and Arkansas. With the help of Friends throughout Ohio and Indiana, Coffin engineered the monumental task of distributing food, clothing, bedding, farming utensils, schoolbooks, and other needed supplies. His work at Vicksburg, Mississippi, was especially remarkable. Thousands of freed blacks had descended upon the Union army in the summer of 1863. Because the army was preoccupied with military maneuvers, the then elderly Quaker philanthropist organized relief camps with the help of Quaker volunteers. In so doing he kept these ex-slaves out of Grant's way during the Mississippi campaign.[35]

In addition to his work in the South, Coffin shouldered similar responsibilities in the North as freed blacks came into Indiana and Ohio. In the fall of 1863 the idea of creating a Freedmen's Bureau was being discussed in Washington. President Abraham Lincoln favored the concept and invited members from the different freedmen's associations in the Northern states to come to the nation's capital and attempt to influence members of Congress in this matter. Therefore, in December 1863 delegates from associations of Boston, New York, Philadelphia, Cincinnati, and Chicago met in Washington; Coffin was one of the representatives from the Cincinnati organization. After one week of meetings with the president, cabinet heads, and members of Congress, these men effectively persuaded several senators and representatives to bring a freedmen's bill before Congress.[36]

Members of the Society of Friends participated in a variety of activities during the Civil War. Some of these ventures were those in which one might expect Quakers to become involved, especially their work among the blacks and caring for sick and wounded soldiers. As the emphasis in the historical literature pertaining to the Quakers in the Civil War is upon these humanitarian efforts, this is certainly understandable. But perhaps just as important and unsuspected were Friends' contributions to the war in ways frowned upon by the monthly meetings. These actions included selling horses to the government for military purposes, paying money into a fund to stimulate enlistments, and other reported activities. Interestingly enough, although several Quakers produced acknowledgments for violating the peace testimony, only one Friend was disowned for a war-related breach of faith.[37] Quaker actions in support of the conflict, largely unforeseen for a religious group that expressed principles of pacifism, show that many Friends, once the war began, would not turn their backs on their fellow man. Unfortunately for historians and others interested in the story of the Quakers in Indiana during the Civil War, the degree to which Friends on the home front supported the hostilities, unlike those who enrolled for military duty and whose records are available, is probably not fully determinable.

# 6

# Quaker Opposition to the War

T HE CONSTITUTIONAL and legal ramifications of the Quaker pacifistic principles survived the first year of the war untested. Sufficient numbers of men, including a sizable contingent from the Society of Friends, volunteered for military duty and obviated the need for conscription. Moreover, contributions of money, clothing, food, and other provisions to support the soldiers were, likewise, not compulsory. Thus, those Quakers who elected to oppose all overt support of the war were not forced to compromise the peace testimony, and their conscientious beliefs were preserved intact.

But the year 1862 proved to be different. Despite predictions for a short war, the fighting continued. As the war dragged on, and the stark realities of death and destruction became all too apparent, enthusiasm for the soldier's life flagged. Ineffective recruitment in the second year of the conflict also resulted from the slow progress of the Union army in the field. The fire of enlistment had ebbed so sharply by the summer of 1862 that the draft became an "imperative necessity" to replenish depleted ranks. Therefore, Congress, on 17 July 1862, passed the Federal Militia Act. This legislation required the enrollment of all able-bodied male citizens between the ages of eighteen and forty-five in the state militia. Although the responsibility for registration belonged to the states, the act provided for the intervention of the president to execute the law in the event that the states were unable to do so. Upon approval of the War Department, Governor Oliver P. Morton, however, modified the method outlined in the federal act and implemented his own plan for registration. Instead of relying upon the local sheriffs as dictated by the militia law, Morton appointed a commissioner for each county and a deputy commissioner for each township to oversee the enlistment.[1]

Shortly thereafter, on 4 August 1862, President Abraham Lincoln issued his third call for troops—300,000 men for nine months' duty. The Hoosier home front rallied but was unable to fill the quota of 21,250 men set by the secretary of war. The federal law provided that if the states failed to meet their assigned allotments deficiencies were to be made up by a special draft of the militia. Several thousand short of its quota, Indiana then had to resort to conscription. Drawn on 6 October 1862, the draft raised 3,003 Hoosier men for military duty. Only 742, however, including one Quaker, were actually assigned as drafted men; the remaining soldiers volunteered in order to avoid the blemish of impressment.[2]

Conspicuously absent from the Militia Act of 1862, however, was a provision for those men who were "conscientiously opposed to bearing arms," or to use the more modern term, conscientious objectors. Likewise, no provision existed for the exclusion of ministers. In spite of the fact that many Quaker men volunteered for military duty, a considerable number of Friends refused to take up arms. The Quaker attitude toward war, although sincere, potentially challenged the authority of the state. Friends repeatedly asserted that they were law-abiding citizens, but if forced to decide between violating their own consciences and the will of God or defying the state, this peace-loving sect believed that the latter was a lesser offense. Moreover, unilateral enforcement of conscription imminently threatened the Quakers' moral autonomy and could ultimately override it. One historian has said that this situation was much like "forcing men at the point of a bayonet to kill other men."[3]

Further complicating matters was a clause in the Indiana Constitution. Article XII, Section 6 of the 1851 document stated that "no person, conscientiously opposed to bearing arms, shall be compelled to do militia duty; but such person shall pay an equivalent for exemption; and the amount to be prescribed by laws." In the absence of state legislation on this matter, Governor Morton on 24 September 1862 asked the secretary of war to decide the question of commutation. After requesting a recommendation from Morton, the assistant adjutant general of the War Department, Brigadier General Catharinus P. Buckingham, fixed the sum at $200. The onerous task of devising a plan to determine how many conscientious Quakers should be forced to pay the exemption then fell to the Indiana General Commissioner's Office headed by John P. Siddall. In resolving the thorny issue Siddall ascertained that the quota assigned to Indiana in proportion to the whole number of militia was 40 percent. Therefore, 40 percent of those who signed the enrollment as "being conscientious against bearing arms" were drafted and required to pay $200 each. The penalty for nonpayment was confiscation and sale of an equivalent amount of the delinquent's property.[4]

The reactions to the decisions of the War Department and the General Commissioner varied. Several newspapers spoke out on this issue. The *New Castle Courier*, for example, a newspaper that served several Quaker communities, opined that the determinations were just. The editor wrote that those Friends who expressed conscientious scruples should contribute minimally some of their property acquired while under the protection of the federal government. While other men either volunteered or were drafted, "it would be no more than justice to draft an equal ratio of the conscientious" from whom a monetary exemption from military service is required. At the same time, however, this Henry County publication estimated that approximately $280,000 would be raised in the draft of the conscientious men: "This is certainly an enormous amount to be raised off of comparatively a few persons."[5]

The *Richmond Jeffersonian* took a different and critical view of the two-hundred-dollar plan. The *Jeffersonian*, published in Wayne County—the home of the largest number of Quaker meetings in Indiana at the time of the war—predictably wrote that the drafting of 40 percent of the conscientious class "don't look like justice and equity" as this category of men is required to do "more than their share." Citing the provision in the Indiana Constitution that excluded those opposed to bearing arms from militia duty, the *Jeffersonian* vehemently assailed the secretary of war for assuming the authority to set the exemption at $200. In part, the editor wrote, the "draft will operate very oppressively in some cases we know of—poor men, who have no money to pay, and but little property." Furthermore, some men would be unable to raise the $200 even had all their property been sold. The publication queried, "What will be done in such cases?"[6]

Other newspapers also sympathized with the plight of the Quakers. A letter to the editor of an Indianapolis journal, for example, supported the views of the *Jeffersonian*. Praising Friends for their willingness to respond promptly to all of the demands of the government, the writer attacked the General Commissioner's decision as "an act of injustice repugnant to the genius of our institutions." The *Indiana True Republican* also expressed compassion for the Friends. The editor wrote that all that the Friends wanted was "fair play and equal rights with their fellow citizens." Extolling the loyalty of the Quakers, the editor emphasized that even "injustice towards themselves cannot alienate them from their country's cause."[7]

Commissioner Siddall's decision did appear to be unjust. Many townships throughout Indiana successfully recruited enough men to fill their quotas by voluntary enrollment, thereby eliminating the need for a regular draft. The draft of the conscientious class, however, was ordered for every township in which this category of men resided regardless of whether or not the quotas had been filled.[8] Thus, some conscientious Friends were penalized prior to any regular draft.

Not surprisingly, the Society of Friends opposed the drafting of those who expressed scruples against war. Writing on behalf of the Quakers, Charles F. Coffin, well known and influential Friend, personally appealed to Governor Morton and clearly outlined Friends' objections to Siddall's plan. First of all, Coffin argued, the clause in the Indiana Constitution that conscientious objectors could not be forced to do militia duty was inserted to protect those who held that view and not to punish them. Secondly, the writers of the state document never intended that conscientious persons should be subject to a fine or pay an equivalent until called upon to perform military duty. Furthermore, no such call was made until the War Department issued an order for a draft upon the militia. If, subsequently, in the regular course of the draft the name of a conscientious person was drawn, then the clause in the Constitution provided a means for his exemption. And, finally, although the Indiana General Assembly had been remiss, Coffin questioned the legality of the federal government's action in designating the exemption fee. He concluded his letter with an assertion that members of the Society of Friends would "submit to their just share of what the Govt. sees proper" but saw the exemption plan as an "unjust share of the public burden."[9]

Barnabas C. Hobbs, a Quaker minister from Parke County, also pleaded the Friends' case in an article written for an Indianapolis newspaper. His argument against this draft, as was Coffin's, was based upon legal and constitutional grounds. Hobbs wrote that General Commissioner Siddall misinterpreted and misapplied Article XII of the Indiana Constitution. Quoting liberally from the state's legal framework, Hobbs contended that conscientious Friends were guaranteed release from any military obligation. Moreover, in mirroring Coffin's views, Hobbs declared that payment of the military exemption fee occurred only when the persons actually claimed it; otherwise, the "inevitable result of [Siddall's] interpretation of the law would be to sell an indulgence to conscientious men for the enjoyment of their opinions."[10]

Hobbs cited other constitutional protections to bolster the Friends' defense. He wrote that according to the Constitution "excessive fines shall not be imposed," that "no law shall be passed the taking effect of which shall depend on any other authority except as provided in the Constitution," and that the "military shall be kept in strict subordination to the civil power." Finally, Hobbs asserted that "all laws shall be general and of uniform operation throughout the State."[11]

Several days later, in response to Hobbs's letter, an unsigned article appeared in the same publication. The writer accused the Quaker minister of ignorance when he cited Hobbs's conclusion that the men of the conscientious class were penalized before they were called upon to perform military service. Charging that Hobbs distorted the truth, the writer proceeded to outline his perception of the facts. He excoriated the Friends for complaining about the draft. He wrote that the government had dealt with the conscientious class with "extreme leniency." The Friends, who had separated themselves into an independent class which enabled them to avoid military duty, owed unpaid debts to the government. The government also guaranteed the Quakers, some of whom had large landholdings, full protection of their property. In addition, the Constitution also protected the "peculiar" religious beliefs of the Society. The writer rhetorically asked, "In return for all this, is there nothing due from them to the Government? Have those who form the conscientious class paid their indebtedness?" His answer to the latter question was an unqualified no: "They have not volunteered; they have refused to be drafted; they have not contributed material aid; they have not encouraged men to enlist, nor in any other way satisfied this indebtedness. It is, therefore, a debt still due. . . . Friend Hobbs would do his country more service and his profession more credit by urging payment than by sowing seeds of dissention."[12]

A few members of the Society of Friends appealed to Governor Morton to try to have the $200 exemption fee rescinded. Both Hobbs and Coffin submitted documents to the state executive opposing the draft of the conscientious men. The latter's statement, written in response to a suggestion by General Commissioner Siddall, was never acted upon by any official body in the Society of Friends. Nevertheless, Coffin ardently believed that it represented the views of most of the Quakers. He sincerely hoped that the question would be "quietly settled without further discussion."[13]

At once Morton referred the legal question involved to the judgment of Assistant Adjutant General Buckingham. The legalities of the dispute focused on a conflict between the Constitution and the laws of Indiana and the Militia Act of 1862, the latter a federal act. The authority by which the draft was made was solely derived from the federal law. Exemption, however, emanated only from the state. Therefore, General Buckingham decided that the War Department had no authority and could confer none on Governor Morton either to enforce the collection of the exemption payment or determine its amount. Consequently, all of the money heretofore collected, approximately $20,000, was refunded to the Friends.[14]

Although no evidence that Quakers reacted favorably to Buckingham's decision was found in monthly or yearly meeting records, Quaker letters and diaries, or newspaper accounts, it seems only logical to conclude that the War

Department's judgment was gladly accepted by and a relief to conscientious Friends. The victory, however, was short lived. In July 1863 the federal government, in need of a more effective draft law as well as additional man power, passed a national conscription law. This new federal draft law effectively excluded the states from the responsibility of deciding who would or would not be subject to conscription. Under the provisions of this act, all able-bodied male citizens between the ages of twenty and forty-five were declared subject to military service. Exemptions included but were not limited to the mentally or physically unfit, selected high officials of both federal and state levels of government, the only son of a dependent widow, and the only son of infirm parents. Conscientious objectors, however, were omitted from the list of exclusions. And just as in the law of 1862, ministers could not claim religious exemption. As the law stood, conscientious objectors as well as nonpacifists could only avoid military service when their names were drawn for the draft by furnishing a substitute or paying commutation money in the amount of $300.[15]

The Society of Friends never sanctioned the payment of military fines. The Western Yearly Meeting of Indiana informed President Lincoln that it was impossible for Friends to "compound, by payment of money, for a service for the performance of which they feel restrained by the commands of our Savior." Absolutists claimed that providing substitutes and paying exemption or commutation fees were equivalent to the service itself; therefore, in good conscience, Quakers could not seek relief from military duty by such means. The Society strongly urged that when a Friend received notice that he had been drafted he should ask for exemption on conscientious grounds. Should he be arrested and sent to military prison, he should submit to all suffering in a manner representative of the Society's peaceable principles, for the "more patient and firm friends are the lighter will the burden of suffering be." This attitude, advocated not only by Quakers in Indiana, was consistent throughout the geographical embrace of the Society.[16]

Quakers in Pennsylvania immediately began to take active measures to protest the offensive clause in the federal conscription act. Prior to the passage of the law these Friends had presented a memorial to Congress stating their views, and now that the law was in force they similarly petitioned the governor and the legislature for relief. When actual drafting commenced, Pennsylvania Quakers increased their level of activity by submitting to the provost marshal a statement of the reasons why Friends could not obey federal impressment.[17]

From June through September 1863 the Provost Marshal General of the War Department issued circulars which upheld the controversial clause of the conscription act. The federal government reiterated time and again that the only way Quakers could be excused from the draft was to follow the requirements of the law. The circular of 1 August 1863 is representative of the official judgment of the War Department:

> Persons having conscientious scruples in regard to bearing arms are not on that account exempt. They are not found in the list of exempted classes, and the act expressly declares that no persons but those enumerated in that list shall be exempt. The Society of Friends, and others entertaining similar sentiments, if drafted, may find relief from their scruples in the employment of substitutes, or in the payment of the $300.[18]

Early in November 1863 Secretary of War Edwin M. Stanton met with two Quakers of the Baltimore Yearly Meeting. Stanton, the son of a Quaker, was sympathetic to the views of Friends. He alerted them to the fact that a larger and more stringent draft law might be passed by Congress. Expressing sincere interest in the work of Quakers among freed blacks, he appeared willing to credit work in this endeavor toward relieving Friends from the draft. Stanton also proffered sound and constructive advice. His suggestion that Friends hold a meeting to consider the payment of $300 for military exemption into a special fund for the freedmen led to the famous Baltimore Conference in December 1863. Even though this gathering of Quakers, which included Friends from New England, New York, Baltimore, Ohio, Indiana, and the Western Yearly Meetings, rejected Stanton's proposal and reasserted their unwillingness to compromise their beliefs and submit to the military penalties outlined in the conscription law, they reassured Stanton that their humanitarian work among blacks and sick and wounded soldiers would continue. Nevertheless, a change was forthcoming. Perhaps coincidentally, very soon after the Baltimore Conference adjourned on 15 December 1863 the War Department issued instructions providing for the parole of the conscientious objectors who had been drafted. The order read, in part, that persons who were "conscientiously opposed to bearing arms and to paying the commutation money for exemption from draft, and that they belong to a religious society whose creed prohibits them to serve in the Army or to pay commutation money, shall when drafted be put on parole by the provost marshal of the district." One historian wrote that this provision was a "distinct victory for Friends and for those who sympathized with their views, and ultimately proved a solution for most of Friends' conscientious difficulties."[19]

Although Friends in Indiana were delighted and relieved with the War Department's decision, in actuality its effect was minimal. The first call for troops under the conscription act was ordered in June 1863. Indiana furnished its quota of four regiments of six months' men without delay by volunteers, and by late summer Indiana had a surplus of 11,011 over all requests for men. The president issued another call on 20 October 1863 for 300,000 soldiers. It was increased to 500,000 on 1 February 1864 and further enlarged to 700,000 on 14 March 1864. Indiana's allotment was 45,529. To fill the apportionment, 37,011 men enlisted as volunteers. Because Indiana had a sufficient surplus of enrollees to cover the remaining number of men called, the state did not have to resort to the draft under the provision of the law of 1863. Thus, Friends in Indiana escaped the draft throughout the third year of the war.[20]

An additional step was taken for the Society of Friends in 1864. The federal government added an amendment to the conscription act of 1863 on 24 February 1864. Drafted conscientious objectors were now considered "non-combatants" and assigned to do hospital duty, care for the freedmen, or pay $300 to be applied to sick and wounded soldiers.[21] This new law then effectively voided the War Department's parole orders of 15 December 1863. No longer would conscientious Friends be forced into military service, and the need for clemency was thereby negated.

Reactions to the new conscription law differed. Although the new provision may have been acceptable to some Quakers, no doubt others rejected the clause because no sweeping exemption on religious grounds was inserted. While the new amendment eliminated forced military service for the Society of Friends, hospital duty and caring for the freedmen were not always satisfactory alternatives. Furthermore, although the money was given to hospitals, the payment of $300 was unacceptable to many Quakers who possessed ardent convictions against any support of the war. An editorial in *The Friend* stated that the choices of drafted Quakers, as delineated in the law of 1864, mirrored the government's assumption of a "right to oblige the subject to violate his conscience, or to exact a penalty if he elects to obey God rather than man."[22]

Now that the drafting of Indiana Friends became a distinct possibility, the Indiana and the Western Yearly Meetings worked quickly to circulate the Society's recommendation for conscripted Quakers. Both meetings generally agreed to leave the decision to choose the proper course of action to the individual himself. The Society as a whole recognized that a certain degree of moral autonomy was important to individual Quakers. This freedom of conscience enabled Friends to follow their own judgment. The Indiana Yearly Meeting acknowledged that some members might feel that it was their religious duty to reject the provision of the law of 1864; others might willingly accept the relief offered by the government. If Friends were drafted, the meeting counseled, other Quakers should avail themselves to "render . . . advice and pecuniary assistance as occasion may require." The Western Yearly Meeting similarly noted that the question of either service or payment was given to each individual "to exercise his own deliberate judgment."[23]

President Lincoln issued two more calls for troops after the amended conscription bill became law on 4 July 1864. In Indiana men were drafted, including at least 117 Quakers, under both requests. Furthermore, these Friends took different courses of action in regard to having been drafted. Reflecting the Society's liberal stance, the majority of conscripted Quakers, 87 in all, paid the commutation fee of $300. At the suggestion of the yearly meetings in Indiana, the Quakers donated money to reimburse those who paid the commutation fee. Occasionally the amounts were raised solely by voluntary contributions, but more often the committees assigned to deal with drafted men designated a ratio and requested Friends to pay their proportions. The meetings, not always successful in compensating Friends, divided what money was raised equally among the draftees. At the Bridgeport Monthly Meeting in Marion County, for example, $1,800 was paid for commutation by the six conscripted

Quakers; only $505, however, was raised by voluntary do-
nations. In Parke County, the Rush Creek Meeting collected
only $590 out of the total of $900 paid by three drafted
Friends. And, infrequently, Quakers staunchly refused to give
any money to repay those members who were conscripted.
At the Plainfield Monthly Meeting in Hendricks County only
$3,097 out of the desired $3,938 was collected. Of the amount
that was not received, $266 was required of Friends who "have
refused to pay."[24]

A few drafted Friends responded in ways not approved by
the Society. Nine men, who declined to pay the exemption
and refused to perform alternative service, hired substitutes.
Nevertheless, once the war ended they all produced offerings
for this breach of faith. In addition, one Quaker from the
Back Creek Meeting acknowledged that he gave five dollars
to a man "who sustained a considerable loss by advancing
money to pay substitutes for the army." Another Friend condemned his behavior for paying the exemption after being
drafted. The remaining twenty-one drafted Quakers, two of
whom later died in the war, rejected all of the options in the
new draft law and enrolled for military duty.[25]

For years historians have written that some Friends suffered
unduly because of the draft laws of 1863 and 1864. Undoubtedly, these scholars have been influenced by the wide circu-
lation of incidents of cruelty that in actuality characterized
neither the general attitude of the military establishment nor
the army's treatment of conscripted Quakers. Probably the
fullest and most significant account of savagery due to conscientious objection was recorded by Cyrus Pringle in his
diary, *The Record of a Quaker Conscience*. As draftees from the
state of Vermont, Pringle and two fellow Quakers staunchly
refused to carry guns or to work in hospitals. Neither threats
nor severe punishments weakened their pacifist commit-
ments. Finally, President Lincoln and the War Department,
having heard their cases, released them from their military

obligation. Similar cases of suffering due to conscription abound. Margaret Bacon, author of *The Quiet Rebels,* for example, wrote that the passage of the conscription bill in 1863 forced Quakers to make a decision about the war. Initial lax enforcement allowed Quakers to avoid federal penalties for noncompliance. Toward the end of the war, however, some Friends were arrested and jailed for refusal to serve in the army. Daisy Newman, author of *A Procession of Friends,* echoed Bacon's assertions.[26]

The fact that some Northern Quakers endured harassment by military authorities is also well chronicled in Edward N. Wright's monumental work, *Conscientious Objectors in the Civil War,* and in a newer work by Peter Brock, *Pacifism in the United States.* Interestingly enough, virtually all of the incidents of distress encountered by Friends involved those from states other than Indiana. Actually, Wright described only two relatively minor episodes involving Hoosier Friends. The first case involved the release of three Quakers drafted in October 1862. In the second instance a Quaker, also drafted, refused to serve in the army. Governor Morton intervened in his behalf, corresponded with President Lincoln, and succeeded in saving the Friend's farm from the auction block.[27]

Research corroborates the findings of Wright and Brock in regard to actual suffering by Indiana Friends at the hands of military authorities during the war. Only one possible additional case was found. William F. Bell of the Raysville Monthly Meeting in Henry County agreed to perform military service after severe punishment. Church minutes are devoid of further details except that Bell condemned all wars and desired to have his membership retained. Perhaps Brock best summed up the frequency of Quaker persecution in the Union army. Although he emphasized that instances of brutality occurred in the war, as in the cases of Pringle and Bell, it was not official policy and was generally of "short duration" meted out by "some local military bully."[28]

Likewise, few Indiana Quakers suffered because of the actions of civilian authorities. The Indiana Yearly Meeting received no such information until 1864 when it heard a report that Quakers from five quarterly meetings had property valued at $683.77 confiscated. The Western Yearly Meeting reported no cases of suffering throughout the entire war. Monthly meeting records show only two cases of civilian harassment during the war. At the Whitewater Monthly Meeting in Wayne County, forty-five dollars was taken illegally from two members who refused to pay the bounty money assessed by their neighbors. And in Randolph County, the Cherry Grove meeting recorded that $903 was appropriated by citizens of the township due to Friends' testimony against war. All other congregations that assigned committees to investigate similar incidents reported yearly that, except for those who were drafted in 1864 and 1865, Friends experienced no suffering due to the maintenance of their peace testimony.[29]

Thus, those Indiana Quakers who refused to compromise their principles in regard to war suffered very little due to the enforcement of the three draft laws during the Civil War. Under the first act, the relatively ineffective Federal Militia Law of 1862, the order that would have created monetary hardship for many conscientious Friends in Indiana was eventually rescinded. In the second, more comprehensive, conscription bill passed in July 1863, although exemption of the conscientious class from military service, as in the act of 1862, was noticeably omitted, no Friends were conscripted. Credit must be given, however, to Hoosier volunteers. In response to Lincoln's calls for troops under this draft law, sufficient numbers of men in Indiana enrolled for military duty to cancel the need for the draft.

Not until the final draft act of the war became law in July 1864 were conscientious Friends forced to make decisions about conscription. Even then the yearly meetings in Indiana granted individual Quakers the freedom to choose the appropriate course of action. Whereas the Society as a whole opposed the payment of military fines, the act of 1864 made it difficult for conscientious Quakers not to choose this alternative in light of the other unsatisfactory options. Hence, most of the drafted Quakers elected to pay the commutation money.

Similarly, conscientious Friends in Indiana suffered only slightly at the hands of either civilian authorities or citizens during the Civil War. Peter Brock contended that in many areas the Quaker peace testimony was "well known and often respected, if not fully understood." And although the practice since colonial times had been to confiscate Friends' property for refusal to fight, by the seventh decade of the nineteenth century rigid enforcement of the law was relaxed by sympathetic neighbors.[30] The infrequency of reported cases of suffering in Indiana undoubtedly strengthens Brock's argument.

On the basis of the current research, then, it is clear that Indiana Quakers encountered only minor harassment from either military or civilian officials between 1862 and 1865. Generally speaking, Quakers who were opposed to war were able to preserve their conscientious scruples without fear of reproach.

# Conclusion

D
URING THE years of the Civil War, 1861-65, the
Society of Friends faced a serious moral dilemma.
Although the formal position of the Quaker church
was that of opposition to all overt support of the war, a large
number of Friends did not remain passive in the highly
charged environment of the conflict between the North and
the South. Even possible estrangement from both family and
the religious community failed to serve as an effective deter-
rent. The yearly meetings in Indiana repeatedly cautioned
their members to remain true to the peace testimony, and the
*Discipline* clearly outlined the potential consequences in
Quaker society for the violation of the group's antiwar stand.

Evidence implies, however, that the nature of the war itself,
rather than any internal disillusionment with the Society, contributed to the defiance of the peace testimony to a large
degree. The exceedingly emotional concepts of Union, emancipation, and patriotism overrode the calm demeanor required
for an idealistic, impartial, and uncompromising stand in regard to war. Given the turbulent climate, it may well have
been impossible to remain nonpartisan. Furthermore, the
American Civil War, unlike the War of 1812 and the Mexican
War, embattled people of the same nation and was, hence,
virtually inescapable in its effects. National conscription, for

example, a first for the relatively young United States, threw into dramatic contours the pervasiveness and directness of the war issue for Quakers. Although not as weighty an issue for Quakers in Indiana as for those in some other states, volunteer enlistments from the general society did not always suffice. Friends were drafted. Morgan's raid also affected many Quakers (and non-Quakers, too) in the southern half of the state.

A more or less direct impact of the war involved the Society's efforts to give material aid to former slaves and white refugees as they fled from the South and came to Indiana. And when bounty money was needed to stimulate enrollments, some Quakers were compelled to pay the required amounts, while others donated willingly. Thus, external factors, most of which lay beyond the control of Indiana Friends, played crucial roles in convincing many Quakers either to join the army or to contribute to the war effort on the home front.

Whatever the circumstances which may have shaped the opinions and actions of individual Friends in regard to the hostilities, Quaker support of the Civil War was not an aberration. Statistics indicate, for example, that at least 1,212 or 21 percent of Indiana Quaker men enrolled for military duty between 1861 and 1865. This percentage, however, reflects only documented cases of Quaker military service. Because the birth and death records of the Quaker monthly meetings are incomplete, the possibility exists that many more Friends may have joined the armed forces than is determinable by these records and the monthly meeting minutes; indeed, the percentage could be as high as 45 percent. And while low in comparison to the 62 percent of all Indiana men in service between the ages of fifteen through forty-nine, all other historians who have written about Quakers in the Civil War have erred in their estimates.

Quaker support of the Civil War in Indiana, then, including Friends' contributions of money and material aid as well as enrollment for military duty, was the rule rather than the exception. In fact, participation in these activities was so extensive that pacifist Friends in Indiana actually suffered very little at the hands of military and civilian authorities during the war years. Early in the war, however, Friends' suffering would have been exacerbated had Governor Morton not intervened on behalf of Indiana Quakers. Prompted by pleas from Charles Coffin and Barnabas Hobbs, Morton requested that the War Department review the legality of the two-hundred-dollar exemption fee in the military draft of 1862; as noted, Friends were released from this obligation. And although Indiana Friends were conscripted in 1864 and 1865, by then federal law stipulated that drafted pacifists could choose alternative service.

In the aftermath of Robert E. Lee's surrender to Ulysses S. Grant in April 1865, the Society of Friends was again faced with an ethical dilemma. This quandary, analogous to historian Henry Steele Commager's statement that the war did not "come to an end, psychologically or emotionally, with Appomattox,"[1] compelled each monthly meeting to decide what should be done in regard to Quaker military service. Statistics show that opinion was anything but unanimous on the treatment of ex-soldiers. During the war itself only a few meetings took disciplinary action against Friends who gave material aid to the federal and state governments for war-related purposes. Quaker military service, however, received much more attention from the meetings, and a sizable number of Friends were reported to their congregations for this offense. Of the 368 ex-soldiers who were reported to their monthly meetings for violations of the peace testimony, 220 Quaker veterans anguished over their military conduct. Fighting in the war and seeing firsthand the destructive effects of warfare served to strengthen their resolve that all wars were unlawful in the eyes of God. These men offered sincere apologies for having strayed from principles of peace and vowed never to raise their hands in violence to their fellow men. The remaining 148 Quakers, however, refused to admit any wrongdoing and were disowned by the Society. But an even larger number of Quaker soldiers avoided disciplinary action by their monthly meetings. Indisputably, the impact of the Civil War was felt not only by active Quaker participants but also by those Friends who remained at home during the war and, upon cessation of hostilities, sat in judgment of their brethren. The larger ramification is that violations of the peace testimony appear to reflect a general breakdown of Quaker discipline and signal a gradual relaxation of the code's application over the next five decades.

Thus, far more Quakers from Indiana fought in the Civil War than has been generally known. In itself this finding is profoundly important. This powerful evidence dispels the myth that has been perpetuated by historians for over one hundred years that Quakers, at least in Indiana, refused to fight in the Civil War. Since Friends were neither to fight nor show any support of the war, historians have assumed that they did not. But scholars' meager attempts to record the Quaker story in America's most wrenching conflict have been hampered by the unavailability of resource material (e.g., monthly meeting minutes and birth and death records), most of which has only recently been made widely available for examination.

It is hoped that this investigation, while limited in scope, may provide the needed incentive to probe more closely the activities of Friends in other states during the Civil War. Only then can historians adequately assess Quaker participation in the war and the war's impact on the entire Society of Friends.

# Appendix A

## Offering of Franklin Elliott[1]

To Milford Monthly Meeting of Friends:

Dear Friends

After much deliberation I have been led to feele that it is my duty to lay open my feelings before friends. I feele that like the Prodigal of old, I have wandered far from thi Father's House; and that it is only with a great effort, and with divine assistance, that I shall be able again to return to it. I, therefore wish, and earnestly ask the Prayers of Friends in my behalf. I confess that it was not true Patriotic motives that led me to take up arms in the War which has so lately been devastateing our land; But I did it manly to gratify a stubborn and rebellious spirit within me. And I am thankful that it has been overruled for good. Many times I felt and saw great power of God; and as often witnessed his unbounded mercies to his rebellious subjects; Many times I felt that it was through a miraculous interposition of Providence that I escaped unharmed where violence seemed inevitable; and I am well satisfied that it is only through the mercy of God that I have been spared to go so far in my <illegible> and wicked course[.] Seeing that I have been the subject of so great mercies of which I am holy unworthy I am determined to serve the Lord with that ability that he may give me and with the help of God, my hands shall no more be raised in violence against my fellow man. believing that all wars and fighting are inconsistent with Christianity; I wish to say here that though I learned many lessons of unestimable value to me, they were dearly bought; and I wish to warn others against pursuing a like course, for in so doing they will invoke upon themselves the <illegible> displeasure of God. Allow me to say in closing that I have expressed my feelings as plainly as I could find words to express them, and as nearly in accordance with the dictates of my conscience as I could. Many have been my prayers to God that I might have wisdom to act in this case as is pleasing in his sight. I am very anxious to retain right of membership amongst Friends. But if this confession is not satisfactory to Friends, all I ask is for them to act as they may feele to be right, and I shall be content therewith. In humble submission to God I am [signed] Franklin Elliott.

# Appendix B

## Summary of Military Service by Meeting

| MEETING | DISOWNMENTS | OFFERINGS | NOT DISCIPLINED | DIED | TOTAL |
|---|---|---|---|---|---|
| BARTHOLOMEW-JACKSON COUNTIES | | | | | |
| Driftwood-Sand Creek | 11 | 4 | 7 | 10 | 32 |
| BOONE COUNTY | | | | | |
| Sugar Plain | 3 | 0 | 2 | 1 | 6 |
| GRANT COUNTY | | | | | |
| Back Creek | 3 | 28 | 23 | 12 | 66 |
| Mississinewa | 6 | 11 | 15 | 6 | 38 |
| Oak Ridge | 3 | 7 | 4 | 2 | 16 |
| Unassigned[1] | 0 | 0 | 3 | 1 | 4 |
| HAMILTON COUNTY | | | | | |
| Westfield | 7 | 12 | 34 | 7 | 60 |
| Greenwood | 1 | 6 | 0 | 0 | 7 |
| Hinkles Creek | 1 | 0 | 15 | 3 | 19 |
| Poplar Ridge | 0 | 2 | 1 | 0 | 3 |
| Richland | 5 | 0 | 2 | 0 | 7 |

[1]Unassigned means that the author could not determine to which meeting the soldier belonged.

| MEETING | DISOWNMENTS | OFFERINGS | NOT DISCIPLINED | DIED | TOTAL |
|---|---|---|---|---|---|
| Westfield Anti-Slavery | 0 | 0 | 1 | 2 | 3 |
| Gray | 0 | 0 | 0 | 1 | 1 |
| Unassigned | 0 | 0 | 1 | 0 | 1 |
| **HENDRICKS COUNTY** | | | | | |
| Fairfield | 1 | 8 | 6 | 2 | 17 |
| Mill Creek | 9 | 7 | 6 | 10 | 32 |
| Plainfield | 7 | 18 | 2 | 4 | 31 |
| West Branch | 0 | 0 | 1 | 0 | 1 |
| Unassigned | 0 | 0 | 1 | 0 | 1 |
| **HENRY COUNTY** | | | | | |
| Spiceland | 0 | 0 | 21 | 2 | 23 |
| Duck Creek | 1 | 0 | 21 | 4 | 26 |
| Hopewell | 3 | 1 | 8 | 7 | 19 |
| Raysville | 3 | 6 | 5 | 0 | 14 |
| Flat Rock | 0 | 0 | 0 | 1 | 1 |
| Elm Grove | 0 | 0 | 2 | 1 | 3 |
| Cadiz | 0 | 0 | 0 | 1 | 1 |
| Unassigned | 0 | 0 | 11 | 3 | 14 |
| **HOWARD COUNTY** | | | | | |
| Union | 0 | 0 | 5 | 1 | 6 |
| Honey Creek | 7 | 8 | 13 | 5 | 33 |
| New Salem | 3 | 0 | 3 | 0 | 6 |
| Pleasant Hill | 2 | 1 | 4 | 1 | 8 |
| Unassigned | 0 | 0 | 2 | 2 | 4 |
| **HUNTINGTON COUNTY** | | | | | |
| Maple Grove (Hicksite) | 0 | 0 | 2 | 3 | 5 |

| | | | | | |
|---|---|---|---|---|---|
| **JAY COUNTY**<br>Camden (Hicksite) | 0 | 0 | 12 | 8 | 20 |
| **JENNINGS COUNTY**<br>Hopewell | 0 | 0 | 0 | 1 | 1 |
| **LAKE COUNTY**<br>Unassigned | 0 | 0 | 1 | 0 | 1 |
| **MADISON COUNTY**<br>Fall Creek (Hicksite) | 18 | 1 | 9 | 4 | 32 |
| **MARION COUNTY**<br>Indianapolis | 0 | 0 | 7 | 0 | 7 |
| Bridgeport | 0 | 0 | 1 | 0 | 1 |
| Beech Grove | 0 | 0 | 0 | 1 | 1 |
| Unassigned | 0 | 0 | 0 | 1 | 1 |
| **MIAMI COUNTY**<br>Pipe Creek | 5 | 4 | 3 | 1 | 13 |
| **MONTGOMERY COUNTY**<br>Sugar River | 0 | 2 | 4 | 2 | 8 |
| **MORGAN COUNTY**<br>White Lick | 11 | 2 | 13 | 9 | 35 |
| West Union | 7 | 4 | 11 | 6 | 28 |
| Unassigned | 0 | 0 | 1 | 0 | 1 |
| **ORANGE COUNTY**<br>Lick Creek[2] | 0 | 0 | 52 | 11 | 63 |

[2]The Men's Minutes for Lick Creek Monthly Meeting have been lost. There were no disownments or offerings noted in the *Abstracts* by Heiss.

| MEETING | DISOWNMENTS | OFFERINGS | NOT DISCIPLINED | DIED | TOTAL |
|---|---|---|---|---|---|
| PARKE COUNTY | | | | | |
| Rocky Run | 1 | 0 | 0 | 0 | 1 |
| Rush Creek | 4 | 3 | 5 | 8 | 20 |
| Bloomfield | 2 | 3 | 35 | 11 | 51 |
| Unassigned | 0 | 0 | 0 | 2 | 2 |
| PORTER COUNTY | | | | | |
| Unassigned | 0 | 0 | 0 | 2 | 2 |
| RANDOLPH COUNTY | | | | | |
| Sparrow Creek | 2 | 0 | 16 | 4 | 22 |
| White River | 0 | 4 | 14 | 3 | 21 |
| Cherry Grove | 0 | 0 | 15 | 6 | 21 |
| Jericho | 0 | 0 | 7 | 6 | 13 |
| Unassigned | 0 | 0 | 2 | 0 | 2 |
| RUSH COUNTY | | | | | |
| Walnut Ridge | 8 | 5 | 11 | 8 | 32 |
| Carthage | 0 | 0 | 0 | 1 | 1 |
| Unassigned | 0 | 0 | 0 | 2 | 2 |
| ST. JOSEPH COUNTY | | | | | |
| Unassigned | 0 | 0 | 1 | 0 | 1 |
| TIPPECANOE COUNTY | | | | | |
| Greenfield | 1 | 0 | 2 | 0 | 3 |
| UNION COUNTY | | | | | |
| Silver Creek-Salem | 3 | 0 | 6 | 5 | 14 |
| VERMILLION COUNTY | | | | | |
| Vermilion | 0 | 0 | 3 | 0 | 3 |

| | | | | |
|---|---|---|---|---|
| **VIGO COUNTY** | | | | |
| Honey Creek (Hicksite) | 2 | 0 | 0 | 2 |
| **WABASH COUNTY** | | | | |
| Wabash | 2 | 1 | 23 | 2 | 28 |
| **WASHINGTON COUNTY** | | | | |
| Blue River | 3 | 3 | 8 | 3 | 17 |
| Blue River (Hicksite) | 2 | 4 | 13 | 3 | 22 |
| **WAYNE COUNTY** | | | | |
| Springfield | 1 | 11 | 31 | 6 | 49 |
| New Garden | 5 | 5 | 13 | 6 | 29 |
| Whitewater | 6 | 0 | 16 | 4 | 26 |
| Dover | 1 | 2 | 7 | 1 | 11 |
| Milford | 4 | 9 | 8 | 4 | 25 |
| Whitewater (Hicksite) | 7 | 4 | 8 | 6 | 25 |
| Chester[3] | 2 | 1 | 3 | 1 | 6 |
| Milford (Hicksite)[3] | 2 | 5 | 4 | 3 | 13 |
| West Grove | 1 | 0 | 7 | 0 | 8 |
| West River | 0 | 0 | 0 | 1 | 1 |
| Nettle Creek | 0 | 0 | 1 | 0 | 1 |
| Center | 0 | 0 | 0 | 1 | 1 |
| Fairfield | 0 | 0 | 0 | 1 | 1 |
| Unassigned | 0 | 0 | 7 | 2 | 9 |
| **COUNTY UNKNOWN** | 0 | 0 | 7 | 0 | 7 |
| TOTAL | 148 | 220 | 608 | 238 | 1,212 |

[3]One soldier is marked twice; he was disowned and later died in the war.

# Appendix C

## Indiana Friends in Military Service

The following list of names is the culmination of a two-year search for members of the Society of Friends from Indiana who took up arms in the Civil War, 1861–65. The names of these Quaker soldiers were determined by several research methods. Those Friends who either produced offerings or were disowned by their respective meetings for military service were identified by a close reading of the monthly meeting minutes, most of which have been microfilmed by the Indiana Historical Society in Indianapolis and are available for examination upon request. A complete list of all the monthly meeting records researched can be found in the bibliography. Unfortunately for the researcher, a few of the original meeting books have been lost or damaged. In cases in which the monthly meeting minutes were not available, the author used the seven-volume work by Willard Heiss, *Abstracts of the Records of the Society of Friends in Indiana*. Since a thorough discussion of the names and locations of monthly meeting records is beyond the scope of this essay, that information can best be obtained by reading the introduction to the first volume of Heiss' monumental work. It includes a list of meetings established in Indiana prior to 1850 as well as guides to finding the locations of the record books and suggestions for further investigation. For a complete list of Friends' meetings in Indiana one should see Heiss' *A List of All the Friends' Meetings That Exist or Ever Have Existed in Indiana.*

The names of those Quakers who either died in the war or were not disciplined by the Society of Friends were determined by checking lists of soldiers from the counties in which Quakers resided against the birth and death records (also included in the Heiss volumes) of the monthly meetings. The soldiers' lists were either obtained from county histories or from W. H. H. Terrell's eight-volume *Report of the Adjutant General of the State of Indiana.* A complete list of county histories utilized in this manner can be found in the bibliography.

Since the birth and death records of the monthly meetings are far from complete, the author examined cemetery records of the counties in which Quakers lived. The Indiana Commission on Public Records, State Archives Division, has a file called "Veterans Graves Registration," an alphabetical card catalog, by county, of Civil War veterans buried within the state of Indiana. Each card includes the name of the cemetery where interment occurred as well as the company and regiment in which the veteran served. This index, compiled only for fifty-one of Indiana's ninety-two counties, was also checked against the birth and death records compiled by Heiss. The counties that were researched by this method include Grant, Morgan, Howard, Huntington, Miami, Jay, Montgomery, Marion, Orange, Washington, Vigo, Vermillion, and Parke. Volume 1 of Terrell's *Report* also lists names of veterans buried within the state of Indiana, but it has the disadvantage of the absence of the names of cemeteries where burial occurred.

The remaining cemetery records, encompassing a wide range of completeness and also checked against soldiers' lists, were either found in county libraries or the Genealogy Division of the Indiana State Library. County records researched by this method include Porter, Bartholomew, Hancock, Rush, Jennings, Jackson, Randolph, Wayne, Henry, Hamilton, Boone, Hendricks, Wabash, and Madison. In addition, the county recorders' offices also have cemetery records; sometimes these are more complete than those found in local libraries. The recorders of Boone and Randolph counties also have burial record books which give the names and locations of graves of Civil War veterans within their respective counties.

Finally, a few names were discovered in letters written by Quakers. This correspondence frequently included names of relatives and friends who had joined the army. A complete list of manuscript sources can be found in the bibliography.

The membership status of each Quaker soldier was ascertained by using Heiss' *Abstracts*. Any Quaker who was disowned prior to the war and who had not been readmitted to the Society before the outbreak of hostilities was not included in the total of 1,212. In the course of the author's research, between 100 and 200 names were deleted for this reason. The only exception to this was if the Quaker was reinstated after the war or was buried in a Quaker cemetery. Such cases, however, were few indeed. Similarly, names of soldiers appearing in the birth and death records who joined the Society of Friends after the war have not been included in the total number. To insure additional accuracy the names and service records of all soldiers were compared with the official record of military service kept by the Indiana Commission on Public Records, State Archives Division. If the age listed on the official record was not the same as the age determined from the Quaker birth and death records, that soldier's name was deleted. This way soldiers with common names could be distinguished as Quakers or non-Quakers. One exception to this was when the Quaker soldier was under the legal military age of eighteen. Obviously some Quaker soldiers lied about their ages in order to enroll for military duty. Thus, their official military record lists them as age eighteen when in reality they were not yet of legal age. In any case, when there was doubt as to whether a soldier was a Quaker or not, the name was dropped. Thus, the total number of 1,212 that the author has documented is the minimum number of Quaker soldiers in Indiana.

The impossibility of footnoting each source as it is used in the following sketches is readily apparent; the reader must consult the bibliography for sources that were used in this endeavor. Inevitably, some information may conflict with that contained in one or more sources. Some references proved reliable for certain kinds of facts but less so for other data. In conflicting situations the information from what the author deemed the most reliable source was used.

Finally, in amassing the following information some errors are unavoidable, but the author is convinced that inaccuracy has been kept to a minimum. What follows explains what kind of information is included in each brief portrait, and how it was obtained. The order in which the following information is explained follows the order in which it appears in the sketches.

*Names*

Wherever possible, both the first and middle names are given for each entry. In cases in which only initials are used it is because no names were located. Since some names lend themselves to several spellings, the spelling used by the Quakers in their birth and death records is preferred. The preferred spelling, whether or not it is a first or last name, is given first and, when necessary, followed by alternatives in parentheses.

*Birth Date*

In most cases the birth date included in each portrait is the one given in the Quaker birth and death records. In the absence of such information reliance was placed upon cemetery records and the "Veterans Graves Registration." When no specific information was located, birth dates were estimated and indicated as: "Born circa 1833."

*Ancestry*

When known, the names of both parents are given. This information was most frequently derived from the Quaker birth and death records, but occasionally county histories included parentage. Cemetery records sometimes listed the names of parents, especially if they were buried in a family plot.

*Monthly Meeting*

In listing birth dates and parents' names, the names of the monthly meetings to which the birth and death records belonged and the counties in which they were located are given. Since the Quakers were mobile people, some names were found in several record books. In these instances, when it could be discerned, the monthly meeting to which the member belonged at the time of the Civil War is recorded.

*War Record*

Initially, the rank, company, and regiment of Quaker soldiers were determined from the lists of soldiers compiled by authors of county histories. To insure accuracy these records were cross-checked with Terrell's *Report of the Adjutant General*, the official record of Civil War soldiers in Indiana regiments. When conflicting data were found, the information from Terrell was preferred. The military records of those Friends who produced offerings or were disowned were ascertained by checking the alphabetical Civil War file located in the Indiana Commission on Public Records, State Archives Division. The absence of this information from the portraits generally indicates that no military record was found. Occasionally there were numerous veterans with the same name, which rendered it impossible to determine the correct regiment; thus, to avoid error, no information is included. Some of the Friends also served in out-of-state regiments, which might explain the absence of their names from the official rolls for Indiana. When known, the out-of-state regiment is included. The author found military records for 1,117 out of 1,212 Quaker veterans.

Most of the regiments raised within the state of Indiana were three-year units; a few, however, were formed for periods of time ranging from sixty days to one year. Unless a specific span of time is entered the unit was designated for three-year service. The rank indicates the highest grade achieved by the soldier. Since most Quakers either remained recruits or privates those ranks are excluded from the individual sketches. If no rank is given, the reader should assume that the veteran in question received no promotion and remained at the lower grade.

When known, other types of information are included in these short biographies. The age given to each soldier is his age at muster-in date, usually derived by subtracting his birth date from the date of muster. When the birth date was not known, the author checked either the veterans' card file in the State Archives Division or cemetery records to find the information.[1] The author was able to determine the ages of 1,016 out of 1,212 documented cases of Quaker military service.

As noted earlier, most veterans volunteered in the armed forces. Occasionally, however, a Quaker soldier was drafted into military service or entered his regiment as a substitute, and this information is recorded. When no information of this type is included the reader should assume that the service was voluntary. Other types of information include reenlistment, desertion, specific kinds of duties, e.g., nurse, cook, musician, etc., and any unusual war experience such as capture and incarceration in a Confederate prison.

If the soldier died in the war the date, place, cause of death, and place of burial, if known, are listed. When a soldier was discharged before his term of service was completed, usually for physical disability, the date of discharge is given. Unless this information is entered, the reader should assume that the soldier was mustered out either at the expiration of his term of service or because the war had ceased. Virtually all of the above information was found in Terrell's *Report of the Adjutant General*, in the official card file located in the State Archives Division, or in the "Veterans Graves Registration." For many of the Wayne County soldiers, supplementary material was found in J. C. Power's *Directory and Soldiers' Register of Wayne County*.

*Disciplinary Action*

As earlier discussed, some soldiers were disciplined by their monthly meetings for participation in military service. If a soldier produced an offering or was disowned for his infraction, this information, gleaned from a reading of the monthly meeting minutes, is given. If the soldier neither died in the war nor was reported to his meeting, the reader should assume that the Quaker received no disciplinary action.

*Death And Burial*

Wherever possible, the date of death and place of burial are included. The Heiss volumes contain some of this information, but county cemetery records and the "Veterans Graves Registration" were often more useful. When conflicting information was discovered, the data in the Heiss volumes were preferred. When necessary, the name of the county of burial is included.

Abbott, John A. Born circa 1840. Company D 26th Regiment; 24 years of age. Died circa 1880; buried West Union, Morgan County.

Addington, Elihu. Born circa 1818 of Joseph Addington; White River, Randolph County. Company A 106th Regiment, 90 days; 45 years of age.

Addington, George W. Born 19 September 1822 of Thomas and Mary Addington; Sparrow Creek, Randolph County. Company L 121st Regiment, 9th Cavalry; Sergeant; 41 years of age.

Addington, Henry T. Born circa 1844; Sparrow Creek, Randolph County. Company A 147th Regiment, 1 year; Corporal; 20 years of age.

Addington, James. Born 12 July 1816 of Thomas and Mary Addington; Sparrow Creek, Randolph County. Company C 8th Regiment, 3 months; 44 years of age; reenlisted Company A 147th Regiment, 1 year.

Addington, Thomas. Born 5 December 1829 of Thomas and Mary Addington; Sparrow Creek, Randolph County. Company A 84th Regiment; Chaplain; 32 years of age.

Addington, Thomas L. Born circa 1828 of Thomas Addington; White River, Randolph County. Company B 106th Regiment, 60 days; Sergeant; 35 years of age.

Alexander, Joseph. Born 18 October 1835; Lick Creek, Orange County. Company A 50th Regiment; Wagoner; 25 years of age. Died 27 November 1906; buried Lick Creek.

Allen, Isaac. Born 18 June 1842 of Charles and Sarah Allen; West Union, Morgan County. Company A 33rd Regiment; 19 years of age. Died 10 January 1862; buried West Union.

Allen, John Philander. Born 8 April 1821 of Harman and Nancy Allen; Walnut Ridge, Rush County. Company G 79th Regiment; Corporal; 41 years of age. Died at Murfreesboro, Tennessee, 3 April 1862.

Allen, Reuben W. Born 12 April 1840 of Daniel and Eliza Allen; Fall Creek (Hicksite), Madison County. Company D 36th Regiment; 21 years of age. Died of disease at Murfreesboro, Tennessee, 22 February 1862.

Allen, William. Born 22 December 1840 of Joseph and Elizabeth Allen; Fairfield, Hendricks County. Company H 20th

Regiment; 20 years of age; discharged for disability August 1862; disowned at Fairfield.

Allison, Leonidas L. Spiceland, Henry County. Company F 6th Regiment, 3 months; Musician.

Allred, Moses. Born circa 1816. Company F 34th Regiment; 45 years of age; discharged for disability 25 January 1862. Died circa 1870; buried Back Creek, Grant County.

Anderson, Joseph M. Born circa 1846 of Wright Anderson; Sugar River, Montgomery County. 16th Regiment; unassigned recruit; 18 years of age.

Anderson, William Penn. Born 8 August 1844 of Elijah and Asenath Anderson; Mill Creek, Hendricks County. Company B 117th Regiment, 6 months; 18 years of age; reenlisted Company H 132nd Regiment, 100 days; produced offering at Mill Creek.

Andrews, William Henry. Born 21 March 1844 of Joseph and Sarah Andrews; West Union, Morgan County. Company E 12th Regiment; 19 years of age; produced offering at West Union. Died 16 May 1918; buried West Union.

Antrim, John Beard. Born 25 November 1833 of James P. and Mary Beard Antrim; Spiceland, Henry County. Company A 36th Regiment; Corporal; 27 years of age; wounded at Missionary Ridge, Tennessee, 25 November 1863.

Armitage, Aaron. Died 17 August 1863; buried Quaker Cemetery, Jay County.

Armitage, Seba. Born circa 1836. Company F 34th Regiment; Corporal; 25 years of age. Died of typhoid fever at Camp Wickliffe, Kentucky, 1 February 1862; buried Quaker Cemetery, Jay County.

Armstrong, Thomas. Born 2 February 1832 of Elizabeth Armstrong; Driftwood, Jackson County. Killed in the war.

Arnett, James H. Born 9 September 1818 of Asbury and Jemima Arnett; Honey Creek, Howard County. Company L 39th Regiment, 8th Cavalry; 47 years of age. Died 5 October 1897; buried Crown Point, Marion County.

Arnett, James H., Jr. Born circa 1845. Company L 39th Regiment; 18 years of age. Died 16 May 1908; buried Crown Point, Marion County.

Arnett, Lindley. Born circa 1832. Company K 47th Regiment; 30 years of age. Died circa 1903; buried Back Creek, Grant County.

Arnett, Valentine M. Born 12 October 1821; Westfield, Hamilton County. Company D 136th Regiment, 100 days; 43 years of age; reenlisted Company G 147th Regiment, 1 year; Sergeant.

Arnold, Calvin W. Born 9 January 1836 of Benjamin and Celia Arnold; New Garden, Wayne County. Company D 57th Regiment; 25 years of age. Killed at Stone's River, Tennessee, 31 December 1862.

Arnold, Joseph W. Born circa 1844. Company G 57th Regiment; 18 years of age. Died of fever at Kokomo, Indiana, 18 May 1862; buried Friends Cemetery, Miami County.

Arnold, Michael F. Born 3 October 1836 of Raiford and Sarah Arnold; White Lick, Morgan County. Company E 12th Regiment; Sergeant; 25 years of age; disowned at White Lick.

Arnold, Nathan. Born 22 June 1833 of Elizabeth Arnold; Pipe Creek, Miami County. Buried Friends Cemetery, Miami County.

Atkinson, Thomas. Born 19 October 1837 of John and Milly Atkinson; Lick Creek, Orange County. Company D 66th Regiment; 24 years of age. Died 13 April 1886; buried Beech Grove, Orange County.

Bailiff, Henry H. Born 9 September 1847 of Daniel and Eliza Ann Bailiff; West Union, Morgan County. Company E 12th Regiment; 16 years of age. Killed at Atlanta, Georgia, 4 August 1864.

Bailiff, William. Born 11 May 1843 of Daniel and Eliza Ann Bailiff; West Union, Morgan County. Company E 12th Regiment; 19 years of age; produced offering at West Union.

Baldwin, Addison. Born 1 August 1841 of Thomas and Lydia Addison; Mississinewa, Grant County. 12th Light Artillery; 22 years of age; produced offering at Mississinewa. Died 24 July 1898; buried IOOF, Grant County.

Baldwin, Calvin. Born 17 August 1835 of Daniel and Charity Baldwin; Springfield, Wayne County. Company H 140th Regiment, 1 year; 28 years of age. Died 28 October 1919.

Baldwin, Elias. Born 11 June 1823 of Daniel and Charity Baldwin; Spiceland, Wayne County. Company H 140th Regiment, 1 year; 41 years of age.

Baldwin, Ira. Born 24 March 1846 of Thomas and Celia Baldwin; Back Creek, Grant County. Company H 8th Regiment; 15 years of age. Died at Sulphur Rock, 23 May 1862.

Baldwin, Jonathan. Born 20 November 1842 of Elwood and Phebe Baldwin; Spiceland, Henry County. Company F 84th Regiment; 21 years of age.

Baldwin, Lancaster. Born 20 September 1843 of Lindsey and Mary Baldwin; Back Creek, Grant County. Company C 89th Regiment; Sergeant; 18 years of age; disowned at Back Creek. Died 25 October 1911.

Baldwin, Sanford T. Born 2 December 1839 of Thomas and Celia Baldwin; Back Creek, Grant County. Company H 118th Regiment, 6 months; 2nd Lieutenant; 22 years of age. Died 22 June 1919; buried IOOF, Grant County.

Bales, Jesse W. Cherry Grove, Randolph County. Company D 105th Regiment; Minute Men; Corporal.

Bales, Joel. Company F 140th Regiment, 1 year. Buried White River, Randolph County.

Bales, William. Born 19 September 1819 of John and Rachel Bales; Mill Creek, Hendricks County. Company F 70th Regiment; transferred to 33rd Regiment; 44 years of age.

Ballard, Alfred H. Born circa 1838. Company E 12th Regiment; 24 years of age. Died of typhoid fever at Snyder's Bluff, Mississippi, 9 June 1863; buried Fairfield, Hendricks County.

Ballard, Asa. Born 13 September 1823 of Joseph Ballard; White Lick, Morgan County. Company E 12th Regiment; 38 years of age. Killed at Richmond, Kentucky, 30 August 1862.

Ballard, Braxton. Company C 130th Regiment. Buried Old Friends Westfield, Hamilton County.

Ballard, Henry C. Born 12 July 1839 of Samuel and Milicent Ballard; White Lick, Morgan County. Comapny G 11th Regiment; Sergeant; 22 years of age. Died circa 1906; buried Mooresville.

Ballard, Jesse H. Company H 21st Regiment, 1st Heavy Artillery. Buried Old Friends Westfield, Hamilton County.

Ballard, John E. Born circa 1834. Company K 115th Regiment, 6 months; 29 years of age. Died 24 October 1864; buried Cherry Grove, Randolph County.

Ballard, Joshua. Born 25 September 1834 of Jesse and Sarah Ballard; West Union, Morgan County. Produced offering at West Union.

Ballard, William. Born circa 1831. Company L 21st Regiment, 1st Heavy Artillery; 32 years of age; discharged for disability 26 August 1865. Died circa 1866; buried West Union.

Ballenger, John. Company B 117th Regiment, 6 months; Corporal; reenlisted Company E 78th Regiment, 60 days; produced offering at Plainfield, Hendricks County.

Bangham, Joseph C. Reported for military service at New Garden, Wayne County.

Barker, Isaac. Born 15 February 1839 of Enoch and Anna Barker; Westfield, Hamilton County. Company G 147th Regiment, 1 year; 26 years of age. Died 17 June 1866; buried Old Friends Westfield.

Barker, Joseph. Born 15 December 1825 of Abel and Margaret Barker; Sugar Plain, Boone County. Disowned for military service at Sugar Plain.

Barnard, Fernando. Born 5 December 1842 of Isaac and Elvira Barnard; Walnut Ridge, Rush County. Company C 16th

Regiment; 19 years of age. Killed at Vicksburg, Mississippi, 22 May 1863.

Barnard, Libni F. Born 21 March 1842 of John and Elizabeth Barnard; Walnut Ridge, Rush County. 3rd Light Artillery; 19 years of age. Killed at Lone Jack, Missouri, 16 August 1862.

Bates, Jonathan. Born 24 April 1838 of Caleb and Rebecca Bates; Union, Howard County. Company G 89th Regiment; 24 years of age. Died 30 January 1912; buried Friends Cemetery, Howard County.

Baynes, James. Born 30 November 1840 of Reezon and Lowry H. Baynes; Blue River (Hicksite), Washington County. Company E 90th Regiment, 5th Cavalry; 21 years of age; produced offering at Blue River (Hicksite).

Baynes, William H. Born 5 November 1842 of Reezon and Lowry H. Baynes; Blue River (Hicksite), Washington County. Company E 53rd Regiment; 19 years of age; produced offering at Blue River (Hicksite). Died 8 July 1924; buried Highland Friends, Washington County.

Beals, Enoch. Born 14 October 1841; Back Creek, Grant County. Company K 28th Regiment, 1st Cavalry; 22 years of age; produced offering at Back Creek. Died 22 January 1892; buried Back Creek.

Beck, Sylvester. Born 11 October 1841 of John and Adah Beck; Wabash, Wabash County. Company K 8th Regiment, 3 months; 20 years of age; reenlisted Company F 41st Regiment, 2nd Cavalry; produced offering at Wabash.

Beeson, Amos C. Born 29 July 1842 of Mahlon H. and Sarah Beeson; Walnut Ridge, Rush County. Company G 79th Regiment; 20 years of age; discharged 7 February 1863; produced offering at Walnut Ridge.

Beeson, David. Born 21 December 1840 of Isaac K. and Rebecca Beeson; Bloomfield, Parke County. Company A 85th Regiment; 21 years of age; discharged 7 October 1863.

Beeson, Isaac N. Born 24 April 1843 of Thomas and Elizabeth Beeson; Springfield, Wayne County. Company C 121st

Regiment, 9th Cavalry; Corporal; 20 years of age; produced offering at Springfield. Died 15 June 1919; buried West River Friends, Wayne County.

Beeson, J. Willis. Company F 9th Regiment; reenlisted same company and regiment. Died 24 February 1864; buried Quakerdom Cemetery, Porter County.

Beeson, John W. Born 18 February 1841 of Thomas and Elizabeth Beeson; Springfield, Wayne County. Company B 90th Regiment, 5th Cavalry; 21 years of age; produced offering at Springfield.

Beeson, Jonathon. Born 28 December 1836 of Thomas and Elizabeth Beeson; Springfield, Wayne County. Company D 69th Regiment; 25 years of age; taken prisoner at Richmond, Kentucky, paroled, and exchanged; produced offering at Springfield.

Beeson, Othniel. Born 7 May 1813 in Guilford County, North Carolina. Militia Enrollment Officer. Died 10 October 1897, Fayette County.

Beeson (Beason), Stephen K. Born 5 March 1844 of David L. and Hannah Beeson; Bloomfield, Parke County. Company K 21st Regiment, 1st Heavy Artillery; 17 years of age; produced offering at Bloomfield. Died 27 November 1916; buried Poplar Grove, Parke County.

Beeson, William. Born 23 May 1825 of William and Mary Beeson; Fairfield, Hendricks County. Company B 117th Regiment, 6 months; 38 years of age. Buried Fairfield.

Bell, Josiah. Born 13 March 1844 of Thomas and Hannah Bell; Hopewell, Henry County. Company I 69th Regiment, 18 years of age. Died at Keokuk, Iowa, 17 February 1863.

Bell, William F. Born 15 September 1832; Raysville, Henry County. Company K 36th Regiment; 29 years of age; produced offering at Raysville.

Benbow, Benjamin F. Born 26 June 1842 of Evan and Margaret Benbow; Back Creek, Grant County. Company I

101st Regiment; 20 years of age. Died at Chattanooga, Tennessee, 2 December 1863.

Benbow, Evan. 13th Light Artillery. Disowned at Pipe Creek, Miami County.

Benbow, Isaac E. Born 30 October 1845 of Aaron and Catharine Benbow; Mississinewa, Grant County. Company C 89th Regiment; 16 years of age; produced offering at Mississinewa. Died 15 March 1900; buried Veterans Facility, Grant County.

Benbow, John S. Born 13 October 1833 of Benjamin and Mary Benbow; Back Creek, Grant County. Produced offering at Back Creek.

Benbow, William. Born 15 March 1842 of Powel and Rachel Benbow; Springfield, Wayne County. Company I 57th Regiment; 19 years of age; reenlisted same company and regiment.

Bennett, Charles E. Born circa 1838. Company C 8th Regiment, 3 months; reenlisted Company F 75th Regiment; Corporal; 24 years of age. Died of disease at Camp Dennison, Ohio, 15 February 1863.

Bennett, Joseph W. Born 12 February 1840 of Solomon and Mary Bennett; Westfield, Hamilton County. Company A 101st Regiment; 22 years of age.

Benson, John M. Born April 1840; White River, Randolph County. Company H 84th Regiment; 21 years of age; deserted 25 September 1862; produced offering at White River.

Bevan, Samuel R. Born 19 January 1838 of Owen and Mary Bevan; Sparrow Creek, Randolph County. Company E 57th Regiment; Corporal; 23 years of age; reenlisted same company and regiment.

Bewly, George. Born 30 May 1825; Sand Creek, Bartholomew County. Disowned at Sand Creek.

Blackledge, Hiram. Cherry Grove, Randolph County. Company C 19th Regiment; wounded.

Blair, Enos. Born 31 March 1824 of Solomon and Nancy Blair; Plainfield, Hendricks County. Company A 103rd Regiment, 6 days; 39 years of age; produced offering at Plainfield.

Blair, Soloman (Solomon). Born 3 February 1829 of Solomon and Nancy Blair; Plainfield, Hendricks County. Company A 103rd Regiment, 6 days; Clerk; 34 years of age; produced offering at Plainfield.

Blizzard, William C. Born 9 November 1844 of Benjamin and Lydia Blizzard; Cherry Grove, Randolph County. Company C 9th Regiment; Substitute; 19 years of age. Died 5 January 1893; buried Cherry Grove.

Bloxson, William. Born 16 January 1842. Company I 11th Regiment; 19 years of age; transferred to Veteran Reserve Corps 13 June 1864 because of wounds received at Champion's Hill, Mississippi. Died 14 November 1864; buried Rush Creek #2, Parke County.

Bogue, Charles. Born circa 1841 of Charles W. and Sarah Bogue; Spiceland, Henry County. Company I 69th Regiment; 21 years of age. Died at Milliken's Bend, Louisiana, April 1863; buried Old Quaker Cemetery, Henry County.

Bogue, Eli. Born 12 October 1840. Died 4 June 1921; buried Friends Cemetery, Parke County.

Bogue, Jonathan. Born circa 1844. Company A 42nd Regiment; Substitute; produced offering at Mississinewa, Grant County. Died 5 October 1885; buried Back Creek, Grant County.

Bond, Enos. Born 26 October 1842 of John and Lucinda Bond; Springfield, Wayne County. Company I 69th Regiment; 19 years of age; produced offering at Springfield. Died 26 April 1868.

Bond, John. Born 8 September 1836 of Joseph and Naomi Bond; Rush Creek, Parke County. 9th Light Artillery; 25 years of age. Died at home 6 July 1864; buried Rush Creek #2.

Bond, John. Born 3 December 1824. Company I 91st Regiment; 37 years of age; discharged 6 August 1865. Died 15 April 1870; buried Lick Creek, Orange County.

Bond, Levi. Born 29 September 1844 of John and Lucinda Bond; Springfield, Wayne County. Company C 36th Regiment; 17 years of age; discharged because of wounds 4 April 1864; produced offering at Springfield.

Bond, Nathan. Born 1 March 1843 of Joseph and Naomi Bond; Rush Creek, Parke County. Company I 31st Regiment; 18 years of age; discharged 14 April 1863; disowned at Rush Creek.

Borton, Eber, Sr. Born 18 June 1815. 8th Ohio Battery. Died 2 March 1908; buried Webster, Wayne County.

Bowman, Jabez H. Born 28 December 1837 of William and Elvira Bowman; Duck Creek, Henry County. Company D 36th Regiment; Corporal; 24 years of age; disowned at Duck Creek.

Bowman, Levi R. Born circa 1841. Company F 10th Regiment; Corporal; 20 years of age; produced offering at Greenwood, Hamilton County.

Bowman, Sheppard. Born 8 September 1838 of Jesse and Mary Bowman; Duck Creek, Henry County. Company D 147th Regiment, 1 year; Corporal; 26 years of age.

Bowman, William H. Born 5 April 1835 of Jesse and Mary Bowman; Duck Creek, Henry County. Company E 139th Regiment, 100 days; 2nd Lieutenant; 29 years of age.

Boyd, Robert Hollowell. Born circa 1846 of Jesse and Elizabeth Boyd; Lick Creek, Orange County. Company B 24th Regiment; 18 years of age. Died circa 1925; buried IOOF, Orange County.

Boyd, Thomas. Company I 153rd Regiment, 1 year; produced offering at Greenwood, Hamilton County. Buried Crownland, Hamilton County.

Boyd, William. Born circa 1843 of Jesse and Elizabeth Boyd; Lick Creek, Orange County. Company B 24th Regiment; 18 years of age. Died circa 1915; buried Lick Creek.

Boyd, Zeno. Born 26 December 1846; Lick Creek, Orange County. Company B 24th Regiment; 17 years of age. Died at home 14 February 1865; buried Lick Creek.

Branson, Jacob. Born 4 May 1844 of Isaiah and Sarah G. Branson; Chester, Wayne County. Company E 87th Ohio Regiment; captured at Harpers Ferry, West Virginia, 15 September 1862; honorably discharged after four months; reenlisted Company B 137th Ohio National Guards; 18 years of age.

Braxton, John M. Born 2 August 1844; Lick Creek, Orange County. Company D 66th Regiment; Musician; 17 years of age. Died 16 January 1897, buried Lick Creek.

Bray, John M. Born 17 September 1844 of Henry and Betsy Jane Bray; Hinkles Creek, Hamilton County. Company B 26th Regiment; 20 years of age; reenlisted Company D 136th Regiment, 100 days. Buried Hinkles Creek.

Brazington, Joseph S. Born 16 June 1825; Pipe Creek, Miami County. Company C 151st Regiment, 1 year; 39 years of age; produced offering at Pipe Creek. Buried Friends Cemetery, Miami County.

Brewer, David W. Born circa 1835. Company A 33rd Regiment; Sergeant; 26 years of age. Died circa 1906; buried West Union, Morgan County.

Brooks, David H. Born 9 May 1842 of Larkin and Laura Brooks; Wabash, Wabash County. Company A 89th Regiment; 21 years of age; transferred to Company E 26th Regiment; Corporal. Died 19 January 1926; buried Friends Cemetery, Wabash County.

Brooks, James S. Born 24 October 1838 of Charles and Elizabeth Brooks; Blue River (Hicksite), Washington County. Company E 90th Regiment, 5th Cavalry; 23 years of age; produced offering at Blue River (Hicksite).

Brooks, John. Born 14 September 1836 of Charles and Elizabeth Brooks; Blue River (Hicksite), Washington County. Company E 90th Regiment, 5th Cavalry; 25 years of age;

discharged 7 November 1864. Buried Highland Friends, Washington County.

Broughman, William H. Born circa 1846. Company C 39th Regiment, 8th Cavalry; 17 years of age. Died 12 April 1866; buried Friends Cemetery, Randolph County.

Brown, Amos K. Company C 34th Regiment.

Brown, Comley. Company A 133rd Regiment, 100 days. Buried West Grove, Wayne County.

Brown, David H. Born 22 January 1841 of Joshua K. and Ann H. Brown; Wabash, Wabash County. Company H 118th Regiment, 6 months; 22 years of age.

Brown, Frank J. Born 12 February 1839; Whitewater, Wayne County. Company A 133rd Regiment, 100 days; 25 years of age. Died 6 July 1914; buried Earlham Cemetery.

Brown, George Henry. Born 29 February 1840; Fall Creek (Hicksite), Madison County. Company B 89th Regiment; 2nd Lieutenant; 22 years of age.

Brown, Isaac H. Born circa 1843. Company I 7th Regiment; 18 years of age. Died at Cumberland, Maryland, 11 February 1862; buried Fairfield Friends, Hendricks County.

Brown, Milton C. Born 29 October 1842 of John and Cyrena Brown; Walnut Ridge, Rush County. Company G 16th Regiment; Sergeant; 19 years of age; produced offering at Walnut Ridge.

Brown, Thomas C. Born 2 August 1842 of Joseph and Elizabeth Brown; Vermilion, Vermilion County, Illinois. Company A 43rd Regiment; 22 years of age; deserted 8 November 1864. Buried Spangler Cemetery, Vermillion County, Indiana.

Bruce, Willis. Born 12 March 1836; West Union, Morgan County. Company F 90th Regiment, 5th Cavalry; 26 years of age; transferred to Veteran Reserve Corps.

Brumley, Samuel. Born 13 April 1832; Back Creek, Grant County. Company F 34th Regiment; 30 years of age.

Budd, Charles C. Born 6 January 1843 of John and Elizabeth Budd; Raysville, Henry County. Company E 139th Regiment, 100 days; 21 years of age.

Bundy, Elias M. Born 18 July 1841 of Jesse and Rachel Bundy; Hopewell, Henry County. Company I 69th Regiment; 21 years of age; wounded at Port Gibson, Mississippi, 1 May 1863.

Bundy, Jorden J. Born 26 July 1838. Company A 110th Regiment, 3 days; 25 years of age. Died 20 October 1864; buried Cadiz, Henry County.

Bundy, Martin L. Born 11 November 1817. Paymaster and Lieutenant Colonel; 44 years of age. Died 17 February 1910; buried Henry County.

Burcham, Levi. Born circa 1848. Company C 43rd Regiment; Corporal; 13 years of age. Died 17 August 1865; buried Sugar Grove, Hendricks County.

Burris, Daniel. Born 7 September 1831; Duck Creek, Henry County. Company F 6th Regiment, 3 months; 29 years of age.

Burris, Daniel H. Son of John H. Burris; Duck Creek, Henry County. Company A 105th Regiment, Minute Men; re-enlisted Company E 139th Regiment, 100 days.

Burris, Jacob. Born 30 July 1836 of Stephen and Hannah Burris; Duck Creek, Henry County. Company A 19th Regiment; 25 years of age; wounded and captured in the Battle of the Wilderness, Virginia, 6 May 1864.

Burris, Jacob. Hinkles Creek, Hamilton County. Company G 147th Regiment, 1 year.

Burt, Joseph H. Born circa 1835. Company A 11th Regiment; 26 years of age. Died 12 June 1863; buried Silver Creek, Union County.

Bush, Jefferson. White River, Randolph County. Company H 124th Regiment; Corporal.

Butler, Amos. Born 23 July 1843 of Joseph J. and Eliza Butler; Walnut Ridge, Rush County. Company F 84th Regiment;

19 years of age. Died of disease 22 April 1863; buried Walnut Ridge.

Butler, Charles M. Born 27 January 1837 of William and Susannah Butler; Raysville, Henry County. 19th Light Artillery; Quartermaster Sergeant; 25 years of age; disowned at Raysville. Died 12 September 1912; buried Glencove Cemetery, Henry County.

Butler, Joel. Born 1 March 1836 of Ansolem and Ruth Butler; Milford, Wayne County. Company D 8th Regiment; 25 years of age; disowned at Milford.

Butler (Buller), John. Born circa 1825. Company K 47th Regiment; 37 years of age; drafted. Died circa 1865; buried Back Creek, Grant County.

Butler, Theodore. Born 27 September 1843 of Ansolem and Ruth Butler; Milford, Wayne County. Company D 8th Regiment; 18 years of age. Died at Ironton, Missouri, 21 October 1862.

Byrkitt, Isaiah. Company F 84th Regiment. Died 1 June 1863; buried Elm Grove, Henry County.

Byrkitt, Jacob. Company F 84th Regiment; discharged 22 December 1863. Buried Elm Grove, Henry County.

Cadwallader, Eli. Born 20 March 1825 of Thomas and Vashti Cadwallader; New Garden, Wayne County. Company C 9th Regiment; 39 years of age; drafted.

Cain (Cane), Alfred M. Company C 102nd Regiment, 8 days; Corporal; disowned at Richland, Hamilton County.

Cammack, David. Born 25 January 1846 of Nathan H. and Priscilla Cammack; Milford, Wayne County. Company K 124th Regiment; 18 years of age; produced offering at Milford.

Cardwell, Peter. Born 20 December 1825. Company G 147th Regiment, 1 year; Captain; 39 years of age.

Carey, Calvin. Born 30 November 1846 of J. B. and M. J. Carey; Fairfield, Hendricks County. 17th Light Artillery; 17 years of age; produced free will offering at Fairfield.

Carey, Charles A. Born 12 December 1845 of John and Eliza Carey; Back Creek, Grant County. Company F 48th Regiment; 18 years of age; deserted 28 June 1865; produced offering at Back Creek. Died 19 June 1876; buried Back Creek.

Carey, Elias. Born 9 November 1836 of John and Eliza Carey; Back Creek, Grant County. Company E 14th Pennsylvania Cavalry; produced offering at Back Creek. Died 30 July 1911; buried Veterans Facility, Grant County.

Carey, Jesse. Born circa 1845. Company C 117th Regiment, 6 months; 18 years of age; reenlisted 17th Light Artillery, produced free will offering at Fairfield, Hendricks County.

Carey, John J. Born 5 June 1841 of Sylvanus and Sarah Carey; Oak Ridge, Grant County. Company H 118th Regiment, 6 months; 22 years of age; produced offering at Oak Ridge.

Carey, Jonathan. Born 10 March 1831 of Zenas and Lydia Carey; Poplar Ridge, Hamilton County. Company D 101st Regiment; 31 years of age; discharged for disability 7 March 1865.

Carey, Samuel W. Born 31 December 1837 of Sylvanus and Sarah Carey; Westfield, Hamilton County. Company D 75th Regiment; 26 years of age; transferred to Company I 42nd Regiment.

Carey (Cary), William. 17th Light Artillery; produced free will offering at Fairfield, Hendricks County.

Carson, Samuel. Company F 6th Regiment, 3 months; reenlisted 2nd Light Artillery. Buried Westfield Antislavery Friends, Hamilton County.

Carter, Amos. Born 29 July 1838 of John D. and Ruth Carter; White Lick, Morgan County. Company E 12th Regiment; 24 years of age; produced offering at White Lick.

Carter, Benajah H. Born 1 September 1844 of Jesse and Nancy Carter; Plainfield, Hendricks County. Company A 103rd Regiment, 8 days; 18 years of age; produced offering at Plainfield.

Carter, Jesse B. Born 28 February 1840 of Jesse and Nancy Carter; Plainfield, Hendricks County. Company B 11th Regiment; 21 years of age; produced offering at Plainfield.

Carter, John. Born 19 April 1847 of William and Mary Carter; Mill Creek, Hendricks County. Company A 26th Regiment; 17 years of age. Died at Donaldsonville, Louisiana, 15 January 1865.

Carter, John B. Born 26 March 1844 of B. A. and Hannah Carter; Kokomo, Howard County. Company B 24th Regiment; 17 years of age.

Carter, John N. Born 17 March 1819; Bloomfield, Parke County. Company A 85th Regiment; 43 years of age. Died 29 September 1912; buried Bloomingdale, Parke County.

Carter, Levi. Born 23 March 1838 of Lindley and Mary Carter; Union, Howard County. Company C 75th Regiment; 24 years of age. Died 20 August 1905; buried New London, Howard County.

Carter, Mason. Son of James and Martha Carter; Lick Creek, Orange County. Company G 49th Regiment. Died at Jeffersonville, Indiana, 14 January 1862.

Carter, Milton. Born 7 August 1821 of Jesse and Nancy Carter; White Lick, Morgan County. Company D 70th Regiment; 1st Sergeant; 41 years of age. Died circa 1870; buried West Union, Morgan County.

Carter, Robert L. Company C 51st Regiment; produced offering at Plainfield, Hendricks County.

Carter, Thomas F. Born 3 October 1842 of Nathaniel and Martha Carter; White Lick, Morgan County. Company E 12th Regiment; 19 years of age. Died of wounds at Chattanooga, Tennessee, 31 May 1863; buried White Lick.

Carter, Vincent. Born 16 July 1840 of John D. and Ruth Carter; White Lick, Morgan County. Company E 12th Regiment; Corporal; 22 years of age; discharged for wounds 2 April 1863; produced offering at White Lick.

Carter, William. Born 12 January 1837 of Jonathan and Mary Carter; Lick Creek, Orange County. Company G 24th Regiment; 27 years of age; discharged for disability 5 March 1865. Buried IOOF, Orange County.

Cavender, William. Son of Abraham and Rebecca Cavender; Milford (Hicksite), Wayne County. Company I 124th Regiment; transferred to Commissary Department.

Chambers, Andrew J. Born 31 May 1828; Sugar Plain, Boone County. Company E 72nd Regiment; 34 years of age.

Chamness, Anthony. Born 14 March 1844 of William and Amy Chamness; Cherry Grove, Randolph County. Company K 16th Regiment; 18 years of age; discharged for wounds received at Richmond, Kentucky, 7 March 1863. Buried White River, Randolph County.

Chamness, Boaz A. Born 19 April 1844 of George and Catherine Chamness. Company C 121st Regiment, 9th Cavalry; 18 years of age. Died 6 August 1865; buried Nettle Creek Friends, Wayne County.

Chamness, Nereus B. Born 23 January 1846; West Union, Morgan County. Company D 70th Regiment; 16 years of age; produced offering at West Union.

Chamness, William. Born 2 March 1847; Cherry Grove, Randolph County. Company D 69th Regiment; transferred to 24th Regiment.

Chance, Cyrus. Born circa 1846. Company C 130th Regiment; 18 years of age; disowned at Westfield, Hamilton County.

Chance, Isaac. Born circa 1843. Company H 57th Regiment; 18 years of age; disowned at Westfield, Hamilton County.

Chapman, George. Born 31 May 1825 of William and Mary Chapman; Bloomfield, Parke County. Company F 126th regiment, 11th Cavalry; 2nd Lieutenant; 38 years of age. Died 19 August 1906; buried Bloomingdale, Parke County.

Chappell, John W. Company K 51st Regiment. Walnut Ridge, Rush County.

Chappell, Thomas. Born 23 September 1843 of John and Elizabeth P. Chappell; Westfield, Hamilton County. Company D 136th Regiment, 100 days; 20 years of age; produced offering at Westfield.

Clark, Caleb C. Company D 101st Regiment; produced offering at Greenwood, Hamilton County.

Clark, William. Born 1 September 1819; Lick Creek, Orange County. Company F 47th Regiment; 42 years of age. Died 22 July 1866; buried Newberry Cemetery, Orange County.

Clawson, Alfred H. Born circa 1841. Whitewater, Wayne County. 55th Regiment, 3 months; reenlisted Company E 107th Regiment, Minute Men; 22 years of age.

Clayton, John Alexander. Born 7 October 1836 of Thomas and Anna Clayton; Westfield, Hamilton County. Company D 101st Regiment; Sergeant; 25 years of age.

Clayton, Thomas. Born 12 November 1841 of Thomas and Anna Clayton; Westfield, Hamilton County. Company D 101st Regiment; 22 years of age; transferred to 58th Regiment 22 June 1864.

Clayton, William. Born 10 October 1839 of Thomas and Anna Clayton; Westfield, Hamilton County. Company K 63rd Regiment; 23 years of age; transferred to 128th Regiment 15 June 1865.

Clayton, William Alexander. Born 12 April 1848 of Simeon and Anna Clayton; Blue River, Washington County. Company F 140th Regiment, 1 year; 16 years of age; reported for military service at Blue River.

Cloud, Eli. Born 27 April 1844 of Mordacai and Jemima Cloud; Poplar Ridge, Hamilton County. Company A 101st Regiment; 18 years of age; produced offering at Poplar Ridge.

Cloud, Enos. Son of Mordacai and Jemima Cloud; Poplar Ridge, Hamilton County. Company A 101st Regiment; produced offering at Poplar Ridge.

Cloud, Joel. Company B 24th Regiment; Sergeant. Buried
Lick Creek, Orange County.

Cloud, Jonathan. Born 21 August 1836 of Mordacai and Jemima Cloud; Westfield, Hamilton County. Company A
101st Regiment; 26 years of age. Died of accidental wounds
16 December 1863; buried Old Friends Westfield.

Cloud, Joseph. Born 5 January 1842 of Joel and Anna Cloud;
Spiceland, Henry County. Company G 147th Regiment, 1
year; 23 years of age.

Cloud, William T. Born 19 December 1846; Lick Creek, Orange County. Company K 53rd Regiment; 15 years of age;
2nd Lieutenant. Died 1 November 1907; buried Lick Creek.

Coats, Elihu. Son of Gabriel and Matilda Coats; Jericho
Friends, Randolph County. Company I 54th Regiment, 1
year.

Coats, Gabriel. Son of John and Charity Coats; Jericho
Friends, Randolph County. Company I 54th Regiment, 1
year; killed at Chickasaw, Alabama, 28 December 1862.

Coble, David. Born 18 May 1816 of Eli and Rebecca Coble;
Wabash, Wabash County. Company I 8th Regiment, Wa-
bash Pioneers; 45 years of age. Died 13 August 1909; buried
Friends Cemetery, Wabash County.

Cockayne (Cokayne), Charles. Born 18 November 1836
of James and Elizabeth Cockayne; Whitewater, Wayne
County. Company A 69th Regiment; 25 years of age; captured in the battle of Richmond, Kentucky, later
exchanged.

Cockayne, Joseph. Born 2 March 1839 of James and Elizabeth
Cockayne; Whitewater, Wayne County. Company C 147th
Regiment, 1 year; Sergeant; 25 years of age.

Coffin, Elihu. Born 24 February 1817 of Moses and Phebe
Coffin; Walnut Ridge, Rush County. Buried Westland
Friends, Hancock County.

Coffin, Joseph L. Born circa 1845. Company B 119th Regiment, 7th Cavalry; Corporal; 18 years of age. Died at In-

dianapolis 12 November 1863; buried White River, Randolph County.

Coffin, Joseph R. Born 24 September 1845 of Samuel and Rachel Coffin; Blue River (Hicksite), Washington County. Company D 38th Regiment; 18 years of age; transferred to Veteran Reserve Corps.

Coffin, William M. Born circa 1834. Company E 90th Regiment, 5th Cavalry; 1st Lieutenant; 28 years of age; discharged for disability 15 May 1865; disowned at Blue River (Hicksite), Washington County.

Coggeshall, Allen. Born 18 October 1843 of John and Nancy Coggeshall; New Garden, Wayne County. Company E 69th Regiment; 18 years of age; produced offering at New Garden.

Coggeshall, Job S. Son of Caleb Coggeshall; New Garden, Wayne County. Company C 41st Regiment, 2nd Cavalry; Hospital Steward.

Coggeshall, Peter. Son of Gayer and Hannah Coggeshall; Milford, Wayne County. Produced offering at Milford.

Collier, Joseph B. Born circa 1823. Company A 52nd Regiment; 39 years of age; discharged for disability 10 July 1863; disowned at Greenwood, Hamilton County.

Collins, Joel. Company E 139th Regiment, 100 days. Buried Hicksite Friends, Henry County.

Comer, John. Born 3 November 1834 of William and Rebecca Comer; Mississinewa, Grant County. Company I 101st Regiment; 27 years of age; deserted 26 April 1864. Died circa 1908; buried IOOF, Grant County.

Comer, Matthew. Born circa 1826. Son of Joseph Comer; White River, Randolph County. Company B 90th Regiment, 5th Cavalry; 36 years of age.

Commons, David M. Born 18 July 1800. Company C 57th Regiment; 61 years of age. Died 1871, Wayne County.

Commons, Joseph A. Born 22 May 1842 of David M. Commons; Wayne County. Company C 106th Regiment, Min-

ute Men; 21 years of age. Died 10 April 1930, Wayne
County.

Commons, Robert D. Born circa 1839 of David M. Commons. Company D 8th Regiment; 22 years of age. Died 14
May 1879; buried West Grove, Wayne County.

Condiff, Robert A. Born circa 1840. Mill Creek, Hendricks
County. Company A 51st Regiment; 21 years of age. Killed
at Columbia, Tennessee, 19 January 1865; buried Columbia, Tennessee.

Conklin, Joseph O. Born circa 1838. Company D 75th Regiment; 24 years of age. Died near Atlanta, Georgia, 7 August 1864; buried Westfield Anti-Slavery Friends, Hamilton
County.

Conley, John. Born 20 March 1848 of Benjamin Conley;
Springfield, Wayne County. Company H 140th Regiment,
1 year; 16 years of age. Died 28 November 1933; buried
Nettle Creek Friends, Wayne County.

Conner, John. Born 8 February 1820 of William and Susannah Conner; Cherry Grove, Randolph County. Company
G 124th Regiment; 43 years of age. Died at Atlanta, Georgia, 4 October 1864.

Cook, Alfred B. Son of E. M. Cook; Whitewater, Wayne
County. Company D 8th Regiment, 3 months; Sergeant-
Major; reenlisted Company B 90th Regiment, 5th Cavalry;
Assistant Quartermaster; taken prisoner in the Stoneman
Raid; disowned at Whitewater.

Cook, Jesse. Born 13 October 1846 of Seth and Luzena Cook;
Westfield, Hamilton County. Company G 147th Regi-
ment, 1 year; 18 years of age; produced offering at
Westfield.

Cook, Jesse M. Fall Creek (Hicksite), Madison County.
Company E 101st Regiment. Died at home 25 December
1862.

Cook, John. Fall Creek (Hicksite), Madison County. Company G 39th Regiment, 8th Cavalry; discharged for dis-

ability 22 February 1865; produced offering at Fall Creek. Died 10 April 1896.

Cook, Jonathan. Born 8 May 1842 of Samuel and Mary Cook; Dover, Wayne County. Company F 124th Regiment; 21 years of age; transferred to Veteran Reserve Corps 14 November 1864. Buried Webster, Wayne County.

Cook, Jonathan S. Born 12 May 1841 of William and Ruth Cook; Mississinewa, Grant County. Company I 23rd Regiment; 22 years of age. Died of disease at New Bern, North Carolina, 14 April 1865.

Cook, William. Born 9 July 1836 of John and Mary Cook; Hopewell, Henry County. Company D 8th Regiment; 27 years of age; discharged for disability 26 January 1864. Died 6 February 1865.

Cook, William P. Company G 147th Regiment, 1 year. Produced offering at Greenwood, Hamilton County.

Cook, Zimri. Disowned at White Lick, Morgan County.

Copeland, Cyrus. Born 9 December 1844 of Simon and Nancy Copeland; Lick Creek, Orange County. Company I 112th Regiment, 8 days; 18 years of age. Died 2 August 1867; buried Beech Grove, Orange County.

Copeland, Exum. Born 22 February 1844; Duck Creek, Henry County. Company D 36th Regiment; 17 years of age; discharged 11 April 1862. Died 31 March 1912; buried Greensboro Township, Henry County.

Coppock, Calvin. Born 2 March 1828; Back Creek, Grant County. Company C 89th Regiment; Corporal; 34 years of age; prisoner of war, paroled at Munfordville, Kentucky, 17 September 1862; disowned at Back Creek. Died circa 1898.

Coppock, Isaac. Born circa 1843. Company A 101st Regiment; 19 years of age. Died of disease at Murfreesboro, Tennessee, 18 February 1863; buried Old Friends Westfield, Hamilton County.

Coppock, Joel H. Born 23 September 1837 of John and Rachel Coppock; Back Creek, Grant County. Company K 28th Regiment, 1st Cavalry; 25 years of age; produced offering at Back Creek. Died 3 November 1916; buried Riverside Cemetery, Grant County.

Corbit, Wiley A. Disowned at New Garden, Wayne County.

Cosand, Robert H. Born 30 April 1832 of Samuel and Mary Cosand; Sugar Plain, Boone County. Company G 11th Regiment; 29 years of age; disowned at Sugar Plain.

Cosand, Samuel W. Born 27 June 1843 of Samuel and Mary Cosand; Sugar Plain, Boone County. Company D 72nd Regiment; 19 years of age; disowned at Sugar Plain.

Cowgill, Jonathan. Born 7 March 1832 of Caleb and Mary Cowgill; New Garden, Wayne County. Company A 69th Regiment; Corporal; 30 years of age. Died of typhoid fever at Memphis, Tennessee, 3 April 1863; buried New Garden.

Cox, Gilbert L. Born circa 1845. Son of George and Zeuriah Cox; Jericho Friends, Randolph County. Company H 124th Regiment; 19 years of age. Died at Altoona, Georgia, 27 June 1864.

Cox, John. Born circa 1830. Company L 126th Regiment, 11th Cavalry; 33 years of age. Died 4 March 1864; buried White River, Randolph County.

Cox, John C. Born circa 1837. Company K 14th Regiment; Sergeant; 24 years of age. Died at Huttonville, Virginia, 2 November 1861; buried Lick Creek, Orange County.

Cox, John K. Born 23 March 1843 of Bennet and Elizabeth Cox; Walnut Ridge, Rush County. Company F 70th Regiment; 19 years of age. Killed at Dallas, Georgia, 25 May 1864.

Cox, John M. Born circa 1838. 9th Light Artillery; 24 years of age. Died circa 1918; buried Poplar Grove, Parke County.

Cox, Lindley. Company C 135th Regiment, 100 days; Sergeant; disowned at Sugar River, Montgomery County.

Cox, Milton. Born 11 November 1833; New Salem, Howard County. Company G 57th Regiment; 28 years of age; discharged for disability 20 April 1863; disowned at New Salem.

Cox, Olinthus. Son of George and Zeuriah Cox; Jericho Friends, Randolph County. Company H 124th Regiment; Corporal.

Cox, Thomas. Disowned at Sugar River, Montgomery County.

Cox, Walter. Born 4 August 1838 of Walter and Pharaby Cox; Sand Creek, Bartholomew County. Company F 39th Regiment, 8th Cavalry; 23 years of age. Killed at Stones River, Tennessee, 31 December 1862; buried Sand Creek Friends.

Cox, William I. Born 22 April 1838; Springfield, Wayne County. Company D 69th Regiment; Corporal; 24 years of age; taken prisoner at Richmond, Kentucky, exchanged, and rejoined his regiment; taken prisoner again at battle of Black River Bridge, exchanged, and rejoined his regiment.

Cox, William M. Company F 134th Regiment, 100 days; Captain. Produced offering at White River, Randolph County.

Crawford, William C. Born 25 November 1842 of Harrison and Olive Crawford; Hopewell, Henry County. Company I 69th Regiment; 19 years of age; discharged for wounds received at Richmond, Kentucky, 30 August 1862; reenlisted Company H 140th Regiment, 1 year.

Crow, Abijah. Camden (Hicksite), Jay County. Company E 119th Regiment, 7th Cavalry.

Crowell, Hugh Walker. Born 2 February 1847 of John and Susannah Crowell; Back Creek, Grant County. Company D 139th Regiment, 100 days; 17 years of age.

Crowell, Milton. Born 9 August 1839 of John and Susannah Crowell; Back Creek, Grant County. Company H 12th Regiment, 1 year; 22 years of age; produced offering at Back Creek. Died 11 April 1892; buried Park Cemetery, Grant County.

Crowell, William P. Born 22 May 1842 of John and Susannah Crowell; Back Creek, Grant County. Company H 12th

Regiment, 1 year; 18 years of age; reenlisted Company K 153rd Regiment, 1 year; 2nd Lieutenant.

Culbertson, James S. Born 9 May 1838; Honey Creek, Howard County. Company C 80th Regiment; Major; 23 years of age. Died 2 September 1875; buried Honey Creek.

Curnutt, William. Born 13 January 1830; White Lick, Morgan County. Company E 12th Regiment; Corporal; 32 years of age. Died near Atlanta, Georgia, 3 August 1864.

Darlington, Ziba. Born 28 May 1838 of Amos and Jane Darlington; Fall Creek (Hicksite), Madison County. Company A 16th Regiment; 24 years of age; discharged for wounds received at Vicksburg, Mississippi, 22 May 1863; produced offering at Fall Creek. Died 23 December 1918; buried Pendleton.

Darnell, Charles. Born 21 July 1827; Fall Creek (Hicksite), Madison County. Company A 156th Regiment, 1 year; produced offering at Fall Creek.

Davenport, William Amos. Born 23 December 1833; Honey Creek, Howard County. Company I 34th Regiment; 28 years of age; discharged for disability 7 October 1862. Died 23 January 1910; buried Friends Cemetery, Howard County.

Davies, Samuel. Born 29 April 1844 of Samuel and Jane Davies; Bloomfield, Parke County. Company F 126th Regiment, 11th Cavalry; Sergeant; 19 years of age. Died 17 February 1932; buried Friends Cemetery, Parke County.

Davis, Amos. Born 4 October 1842 of Spencer and Amelia Davis; Springfield, Wayne County. Company E 9th Regiment; 21 years of age; drafted; produced offering at Springfield.

Davis, Charles. Born 6 January 1841 of Joseph and Hannah Davis; West Grove, Wayne County. Company B 19th Regiment; Sergeant; 20 years of age; wounded in thigh at Sulphur Springs; transferred to 20th Regiment; Lieutenant.

Davis, Harmon. Born 31 July 1843 of Joseph and Hannah Davis; West Grove, Wayne County. Company C 41st Regiment, 2nd Cavalry; Corporal; 18 years of age. Buried Fair-field Cemetery, Wayne County.

Davis, John M. Born 12 February 1835 of Joseph and Judith Davis; Walnut Ridge, Rush County. Jackson Guards; 28 years of age.

Davis, Martin L. Born 1 September 1845 of Martin and Mary Davis; Westfield, Hamilton County. Company D 136th Regiment, 100 days; 19 years of age.

Davis, Nathan. Born 16 December 1840 of Wyllis and Ann Davis; Mississinewa, Grant County. Company H 12th Regiment, 1 year; Corporal; 20 years of age; disowned at Mississinewa.

Davis, Samuel. Born circa 1847. Company I 153rd Regiment, 1 year; 18 years of age. Died of disease at Indianapolis 10 March 1865; buried Gray Friends, Hamilton County.

Davis, Washington. Born 26 July 1833; Fall Creek (Hicksite), Madison County. Produced offering at Fall Creek. Died 23 May 1912; buried Fall Creek.

Davis, William. Born 22 September 1838 of Joseph and Hannah Davis; West Grove, Wayne County. 19th Light Artillery; 23 years of age.

Davis, William. Born circa 1839. Company A 36th Regiment; Corporal; 22 years of age; discharged for disability 22 May 1862; produced offering at Springfield, Wayne County.

Davis, William B. Born 8 November 1843 of Pennington and Hannah Davis; Fall Creek (Hicksite), Madison County. Company D 34th Regiment; 20 years of age.

Davis, William S. Born 12 March 1839 of Hiram and Mary Davis; Deer Creek, Grant County. Died 1 March 1930; buried IOOF, Grant County.

Dawes, Edwin. Born 27 August 1835 of Edwin and Sarah Dawes; Wabash, Wabash County. Died 19 December 1923; buried Friends Cemetery, Wabash County.

Day, Caleb. Born 10 May 1838 of John and Edith Day; White Lick, Morgan County. Company E 12th Regiment; 2nd

Lieutenant; 24 years of age. Died at Richmond, Kentucky, 20 September 1862.

Day, Evan. Born 9 August 1842 of William and Ann Day; White Lick, Morgan County. Company E 12th Regiment; 20 years of age. Died at Iuka, Mississippi, 27 October 1863.

Day, Warner L. Born 5 July 1835 of John and Edith Day; White Lick, Morgan County. Company E 12th Regiment; 27 years of age. Died 30 September 1871; buried Mooresville.

Dennis, Thomas Pool. Born 26 August 1841 of Benjamin and Clarky Dennis; Hopewell, Henry County. Company I 69th Regiment; 20 years of age. Died at Young's Point, Louisiana, 6 March 1863.

Dering, John. Born 8 March 1831 of Anton and Josie Dering; Springfield, Wayne County. Company D 38th Regiment; Substitute; 33 years of age. Died 13 August 1916.

Deverter, John M. Born 10 May 1838. Company A 85th Regiment; Musician; 24 years of age. Died at Danville, Kentucky, 7 February 1863; buried Friends Cemetery, Parke County.

Dewees, Leander. Born 15 January 1847 of David and Hannah H. Dewees; West Union, Morgan County. Company D 70th Regiment; 15 years of age; transferred to 33rd Regiment.

Dick, Mahlon L. Born 3 March 1843 of Isaac and Maria Dick; Union, Howard County. Company C 10th Regiment; 18 years of age. Died 2 September 1923; buried Friends Cemetery, Howard County.

Dicks, Robert H. Born 11 December 1838 of Achilles and Hannah Dicks; Bloomfield, Parke County. Company A 31st Regiment; 22 years of age. Died 13 September 1905; buried Rush Creek #2, Parke County.

Diggs, Allen C. White River, Randolph County. Company I 105th Regiment, Minute Men; Corporal.

Dillinger, Rodolphus S. Born 18 February 1832; Lick Creek, Orange County. Company A 38th Regiment; Corporal; 29 years of age. Died 17 December 1901; buried Lick Creek.

Dillon, William. Born 23 September 1835 of Jesse and Mary Dillon; Back Creek, Grant County. Company I 57th Regiment; 26 years of age; deserted 5 November 1862; produced offering at Back Creek.

Dixon, Addison. Born 26 December 1842 of Elihu and Jane Dixon; Mill Creek, Hendricks County. Company B 117th Regiment, 6 months; 20 years of age; produced offering at Mill Creek.

Dixon, Calvin. Born 17 November 1842 of Phineas and Sarah Dixon; Mill Creek, Hendricks County. Company E 78th Regiment, 60 days; 19 years of age; produced offering at Mill Creek.

Dixon, Nathan F. Born circa 1826. Son of Silas and Mary Dixon; Lick Creek, Orange County. Company G 49th Regiment; 35 years of age; discharged 22 October 1863.

Dixon, William. Born 8 August 1838 of Elihu and Jane Dixon; Bloomfield, Parke County. Company I 137th Regiment, 100 days; 25 years of age. Died 17 January 1906; buried Friends Cemetery, Parke County.

Dixon, Zimri. Company K 43rd Regiment; disowned at Bloomfield, Parke County.

Doan, Charles R. Born 6 August 1846 of Washington and Elizabeth Doan; Plainfield, Hendricks County. 2nd Light Artillery; 19 years of age; produced offering at Plainfield.

Doan, James E. Born 16 October 1842 of Washington and Elizabeth Doan; Plainfield, Hendricks County. Company B 54th Regiment, 3 months; 20 years of age; produced offering at Plainfield.

Doan, Thomas J. Born 13 April 1840 of William and Sophia Doan; White Lick, Morgan County. Company D 70th Regiment; 22 years of age; discharged 10 December 1863.

Draper, Eli. Born 5 August 1841 of David T. and Priscilla Draper; Sand Creek, Bartholomew County. Company D 67th Regiment; 21 years of age; disowned at Sand Creek.

Dwiggins, Thomas B. Born 30 March 1847; New Garden, Wayne County. Company F 124th Regiment; 16 years of age.

Edgerton, Samuel. Born 5 June 1839 of Thomas and Mary Edgerton; West Grove, Wayne County. Company E 54th Regiment, 1 year; 23 years of age.

Edwards, Nathaniel. Company D 150th Regiment, 1 year; Sergeant; produced offering in Kansas for Plainfield, Hendricks County.

Elliott, David (Daniel). Whitewater, Wayne County. 19th Light Artillery; Artificer; discharged for disability 20 March 1863; reenlisted Company I 147th Regiment, 1 year; 2nd Lieutenant.

Elliott, Elisha. Born 18 December 1841 of Isaac and Rachel Elliott; Mississinewa, Grant County. Company C 89th Regiment; 20 years of age. Died of wounds at Pleasant Hill, Louisiana, 3 May 1864.

Elliott, Franklin. Born 13 July 1842 of Solomon and Penelope Elliott; Milford, Wayne County. Company A 36th Regiment; Corporal; 19 years of age; wounded at Stones River, Tennessee, 21 September 1862; produced offering at Milford.

Elliott, Jacob C. Born 20 October 1840 of Jonathan and Amelia Elliott; Milford, Wayne County. Company C 84th Regiment; 21 years of age; wounded at Chickamauga, Georgia; transferred to Veteran Reserve Corps; produced offering at Milford.

Elliott, Joel H. Born 27 October 1840 of Mark and Mary Elliott; West Grove, Wayne County. Company C 41st Regiment, 2nd Cavalry; 20 years of age; bodyguard on General Alexander McCook's staff; assisted in raising Company E 119th Regiment, 7th Cavalry; 1st Lieutenant; disowned at West Grove.

Elliott, John. Born circa 1829. Sugar River, Montgomery County. Company G 10th Regiment, 3 months; 32 years of age.

Elliott, William. Born 28 January 1844 of Reuben and Rebecca Elliott; Mississinewa, Grant County. Company I 101st Regiment; 18 years of age. Died at Munfordville, Kentucky, 5 December 1862; buried Park Cemetery, Grant County.

Elliott, William S. Mississinewa, Grant County. Company C 89th Regiment; Corporal.

Ellis, James W. Born 9 February 1807 of Daniel and Abigail Ellis; Lick Creek, Orange County. Company A 49th Regiment; 54 years of age; discharged 26 November 1862. Died 13 July 1890; buried Ames Cemetery, Orange County.

Ellis, Jehu. Born 22 March 1833 of Robert and Ann Ellis; Back Creek, Grant County. Company I 101st Regiment; 1st Lieutenant; 29 years of age. Died at Chattanooga, Tennessee, 20 October 1863.

Ellis, Richard E. Born 3 November 1838 of Levi and Mary Ellis; Vermilion, Illinois. Company K 97th Regiment; Sergeant; 23 years of age; discharged 3 February 1863. Died 25 November 1872; buried Grondyke #2, Vermillion County, Indiana.

Elmore, Thomas. Born 10 March 1839 of Elizabeth Elmore; White Lick, Morgan County. Produced offering for military service and hiring a substitute at White Lick.

Engle, John S. Born 23 August 1834 of Joshua Jr. and Rachel Engle; Bloomfield, Parke County. Company A 85th Regiment; 28 years of age.

English, Hugh L. Born 1 January 1843 of Hugh Sr. and Mary Ann English; Spiceland, Henry County. Company B 19th Regiment; 18 years of age; wounded at Gainesville, Virginia, 28 August 1862.

Evans, Owen D. Spiceland, Henry County. Company A 69th Regiment.

Farlow, Nathan. Born 29 May 1810 of Joseph and Ruth Farlow; Lick Creek, Orange County. Company F 131st Regiment, 13th Cavalry; Commissary Sergeant; 53 years of age. Died 14 April 1890; buried Beech Grove, Orange County.

Farlow, Thomas. Born 2 February 1840 of Jonathan and Ruth Farlow; Lick Creek, Orange County. Company I 112th Regiment, Minute Men; 23 years of age. Died 3 January 1884; buried Beech Grove, Orange County.

Farlow, William S. Born 27 August 1832 of Enoch and Mary Farlow; Springfield, Wayne County. Company A 17th Regiment; 31 years of age; produced offering at Springfield.

Fawcett (Faucett), Isaac T. Born 14 May 1837 of Jonathan and Mary Fawcett; Blue River, Washington County; disowned at Blue River.

Fawcett, Joseph. Born circa 1836 of Nancy Fawcett; Duck Creek, Henry County. 20th Regiment; Hospital Steward; 25 years of age; discharged for disability 5 November 1862.

Fentress, William H. Born 24 May 1832; Duck Creek, Henry County. Company D 36th Regiment; 2nd Lieutenant; 28 years of age. Killed near Dallas, Georgia, 31 May 1864; buried Greensboro Township Cemetery, Henry County.

Ferree, John H. Born 17 December 1828; Oak Ridge, Grant County. Company H 54th Regiment, 1 year; Captain; 33 years of age. Buried IOOF Cemetery, Converse, Indiana.

Ferris, William. Born 11 March 1832 of Joseph and Deborah Ferris; Milford (Hicksite), Wayne County. Produced offering at Milford (Hicksite).

Fisher, George W. Born circa 1839. White River, Randolph County. Company C 8th Regiment, 3 months; 22 years of age; reenlisted Company G 8th Regiment; discharged for disability 16 October 1862; reenlisted Company H 124th Regiment; Corporal.

Fisher, James R. Born circa 1842. Company F 63rd Regiment; 20 years of age. Died at Terre Haute 12 September 1863; buried Westfield Anti-Slavery Friends, Hamilton County.

Fodrea, Alfred. Born 3 June 1843 of David and Tamier Fodrea; Westfield, Hamilton County. Company A 101st Regiment; 18 years of age; discharged 11 January 1864; reenlisted Company G 147th Regiment, 1 year; produced offering at Westfield.

Fodrea, Levi. Born 11 November 1844 of David and Tamier Fodrea; Westfield, Hamilton County. Company A 101st Regiment; 17 years of age; produced offering at Westfield.

Fodrea, Pennington. Born 8 September 1836 of Nathan and Hannah Fodrea; Sand Creek, Bartholomew County. Company F 39th Regiment, 8th Cavalry; 24 years of age; discharged for disability 17 October 1862. Buried Sand Creek.

Frampton, Elishua D. Born April 1844; Fall Creek (Hicksite), Madison County. Company I 110th Regiment, 5 days; 19 years of age. Died 26 September 1864.

Frampton, William. Born circa 1848; Fall Creek (Hicksite), Madison County. Produced offering at Fall Creek. Died 21 January 1929; buried Grovelawn Cemetery, Pendleton, Indiana.

Franklin, Bartley. Born 7 November 1831 of Shenrod and Meeky Franklin; Cherry Grove, Randolph County. Company D 105th Regiment, Minute Men; 31 years of age.

Frazier, Cyrus. Born March 1839 of John and Louisa Frazier; Bloomfield, Parke County. Company K 43rd Regiment; 22 years of age.

Fulghum, Enos. Company K 124th Regiment; disowned at New Garden, Wayne County.

Fussell, Joshua L. Born 9 June 1827; Fall Creek (Hicksite), Madison County. Company D 34th Regiment; 2nd Lieutenant; 34 years of age; produced offering at Fall Creek. Died 1 March 1915.

Gardner, Paul. Born 16 February 1825 of Paul and Rebecca Gardner; Silver Creek-Salem, Union County. Company D 121st Regiment, 9th Cavalry; Sergeant; 38 years of age. Died 20 March 1909; buried Salem Cemetery.

Garretson, Joel. Born 6 February 1818 of Amos and Mary Garretson; Fall Creek (Hicksite), Madison County. Produced offering at Fall Creek. Died 8 July 1892.

Gason, William. Died 4 November 1865; buried Silver Creek, Union County.

Gause, Stephen. Born 8 March 1848 of Eli and Lydia Gause; Westfield, Hamilton County. Company E 109th Regiment, 8 days; 15 years of age; disowned at Westfield.

Gifford, Bedford W. Born 13 November 1826 of William and Esther Gifford; Honey Creek, Howard County. Company G 89th Regiment; Captain; 35 years of age. Killed in Battle of Yellow-Bayou, Louisiana, 18 May 1864; buried Friends Graveyard at New London, Howard County.

Gifford, William M. Born 10 June 1845 of William and Esther Gifford; Honey Creek, Howard County. Company G 89th Regiment; Corporal; 17 years of age; discharged for wounds 27 March 1864; disowned at Honey Creek.

Gilbert, Joel M. Born 14 October 1830 of Aaron and Margaret Gilbert; Milford, Wayne County. Company C 84th Regiment; 1st Sergeant; 31 years of age.

Gilbert, Jonathan N. Born circa 1840 of Thomas and Catharine Gilbert; Milford, Wayne County. Company C 84th Regiment; 22 years of age; discharged for disability 6 May 1864; produced offering at Milford.

Gilbert, Josiah B. Born 23 October 1834 of Josiah and Abigail Gilbert; Hopewell, Henry County. Company C 84th Regiment; Corporal; 27 years of age; transferred to Engineer Corps.

Gilbert, Oliver. Born circa 1844 of Thomas and Catharine Gilbert; Milford, Wayne County. Company C 84th Regiment; 18 years of age; produced offering at Milford.

Gilbert, William T. Born circa 1841 in Henry County. Company C 51st Regiment; 21 years of age; reenlisted same regiment.

Goodrich, Andrew H. Born 8 May 1840; Deer Creek, Grant County. Company C 12th Regiment; 22 years of age; discharged 29 October 1863. Died 9 January 1917; buried IOOF, Grant County.

Gordon, Clarkson. Born 4 August 1841 of Charles and Lydia Gordon; Spiceland, Henry County. Company A 36th Regiment; 20 years of age; wounded at Chickamauga, Georgia, 19 September 1863, and at Resaca, Georgia, 16 May 1864; reenlisted Company A 4th Regiment, 1st Army Corps U.S. Veteran Volunteers (Hancock's Corps).

Gordon, Micajah C. Born 28 March 1828 of Charles and Lydia Gordon; Spiceland, Henry County. Company D 36th Regiment; 1st Sergeant; 33 years of age; discharged for disability 25 July 1862.

Gordon, Oliver C. Born 14 November 1845 of Charles and Lydia Gordon; Spiceland, Henry County. Company E 69th Regiment; 19 years of age; transferred to 24th Regiment.

Gordon, Robert. Born 11 November 1834 of Charles and Lydia Gordon; Spiceland, Henry County. Company A 36th Regiment; Sergeant; 26 years of age.

Gordon, William M. Born circa 1813. Served in the war from Boone County.

Grave, Allen W. Born 9 October 1840 of David and Jane Grave; Richmond, Indiana. Company B 16th Regiment, 1 year; reenlisted Company F 69th Regiment; 21 years of age; Sergeant. Died 24 July 1915; buried Earlham Cemetery, Richmond, Indiana.

Grave, Alvin (Alvan) S. Born circa 1845 of David Isaac and Eliza Hartley Grave; Wayne County, Indiana. Company D 70th Regiment; transferred to 33rd Regiment; 18 years of age.

Grave (Graves), Charles B. Born in Indiana; enrolled in Kansas.

Grave, Curtis.

Grave, Dixon (Dickenson). 36th Regiment; Wagon Master; prisoner of war captured on return from Bridgeport, Alabama, where he had conveyed the remains of his brother George M. Grave.

Grave (Graves), George M. 2nd Cavalry; transferred to Company I 36th Regiment; Captain. Died September 1863 at Chickamauga, Georgia; buried Maple Grove Cemetery, Richmond, Indiana.

Grave, Henry H. Born 5 July 1838 of David Isaac and Eliza Hartley Grave; Whitewater, Wayne County. 12th Regiment; reenlisted Company C 29th Regiment; 1st Lieutenant; 25 years of age. Killed in battle.

Grave, Jesse. Born 2 July 1836 of David Isaac and Eliza Hartley Grave; Whitewater, Wayne County. Company E 13th Regiment; 26 years of age; disowned at West Union, Morgan County. Died 11 May 1876; buried Monical Cemetery, Morgan County.

Grave, Joseph C.

Grave, Joseph K.

Grave, Levi. Company A 133rd Regiment, 100 days.

Grave, Milton.

Grave, Thomas Clarkson. Born 13 September 1840 of David Isaac and Eliza Hartley Grave; West Union, Morgan County. Company K 33rd Regiment; 2nd Lieutenant; 21 years of age. Produced offering at West Union. Died circa 1924; buried West Union.

Gray, Elias. Born circa 1821. Jericho Friends, Randolph County. Company H 84th Regiment; 41 years of age; discharged 17 August 1863.

Gray, Jesse. Born circa 1822. Company G 153rd Regiment, 1 year; 43 years of age. Died 17 August 1870; buried Quaker Cemetery, Jay County.

Green, Ed. Buried Hinkles Creek, Hamilton County.

Green, Eli. Born 9 September 1844 of Joseph and Ann Green; Poplar Ridge, Hamilton County. Company F 63rd Regiment; 17 years of age.

Green, Isaac J. Born circa 1843. Company A 153rd Regiment, 1 year; 22 years of age; disowned at Richland, Hamilton County. Buried West Grove, Hamilton County.

Green, John W. Born circa 1844. Sparrow Creek, Randolph County. Company C 69th Regiment; 18 years of age.

Gregg, Salathiel. Son of Eli and Martha Gregg; Milford (Hicksite), Wayne County. Company A 8th Regiment, 3 months; reported for military service at Milford (Hicksite).

Gregory, John H. Born circa 1845. Company H 70th Regiment; 17 years of age. Died circa 1921; buried West Union, Morgan County.

Griffin, Elihu. Born 23 March 1830; Spiceland, Henry County. Enrolling Commissioner for Lake County; U.S. Volunteers; Major Paymaster, 1862–65; 32 years of age. Died 1887, Lake County.

Griffith, John. Born circa 1823. Company D 57th Regiment; 38 years of age; discharged for disability 29 August 1864; disowned at Whitewater (Hicksite).

Grimes, Jacob S. Born 20 March 1844 of George M. and Susannah Grimes; Honey Creek, Howard County. Company A 139th Regiment, 100 days; 20 years of age.

Grimes, William P. Born 9 July 1830 of John and Mary Grimes; Bloomfield, Parke County. Company A 85th Regiment; 33 years of age; transferred to Company K 33rd Regiment; Corporal. Died 9 March 1897; buried Ephlin Cemetery, Parke County.

Hadley, Albert. Born 5 July 1842 of Washington and Naomi Hadley; Bloomfield, Parke County. Company I 137th Regiment, 100 days; 21 years of age.

Hadley, Alvin. Born 12 February 1844 of William and Achsah Hadley; Rush Creek, Parke County. Company H 150th Regiment, 1 year; 20 years of age; produced free will offering at Rush Creek. Died 14 August 1878; buried Rush Creek #2.

Hadley, Charles. Born 27 June 1845 of William and Achsah Hadley; Rush Creek, Parke County. Company H 150th

Regiment, 1 year; 19 years of age; produced free will offering at Rush Creek.

Hadley, Daniel. Born 13 January 1843 of William T. and Beulah Hadley; Mill Creek, Hendricks County. Company I 154th Regiment, 1 year; 19 years of age. Died 2 August 1865; buried Harpers Ferry, West Virginia.

Hadley, David. Born 23 June 1835 of Joshua and Sarah Hadley; West Union, Morgan County. Company E 12th Regiment; 29 years of age. Died of chronic diarrhea at Memphis, Tennessee, 2 June 1863.

Hadley, Eli. Born 9 February 1842 of William and Ann Hadley; White Lick, Morgan County. Company K 21st Regiment, 1st Heavy Artillery; Corporal; 21 years of age; produced offering at White Lick. Died 10 July 1919; buried West White Lick.

Hadley, Enos C. Born circa 1840; West Union, Morgan County. Company C 33rd Regiment; 21 years of age. Died in Tennessee.

Hadley, James W. Born 29 March 1843 of Jonathan and Rebecca Hadley; Bloomfield, Parke County. Company K 43rd Regiment; Sergeant; 18 years of age.

Hadley, Levi A. Born 30 October 1836 of Simon B. and Sarah Hadley; White Lick, Morgan County. Company E 26th Regiment; 24 years of age. Died 13 March 1891; buried West White Lick.

Hadley, Nathan. Born 2 October 1832 of Lot M. and Eunice Hadley; West Union, Morgan County; disowned at West Union.

Hadley, Noah. Born 29 January 1825; White Lick, Morgan County. Company C 33rd Regiment; 36 years of age. Died in Libby Prison, Richmond, Virginia, 1863.

Hadley, Samuel Smith. Born 23 January 1845 of Jeremiah and Esther Hadley; Whitewater, Wayne County. Company H 140th Regiment, 1 year; Quartermaster; 19 years of age. Died 25 August 1890.

Hadley, Uriah. Born 4 April 1839 of John D. and Mary Hadley; Bloomfield, Parke County. 9th Light Artillery; 22 years of age. Died at Pittsburg Landing (Shiloh), Tennessee, 30 May 1862.

Hadley, William. Born 26 August 1845 of David and Hannah Hadley; Honey Creek, Howard County. Company L 126th Regiment, 11th Cavalry; 18 years of age; produced offering in Kansas for Honey Creek. Buried Russiaville, Howard County.

Haines, Aaron. Born 20 October 1839 of Charles and Ann Haines; Fall Creek (Hicksite), Madison County; produced offering at Fall Creek.

Haines, Clark. Son of John and Jemima Haines; Fall Creek (Hicksite), Madison County. Produced offering at Fall Creek. Died 17 October 1874.

Haines, Eli C. Born 15 July 1846 of Levi and Charlotte Haines; Wabash, Wabash County. Company A 153rd Regiment, 1 year; 18 years of age.

Haines, Noah C. Born 9 April 1842; Fall Creek (Hicksite), Madison County. Company K 8th Regiment; 20 years of age. Died 30 December 1910.

Haisley, Jesse. Born 7 August 1842 of Ira and Rebecca Haisley; Oak Ridge, Grant County. Company D 139th Regiment, 100 days; 22 years of age; produced offering at Oak Ridge. Died 11 January 1928; buried Park Cemetery, Grant County.

Hall, Alfred. Born 19 January 1845 of Moses and Sarah Hall; Cherry Grove, Randolph County. Company B 119th Regiment, 7th Cavalry; 18 years of age. Died at Memphis, Tennessee, 17 March 1864.

Hall, Elwood. Born 16 January 1843 of Moses and Sarah Hall; Cherry Grove, Randolph County. Company B 90th Regiment, 5th Cavalry; 19 years of age. Died at Indianapolis 29 November 1862.

Hall, John E. Born 3 December 1821 of Richard and Mary Hall; Lick Creek, Orange County. Company G 24th Regiment; 39 years of age. Died 19 November 1907; buried Beech Grove, Orange County.

Hall, Robert. Born circa 1842 in Henry County. Company A 36th Regiment; 19 years of age; wounded at Chickamauga, Georgia, 19 September 1863.

Hall, Robert M. Born circa 1844 of John E. and Margaret Hall; Lick Creek, Orange County. Company D 66th Regiment; 18 years of age; discharged for disability 8 March 1863. Died 11 March 1863; buried Lick Creek.

Hall, William. Born 10 December 1843 of John and Elizabeth Hall; Driftwood, Jackson County. Produced offering at Driftwood.

Hall, William Cartwright. Born circa 1840 in Henry County. Company A 36th Regiment; 21 years of age; discharged for disability 30 June 1862.

Hampton, Haines. Born 16 July 1833 of Jehiel and Sarah Hampton; Dover, Wayne County. Company I 84th Regiment; 29 years of age; wounded at Chickamauga, Georgia. Died at Madison, Indiana, 5 March 1864.

Hardy, Solomon F. Born 19 October 1838 of Neal and Elizabeth R. Hardy; Fall Creek (Hicksite), Madison County. Company A 16th Regiment; Sergeant; 22 years of age; wounded in battle of Richmond, Kentucky, 30 August 1862. Died 29 June 1909; buried Fall Creek.

Hardy, Thomas M. Born 4 February 1840; Fall Creek (Hicksite), Madison County. Company A 16th Regiment; Sergeant; 22 years of age; wounded at Arkansas Post. Died 31 May 1915; buried Fall Creek.

Harlan, Enoch. Born 8 October 1838 of Enoch and Rachel Harlan; Mill Creek, Hendricks County. Company B 117th Regiment, 6 months; Sergeant; 24 years of age; disowned at Mill Creek.

Harris, Albanus. Born 3 September 1845 of Jesse M. and Gulielma Harris; New Garden, Wayne County. Company A 133rd Regiment, 100 days; 18 years of age; produced offering at New Garden.

Harris, Elwood. Born 13 December 1848 of Elijah Harris; New Garden, Wayne County. Company C 121st Regiment, 9th Cavalry; 15 years of age; produced offering at New Garden.

Harris, George W. Born 9 December 1843 of John S. and Sarah Harris; Mississinewa, Grant County. Company E 28th Regiment, United States Colored Troops; 19 years of age; discharged 9 June 1865. Died 29 January 1921; buried Veterans Facility, Grant County.

Harris, Henderson C. Born circa 1839 of Elijah Harris; New Garden, Wayne County. Company I 57th Regiment; 23 years of age. Died at St Louis, Missouri, 7 May 1862.

Harris, Jonathan C. Born 23 May 1833 of Benjamin and Abigail Harris; Sparrow Creek, Randolph County. Company H 84th Regiment; 29 years of age.

Harris, Lewis K. Whitewater (Hicksite), Wayne County. Company C 8th Regiment, 3 months; reenlisted Company F 36th Regiment; 2nd Lieutenant; resigned for physical disability 9 June 1862; reenlisted Company F 69th Regiment; transferred to Company B 69th Regiment, Residuary Battalion; Captain.

Harris, Milton. Born 16 June 1841 of William and Mary Harris; New Garden, Wayne County. Company I 84th Regiment; 21 years of age. Died 14 November 1872.

Harris, Mordecai. Born 24 December 1839 of Benjamin and Abigail Harris; Poplar Run, Randolph County. Company F 55th Regiment, 3 months; 22 years of age; reenlisted Company B 119th Regiment, 7th Cavalry; Sergeant; disowned at Poplar Run.

Harris, Robert. Chester, Wayne County. 19th Light Artillery. Died at Murfreesboro, Tennessee, 27 November 1863.

Harris, Thomas. Born 19 February 1830 of David M. and Rachel Harris; Cherry Grove, Randolph County. Company E 20th Regiment; 31 years of age.

Harter, Joseph L. Born 8 October 1834 of Joseph C. and Catherine Harter; Springfield, Wayne County. Company H 147th Regiment, 1 year; 30 years of age. Died circa 1919; buried Nettle Creek Friends, Wayne County.

Harvey, Cyrus W. Born 30 October 1843 of Jesse and Lydia Harvey; Back Creek, Grant County. Company C 89th Regiment; Sergeant; 18 years of age; produced offering at Back Creek.

Harvey, Edward M. Born 2 October 1840 of Harlan and Ruth Harvey; Plainfield, Hendricks County. Company B 54th Regiment, 3 months; 21 years of age; disowned at Plainfield.

Harvey, Elias F. Born 24 April 1841 of Levi and Anna Harvey; Rush Creek, Parke County. Company E 115th Regiment, 6 months; 22 years of age; produced offering at Rush Creek.

Harvey, Isaac. Born 3 June 1849 of Asahel and Sarah Harvey; Bloomfield, Parke County. Company I 137th Regiment, 100 days; 14 years of age. Died circa 1930; buried Poplar Grove, Parke County.

Harvey, John. Born 9 January 1833 of John and Lydia Harvey; Wabash, Wabash County. Died 28 July 1907; buried Friends Cemetery, Wabash County.

Harvey, Milton. Born 12 April 1825 of Harlan and Ruth Harvey; Bloomfield, Parke County. Company G 71st Regiment; Corporal; 37 years of age; discharged 28 November 1862. Buried Rush Creek #2, Parke County.

Harvey, Silas. Born circa 1830 of Caleb and Bathsheba Harvey; Westfield, Hamilton County. Company A 101st Regiment; 32 years of age.

Harvey, Thomas B. Born 29 November 1837 of Jesse and Elizabeth Harvey; Plainfield, Hendricks County. Produced offering at Plainfield for serving as a surgeon and medical examiner of the army.

Harvey, William. Born 18 November 1838 of Harlan and Ruth Harvey; Plainfield, Hendricks County. Company A 51st Regiment; 2nd Lieutenant; 22 years of age; disowned at Plainfield.

Harvey, Wilson. Born 8 August 1842 of Harlan and Ruth Harvey; Plainfield, Hendricks County. Company B 117th Regiment, 6 months; Corporal; 20 years of age; disowned at Plainfield.

Haskett, Albert A. Born circa 1843 of Daniel Haskett; Hinkles Creek, Hamilton County. Company H 57th Regiment; 1st Lieutenant; 18 years of age; reenlisted same regiment.

Hastings, Joshua. Born 19 December 1841 of Aaron and Margaret Hastings; Milford, Wayne County. Company H 25th Regiment; 1st Lieutenant; 20 years of age; wounded in battle of Stones River, Tennessee, and transferred to Veteran Reserve Corps.

Hastings, William. Born 12 July 1833 of Aaron and Margaret Hastings; Milford, Wayne County. Company H 70th Regiment; 28 years of age; transferred to Company C 33rd Regiment; produced offering at Milford.

Hawkins, Alexander Franklin. Disowned at Richland, Hamilton County.

Hawkins, Elihu. Born circa 1846. Company D 136th Regiment, 100 days; 18 years of age. Disowned at Richland, Hamilton County.

Haworth, Eli. Born circa 1836. Company H 84th Regiment; Corporal; 26 years of age. Died 23 January 1916; buried White River, Randolph County.

Haworth, Jonathan L. Born circa 1841; Westfield, Hamilton County. Company C 130th Regiment; Sergeant; 23 years of age.

Haworth, Richard M. Born 14 October 1821; Union County. Union County Draft Commissioner; Indiana Legion.

Haworth, William. Born circa 1846. Company H 43rd Regiment, 1 year; 18 years of age; produced offering at Plainfield, Hendricks County.

Haworth, William C. Born circa 1842. Company A 147th Regiment, 1 year; 23 years of age; Sergeant; produced offering at White River, Randolph County.

Hayworth, Lewis C. Born circa 1843; Lick Creek, Orange County. Company D 66th Regiment; 19 years of age. Died circa 1935; buried Lick Creek.

Heacock, Daniel. Produced offering at Milford (Hicksite), Wayne County. Died 3 August 1892.

Heacock, Jesse D. Son of Davis and Mary Heacock; Blue River (Hicksite), Washington County. Company D 38th Regiment; produced offering at Blue River (Hicksite).

Heacock, Jonah. Born circa 1841. From Wabash County. Company G 118th Regiment, 6 months; 22 years of age.

Heise, Ernst. Born 20 March 1833; Lick Creek, Orange County. Died circa 1916; buried IOOF, Orange County.

Henby, John D. Born 8 March 1840 of Elijah and Elizabeth Henby; Walnut Ridge, Rush County. Company F 51st Regiment; 21 years of age; discharged for wounds 25 April 1865.

Hendrickson, Jacob W. Born circa 1838. Pleasant Hill, Howard County. Company G 89th Regiment; 24 years of age.

Henley (Henly), Alphus (Alpheus) W. Born 21 July 1836 of Phinehas and Mary Henley; Back Creek, Grant County. 79th Regiment; 1 year; 27 years of age; drafted; produced offering at Back Creek.

Henley, Cyrus. Born 20 April 1841 of Hezekiah and Ann Henley; Walnut Ridge, Rush County. Company G 16th Regiment; Sergeant; 21 years of age. Died 14 November 1864.

Henley, Elias. Born 1 January 1825 of Elias and Jane Henley; Walnut Ridge, Rush County. 22nd Light Artillery; 37 years of age.

Henley (Henby), William. Produced offering at Walnut Ridge, Rush County.

Henly (Henley), John R. Born 29 June 1829 of Phinehas and Mary Henly; Back Creek, Grant County. Company I 101st Regiment; 33 years of age.

Herrington (Harrington), Samuel P. Born circa 1839. New Garden, Wayne County. Company D 8th Regiment; Sergeant; 22 years of age.

Heston, George B. Born circa 1850. Company A 153rd Regiment, 1 year; 14 years of age. Died 16 September 1866; buried Friends Cemetery, Wabash County.

Hiatt, Eli. Born 28 January 1843 of Curtis and Salina Hiatt; Westfield, Hamilton County. Company E 52nd Regiment; 19 years of age; reenlisted and transferred to Company I 52nd Regiment; produced offering at Westfield. Buried Crownland Cemetery, Hamilton County.

Hiatt, Eli. Born 26 November 1842 of Lewis and Charity Hiatt; Sparrow Creek, Randolph County. Company E 57th Regiment; 19 years of age. Died at Shiloh (Pittsburg Landing), Tennessee, 15 May 1862.

Hiatt, Enos. Born circa 1823. Hinkles Creek, Hamilton County. Company G 147th Regiment, 1 year; Corporal; 42 years of age; buried Chester Friends, Hamilton County.

Hiatt, Isaac H. Born 19 July 1841 of Eliel and Mary Hiatt; Westfield, Hamilton County. Company A 101st Regiment; 21 years of age; buried Crownland Cemetery, Hamilton County.

Hiatt, Levi. Born 9 March 1840 of David and Lydia Hiatt; Back Creek, Grant County. Company F 34th Regiment; 21 years of age; disowned at Back Creek.

Hiatt, Nathan. Born 18 March 1843 of Eli and Mary Hiatt; Sparrow Creek, Randolph County. Company A 84th Regiment; 19 years of age. Killed at Chickamauga, Georgia, 20 September 1863.

Hiatt, Pleasant. Born circa 1829. White River, Randolph County. Company A 106th Regiment, Minute Men; 34 years of age.

Hiatt, Sylvester. Born circa 1837. Company B 34th Regiment; Sergeant; 24 years of age. Died of typhoid fever at Winchester, Indiana, 28 March 1862; buried Quaker Cemetery, Jay County.

Hiatt, William P. Born 22 January 1844 of Eliel and Mary Hiatt; Westfield, Hamilton County. Company H 57th Regiment; 17 years of age; reenlisted same regiment. Died of wounds at Nashville, Tennessee, 7 December 1864.

Hibberd, Edgar G. Whitewater, Wayne County. Company A 133rd Regiment, 100 days.

Hill, Allen. Born 15 December 1832 of Henry B. and Lucretia Hill; Walnut Ridge, Rush County. Company G 16th Regiment; 1st Sergeant; 29 years of age; discharged for disability 1 February 1863; reenlisted Company F 146th Regiment, 1 year; Adjutant; disowned at Walnut Ridge.

Hill, Benonia. Born 12 September 1826 of Aaron and Nancy Hill; Back Creek, Grant County. Company H 84th Regiment; Sergeant; 35 years of age; produced offering at White River, Randolph County.

Hill, Daniel. Born 23 December 1840 of Aaron and Nancy Hill; Back Creek, Grant County. Company C 89th Regiment; 21 years of age. Died at Ft. De Russy, Louisiana, 9 April 1864; buried at Weaver Cemetery, Grant County.

Hill, Daniel C. Born 26 September 1843 of Charles and Jemima Hill; Whitewater, Wayne County. Company A 133rd Regiment, 100 days; 18 years of age.

Hill, Henry. Born 7 January 1838 of Henry and Avis Hill; New Garden, Wayne County. Company E 69th Regiment; 24 years of age. Died at St. Louis, Missouri, 5 February 1863.

Hill, Henry B. Born 1 July 1809; Walnut Ridge, Rush County. Company F 16th Regiment, 1 year; Quartermaster; 51 years of age; reenlisted Company C 16th Regiment; Quartermaster; U.S. Draft Commissioner, 4th District, Indiana; Provost Marshal 4th District, Indiana, 1864–65; disowned at Walnut Ridge. Died 17 November 1874, Rush County.

Hill, James H. Born 15 June 1839 of Nathan and Elizabeth Hill; Walnut Ridge, Rush County. Company E 121st Regiment, 9th Cavalry; 24 years of age; Blacksmith; disowned at Walnut Ridge.

Hill, Joseph. Born circa 1835 of William and Sarah Hill; Lick Creek, Orange County. Company F 131st Regiment, 13th Cavalry; Corporal; 29 years of age.

Hill, Milton. Born 19 July 1822 of Thomas and Tamer Hill; Walnut Ridge, Rush County. Company E 121st Regiment, 9th Cavalry; 41 years of age.

Hill, Nathan F. Born 19 September 1821 of Christopher and Mourning Hill; Lick Creek, Orange County. Company F 131st Regiment, 13th Cavalry; 42 years of age; buried Newberry Cemetery, Orange County.

Hill, Nathan V. Born 27 April 1842 of William and Achsah Hill; Bloomfield, Parke County. Company C 21st Regiment, 1st Heavy Artillery; 22 years of age.

Hill, Seth. Born 18 August 1846 of Aaron and Nancy Hill; Back Creek, Grant County. Company B 152nd Regiment, 1 year; 19 years of age.

Hill, Thomas C. Born 15 July 1845 of Milton and Amanda Hill; Walnut Ridge, Rush County. Company E 121st Regiment, 9th Cavalry; 17 years of age; produced offering at Walnut Ridge.

Hill, Thomas Elwood. Born 9 September 1836 of Henry B. and Lucretia Hill; Walnut Ridge, Rush County. Disowned at Walnut Ridge.

Hinshaw, Henry B. Born 19 May 1848 of William B. and Hannah Hinshaw; Springfield, Wayne County. Company G 21st Regiment, 1st Heavy Artillery; 16 years of age.

Hinshaw, William Henry. Born 29 January 1845 of Seth and Sarah Hinshaw; Duck Creek, Henry County. Company E 139th Regiment, 100 days; 18 years of age.

Hitchcock, Barney C. Born 20 September 1842 of Joshua and Mary Hitchcock; Blue River (Hicksite), Washington County. Company G 13th Regiment; 18 years of age.

Hobbs, Ansalem. Born 22 October 1841 of Elisha and Deborah Hobbs; Plainfield, Hendricks County. Company B 11th Regiment; 19 years of age; discharged for promotion in United States Colored Troops; disowned at Plainfield.

Hobbs, Harvey. Born 8 October 1839 of Elisha and Deborah Hobbs; Plainfield, Hendricks County. Company D 19th Regiment; 22 years of age. Died near Petersburg, Virginia, 21 July 1864; buried Sugar Grove, Hendricks County.

Hobbs, Marmaduke. Born 20 March 1829 of Elisha and Lydia Hobbs; Blue River (Hicksite), Washington County. 80th Regiment; Chaplain; 34 years of age; resigned at Cincinnati, Ohio, 24 January 1863; recommissioned Chaplain 4 March 1863, discharged for disability 29 October 1864. Died 5 January 1907; buried Old Blue River.

Hobbs, Orville W. Born 6 January 1848 of Wilson and Zalinda Hobbs; Bloomfield, Parke County. Company G 133rd Regiment, 100 days; 16 years of age.

Hobbs, Seth. Born 27 April 1844 of Matthew and Mary Hobbs; Blue River (Hicksite), Washington County. Company G 18th Regiment; 17 years of age. Died 28 November 1861; buried Old Blue River.

Hobbs, Wilson. Born 21 August 1823 of Samuel and Ruth Hobbs; Bloomfield, Parke County. 85th Regiment; Surgeon; 39 years of age; produced free will offering at Bloomfield.

Hobson, Aaron. Born 11 May 1845 of Jesse and Lydia Hobson; Bloomfield, Parke County. Company K 21st Regiment, 1st Heavy Artillery; 18 years of age. Died of disease at New Orleans, Louisiana, 14 January 1865.

Hobson, David A. Born 19 August 1843; Rush Creek, Parke
County. Company I 31st Regiment; 18 years of age. Died
at home 20 June 1863; buried Rush Creek #2.

Hobson, James M. Born 6 March 1817; Lick Creek, Orange
County. Company D 66th Regiment; 1st Lieutenant; 48
years of age. Died 28 September 1894; buried Lick Creek.

Hockett, Eli. Born 10 November 1836; Mississinewa, Grant
County. Company I 101st Regiment; 25 years of age; pro-
duced offering at Mississinewa. Died 9 August 1916; buried
IOOF, Grant County.

Hockett, Evan. Born 19 February 1825 of Nathan and Rachel
Hockett; Cherry Grove, Randolph County. Company D
69th Regiment; 37 years of age; transferred to Veteran Reserve Corps 10 February 1863.

Hockett, Joseph. Born 19 September 1841 of Josiah and Mary
Hockett; Oak Ridge, Grant County. Company D 139th
Regiment, 100 days; 22 years of age. Died 28 March 1905;
buried Park Cemetery, Grant County.

Hockett, Joseph A. Born 26 December 1843 of Zimri and
Susanna Hockett; Wabash, Wabash County. Company I
23rd Regiment; 20 years of age; drafted. Died 20 October
1919; buried Friends Cemetery, Wabash County.

Hockett, Nathan. Born 1 July 1830 of Joseph and Martha
Hockett; Cherry Grove, Randolph County. Company D
105th Regiment, Minute Men; 33 years of age.

Hodgin, Jesse J. Born 10 August 1844 of Benjamin and Elis-
abeth Hodgin; New Garden, Wayne County. Company E
69th Regiment; 17 years of age.

Hodson, Eli B. Born circa 1845. Mill Creek, Hendricks
County. Company C 51st Regiment; 18 years of age.

Hodson, Francis H. C. Born circa 1839. Company B 8th
Regiment; 23 years of age; reenlisted same regiment. Buried
Old Quaker Graveyard, Henry County.

Hodson, Joel. Born 15 June 1848 of Zachariah and Jenny
Hodson; New Salem, Howard County. Company C 137th

Regiment, 100 days; 15 years of age; disowned at Bangor Monthly Meeting in Iowa for New Salem.

Hodson, John B. Born 20 September 1828 of Robert and Anna Hodson; Spiceland, Henry County. Company E 8th Regiment; 32 years of age; discharged for disability 1 April 1864.

Hodson, Zachariah. Born 14 August 1829; New Salem, Howard County; disowned at Bangor Monthly Meeting in Iowa for New Salem.

Holiday, Lindus. Company A 85th Regiment; Corporal. Died at Nicholasville, Kentucky, 10 December 1862; buried Rush Creek #2, Parke County.

Holiday, William C. Born 27 June 1826; Rush Creek, Parke County. Disowned at Rush Creek.

Hollingsworth, Benjamin S. Born 3 July 1839 of James and Lydia Hollingsworth; Raysville, Henry County. 19th Light Artillery; 23 years of age; produced offering at Raysville.

Hollingsworth, Gilmore. Born 18 August 1838; Back Creek, Grant County. Company H 12th Regiment, 1 year; Musician; 22 years of age; reenlisted Company G 140th Regiment, 1 year; Musician. Died circa 1884; buried Back Creek.

Hollingsworth, Isaac I. Born 19 August 1841 of Isaac and Jane Hollingsworth; Mississinewa, Grant County. Company L 45th Regiment, 3rd Cavalry; 21 years of age; produced offering at Mississinewa.

Hollingsworth, Joel. Born 21 February 1841 of Absalom and Anna Hollingsworth; Honey Creek, Howard County. Company G 89th Regiment; 20 years of age; discharged 9 July 1863; disowned at Honey Creek. Buried Old Friends New London, Howard County.

Holloway, Abner. Born 6 December 1830; Back Creek, Grant County. Company E 83rd Regiment; 33 years of age; drafted.

Holloway, Amos. Born 29 August 1834; Back Creek, Grant County. Company G 153rd Regiment, 1 year; 30 years of age; produced offering at Back Creek. Died 30 November 1914; buried Puckett Cemetery, Grant County.

Holloway, Jesse. Born circa 1844 of Jason and Jane Holloway; Fall Creek (Hicksite), Madison County. Company I 75th Regiment; 18 years of age; transferred to Veteran Reserve Corps 26 January 1864.

Hollowell, Abraham. Born circa 1821 of Thomas and Achsah Hollowell; Blue River, Washington County. Company E 53rd Regiment; 43 years of age; drafted.

Hollowell, Lindley. Born 14 December 1826; Lick Creek, Orange County. Company D 66th Regiment; 35 years of age. Died 12 February 1881; buried Liberty Cemetery, Orange County.

Hollowell, Nathan. Born circa 1846. Lick Creek, Orange County. Company D 66th Regiment; 16 years of age; discharged for disability 6 December 1862; reenlisted Company B 24th Regiment.

Hollowell, Robert T. Born circa 1842 of James and Celia Hollowell; Lick Creek, Orange County. Company D 66th Regiment; 20 years of age; discharged for disability 8 January 1863. Died 27 September 1867; buried Blue River, Washington County.

Hollowell, William. Born 14 February 1832 of Nathan and Nancy Ann Hollowell; Lick Creek, Orange County. Company D 66th Regiment; Corporal; 30 years of age. Killed at Atlanta, Georgia, 22 July 1864.

Holstein, Francis M. Born circa 1841. Company K 39th Regiment, 8th Cavalry; 20 years of age. Died at Camp Nevin, Kentucky, 10 December 1861; buried Friends Cemetery, Parke County.

Hoover, David Y. Born 8 December 1830; Fairmount, Grant County. Company A 89th Regiment; 31 years of age. Died 24 April 1900; buried Little Ridge Cemetery, Grant County.

Hoover, Henry. Born circa 1845 of Matilda Hoover; Whitewater, Wayne County. Company L 71st Regiment, 6th

Cavalry; Corporal; 18 years of age; disowned at White-water.

Hoover, James M. Born 8 February 1843 of John Y. Hoover; Camden (Hicksite), Jay County. Company B 34th Regiment; 18 years of age; discharged for disability 4 April 1863; reenlisted Company G 153rd Regiment, 1 year; Corporal; buried Daugherty Cemetery, Jay County.

Hoover, Richard D. Born 22 December 1847 of John Y. Hoover; Camden (Hicksite), Jay County. Company E 119th Regiment, 7th Cavalry; 15 years of age; transferred to Company E 119th Regiment Reorganized.

Hopkins, William G. Camden (Hicksite), Jay County. Died 24 January 1869; buried Quaker Cemetery, Jay County.

Horner, Jacob. Born 31 January 1828 of Jacob and Lydia Horner; Mill Creek, Hendricks County. Company D 103rd Regiment, 7 days; 35 years of age; buried Mill Creek.

Horney, Jesse. Born 29 July 1843 of Stephen and Nancy Horney; West Grove, Wayne County. Company C 121st Regiment, 9th Cavalry; 20 years of age.

Horton, John. Born circa 1842. Company E 26th Regiment; 19 years of age. Died from accidental wound 6 February 1863; buried Old Quaker Church, Marion County.

Hoskins, Stephen M. Produced offering at Fairfield, Hendricks County.

Howell, Charles. Born 2 August 1845 of Jeremiah and Sarah J. Howell; Oak Ridge, Grant County. Company F 34th Regiment; 18 years of age; produced offering at Oak Ridge. Died 2 September 1911; buried IOOF, Grant County.

Hubbard, Alonzo. Born 3 August 1837; Raysville, Henry County. Company F 6th Regiment, 3 months; 23 years of age.

Hubbard, George. Son of Richard J. and Sarah Hubbard; Milford, Wayne County. Company C 84th Regiment; Corporal; produced offering at Milford.

Hubbard, Harrison. Born 26 November 1840; White Lick, Morgan County. Company I 17th Regiment; Corporal; 20 years of age. Died circa 1910; buried Mooresville.

Hubbard, Henry. Born circa 1842 of Richard J. and Sarah Hubbard; Milford, Wayne County. Company A 8th Regiment, 3 months; reenlisted Company C 41st Regiment, 2nd Cavalry; reenlisted same regiment; Sergeant; 19 years of age. Killed at Knoxville, Tennessee, 16 December 1864.

Hubbard, Joseph B. Born circa 1843 of Richard J. and Sarah Hubbard; Milford, Wayne County. Company D 8th Regiment; Sergeant; 18 years of age; wounded in leg, arm, and hip at Vicksburg, Mississippi; furloughed home. Died of consumption 26 May 1865.

Hubbard, W. Edwin. Born 24 October 1827 of Richard J. and Sarah Hubbard; Milford, Wayne County. Company H 69th Regiment; 34 years of age. Died 29 October 1887; buried Raysville, Henry County.

Hunnicutt, William H. Born circa 1842. Company A 57th Regiment; 19 years of age; deserted 31 December 1862; produced offering at Raysville, Henry County.

Hunt, [first name not legible]. Reported for military service at Westfield, Hamilton County.

Hunt, Calvin. Born 11 February 1823 of John and Catherine Hunt; Westfield, Hamilton County. Company H 57th Regiment; 38 years of age; reenlisted same regiment. Died at Nashville, Tennessee, 22 July 1864.

Hunt, Clayton B. Born 23 November 1845 of Clayton and Elizabeth Hunt; Whitewater, Wayne County. Company A 133rd Regiment, 100 days; 18 years of age.

Hunt, Cyrus E. Born 2 July 1839 of Newby and Sarah Hunt; Bloomfield, Parke County. Company H 21st Regiment, 1st Heavy Artillery; Sergeant; 22 years of age; buried Ephlin Cemetery, Parke County.

Hunt, John W. Born 4 January 1840; Sparrow Creek, Randolph County. Company D 69th Regiment; 22 years of age; disowned at Poplar Run; buried Poplar Run, Randolph County.

Hunt, Joseph. Born 11 December 1843 of Solomon and Sarah Hunt; Mill Creek, Hendricks County. 11th Regiment; Musician; 18 years of age; disowned at Cincinnati Monthly Meeting for Mill Creek.

Hunt, Libni. Born circa 1841. Company H 29th Regiment; Corporal; 20 years of age; reenlisted and transferred to Company I 29th Regiment; Sergeant; produced offering at Blue River, Washington County, for Westfield, Hamilton County.

Hunt, Nathan A. Born 10 August 1830 of Hiram and Sally Hunt; Mill Creek, Hendricks County. Company E 12th Regiment; Musician; 32 years of age; discharged for disability 28 February 1863. Buried Friends Cemetery, Hendricks County.

Hunt, Quincy A. Born circa 1846 of Nathan and Esther Hunt; Bloomfield, Parke County. Company A 57th Regiment, 1 year; 18 years of age; Substitute.

Hunt, William. Born 31 July 1845 of Albert and Anna Hunt; Mill Creek, Hendricks County. Company B 117th Regiment, 6 months; 17 years of age; produced offering at Mill Creek.

Hunt, William A. Born 1 May 1838 of Isam and Susannah Hunt; Honey Creek, Howard County. Company G 89th Regiment; 1st Sergeant; 23 years of age. Killed by guerrillas near Memphis, Tennessee, 23 June 1864.

Hussey, John. Born 30 June 1843 of Thomas and Aletha Hussey; White Lick, Morgan County. Company I 27th Regiment; 17 years of age. Died of disease 22 April 1862.

Hussey, William. Born 18 August 1839 of Thomas and Aletha Hussey; Mill Creek, Hendricks County. Company B 7th Regiment; Sergeant; 22 years of age.

Hutchens, Allen. Born 2 June 1834 of Vestal and Elizabeth Hutchens; Wabash, Wasbash County. Died 28 December 1871; buried Friends Cemetery, Wabash County.

Hutchins, Eli. Born 9 April 1841 of Tommy and Anna Hutchins; Wabash, Wabash County. Died 2 October 1918; buried Friends Cemetery, Wabash County.

Hutchins (Hutchens), Theodore. Born 3 May 1840 of Vestal and Elizabeth Hutchins; Wabash, Wabash County. Company D 47th Regiment; 1st Sergeant; 21 years of age.

Hutchins, Thomas Elliott. Born 19 October 1844 of Meredith and Elizabeth Hutchins; Wabash, Wabash County. Company H 20th Regiment; Sergeant; 18 years of age; transferred to 20th Regiment Reorganized; disowned at Wabash.

Hutchins, William. Born circa 1843. Company A 36th Regiment; 18 years of age. Died at Nelson Furnace, Kentucky, 1 March 1862; buried Flat Rock Friends, Henry County.

Hyatt, Eleazer B. Born 24 June 1839 of Asher and Sarah Hyatt; Westfield, Hamilton County. Company E 52nd Regiment; 23 years of age; buried Crownland Cemetery, Hamilton County.

Inman, Daniel. Born circa 1833. Company A 101st Regiment; 29 years of age; discharged for disability 3 May 1863. Died 15 December 1867; buried Westfield Anti-Slavery Friends, Hamilton County.

Inman, Jonathan. Born circa 1839. Company A 101st Regiment; 23 years of age; discharged for disability 7 May 1864. Died 1 September 1865; buried Old Friends Westfield, Hamilton County.

Jackson, Jehu. Born 18 May 1818 of Elihu and Priscilla Jackson; Fairfield, Hendricks County.

Jackson, William. Born circa 1845 of Joseph and Nancy Jackson; Fairfield, Hendricks County. Company I 121st Regiment, 9th Cavalry; 19 years of age. Died 30 August 1865; buried Fairfield.

James, Charles R. Born 13 January 1844 of Joshua and Sarah Ann James; Fall Creek (Hicksite), Madison County. Company A 16th Regiment; Corporal; 18 years of age; produced offering Fall Creek. Died 29 July 1906; buried Fall Creek.

James, Henry. Born circa 1841 of Jesse K. and Mary James; Maple Grove (Hicksite), Huntington County. Company A 75th Regiment; Corporal; 21 years of age. Killed at Chickamauga, Georgia, 19 September 1863; buried Chickamauga.

James, Joseph Evan. Born 16 June 1842 of Joshua and Sarah Ann James; Fall Creek (Hicksite), Madison County. Company A 16th Regiment; 20 years of age; discharged for disability 2 July 1863. Died 9 July 1863; buried Fall Creek.

James, Samuel. Born circa 1844 of Jesse K. and Mary James; Maple Grove (Hicksite), Huntington County. Company G 118th Regiment, 6 months; Corporal; 19 years of age. Died 20 October 1863; buried Knoxville, Tennessee.

Jay, Elijah. Born 1 April 1829 of William and Stacy Jay; Miami County. Company A 33rd Regiment; 32 years of age; buried in Marion County.

Jay, Isaac. Born 10 October 1836 of Martha Jay; Wabash, Wabash County. 14th Light Artillery; 27 years of age; lost leg and captured at Guntown, Mississippi, 10 June 1864.

Jay, Thomas. Born 1 March 1845 of David and Sarah Jay; Back Creek, Grant County. Company K 28th Regiment, 1st Cavalry; 17 years of age. Died 24 October 1863.

Jay, William F. Born circa 1845. Company B 90th Regiment, 5th Cavalry; transferred to Company H 71st Regiment, 6th Cavalry; 18 years of age; disowned at Milford, Wayne County.

Jefferies, Calvin. Company A 101st Regiment. Buried Old Friends Westfield, Hamilton County.

Jenkins, Anderson T. Born 17 September 1844 of Benjamin and Frances C. Jenkins; Wabash, Wabash County. Company G 138th Regiment, 100 days; Corporal; 19 years of age.

Jennings, Joseph. Born 10 January 1844 of Thomas and Margaret Jennings; Hinkles Creek, Hamilton County. Company D 136th Regiment, 100 days; 20 years of age. Died circa 1929; buried Hinkles Creek.

Jessop (Jessup), Elwood. Born 28 November 1846 of Jehu and Mary Ann Jessop; Dover, Wayne County. Company C 147th Regiment, 1 year; 18 years of age.

Jessup, Elial. Born 8 September 1826 of Enoch and Anna Jessup; Westfield, Hamilton County. Company G 147th Regiment, 1 year; Corporal; 38 years of age.

Jessup, Elwood. Born circa 1844 of Jabez M. Jessup; Hinkles Creek, Hamilton County. Company A 101st Regiment; 18 years of age. Died circa 1914; buried West Grove Friends, Hamilton County.

Jessup, Jackson. Born circa 1844. Company A 101st Regiment; 18 years of age. Died of disease at Murfreesboro, Tennessee, 18 April 1863; buried Old Friends Westfield, Hamilton County.

Jessup, John P. Born circa 1841. Hinkles Creek, Hamilton County. Company G 147th Regiment, 1 year; Corporal; 24 years of age; buried Crownland Cemetery, Hamilton County.

Johns, Samuel. Born circa 1831. White Lick, Morgan County. Company E 12th Regiment; 31 years of age; deserted at Resaca, Georgia, 13 May 1864.

Johnson, Calvin. Born 20 June 1835; West Union, Morgan County. Company D 70th Regiment; Sergeant; 27 years of age. Died at Gallatin, Tennessee, 9 March 1863; buried West Union.

Johnson, Jabin (Jaben). Born 25 May 1837 of John and Phebe Johnson; Westfield, Hamilton County. Company B 39th Regiment, 8th Cavalry; 2nd Lieutenant; 24 years of age.

Johnson, Job. Born circa 1844. Company A 101st Regiment; 18 years of age; disowned at Hinkles Creek, Hamilton County.

Johnson, John W. Born circa 1850 of Caleb and Lydia Johnson; Fairfield, Hendricks County. Died circa 1928; buried West Newton, Marion County.

Johnson, Philip. Born 21 June 1804 of William and Elizabeth Johnson; West Union, Morgan County. Company E 33rd

Regiment; Sergeant; 59 years of age. Died circa 1879; buried West Union.

Johnson, Reuben E. Born 1 June 1848 of Isaac W. and Elizabeth Johnson; Honey Creek, Howard County. Company G 89th Regiment; 14 years of age. Died at Nashville, Tennessee, 8 December 1864.

Johnson, Robert. Born circa 1845; West Union, Morgan County. Company D 70th Regiment; 18 years of age; wounded at the battle of Peach Tree Creek, Georgia, right leg amputated above knee. Died circa 1867; buried West Union.

Johnson, Thomas H. Born 3 August 1845; Pipe Creek, Miami County. Company K 130th Regiment; 18 years of age; produced offering at Pipe Creek.

Johnson, William H. Born 16 November 1837; Cherry Grove, Randolph County. Company H 6th Regiment; 23 years of age; wounded at Chickamauga, Georgia, 20 September 1863; reenlisted Company H 124th Regiment.

Johnson, William S. Born 15 April 1835 of Richard W. and Edna Johnson; Walnut Ridge, Rush County. Company K 134th Regiment, 100 days; 29 years of age.

Johnson, William Thomas Elwood. Born 30 September 1843 of William G. and Anna M. Johnson; Plainfield, Hendricks County. Produced offering at Plainfield.

Johnson, Zeno (Zemo). Born 13 March 1840 of John and Phebe Johnson; Westfield, Hamilton County. Company H 57th Regiment; 21 years of age; discharged for disability 21 May 1863.

Jones, Abner P. Born 30 January 1844; Wabash, Wabash County. Died 26 February 1870; buried Friends Cemetery, Wabash County.

Jones, Daniel. Born 23 June 1825 of Daniel and Elizabeth Jones; New Garden, Wayne County. Company I 147th Regiment, 1 year; 39 years of age.

Jones, Eleazer. Born 9 March 1841 of Eli and Dianna Jones; White Lick, Morgan County. Company E 12th Regiment; 21 years of age.

Jones, Francis M. Born 10 March 1834 of Daniel and Elizabeth Jones; Mississinewa, Grant County. Company D 26th Regiment; 30 years of age. Died 26 February 1926; buried IOOF, Grant County.

Jones, Isaac M. Born 14 December 1845 of Allen M. and Eliza J. Jones; Indianapolis, Marion County. Company B 147th Regiment, 1 year; Corporal; 19 years of age. Died circa 1902; buried Crown Hill Cemetery, Marion County.

Jones, James. Born 19 October 1837; Lick Creek, Orange County. Company F 131st Regiment, 13th Cavalry; Lieutenant; 26 years of age; resigned 11 August 1864. Died 27 September 1902; buried Beech Grove, Orange County.

Jones, Jesse E. Born circa 1843 of Anna Jones; New Garden, Wayne County. Company B 19th Regiment; Sergeant; 18 years of age; wounded at the Battle of the Wilderness 5 May 1864; disowned at New Garden.

Jones, John Franklin. Born 16 February 1839 of William Jones; Mississinewa, Grant County. Company H 12th Regiment, 1 year; 21 years of age; reenlisted Company C 89th Regiment; Captain; disowned at Mississinewa. Died 16 April 1913; buried Park Cemetery, Grant County.

Jones, John W. Born 13 February 1839 of William Jones; Mississinewa, Grant County. Company C 89th Regiment; 23 years of age. Died 14 January 1898; buried Park Cemetery, Grant County.

Jones, Lewis. Born 6 March 1845; Oak Ridge, Grant County. Company F 34th Regiment; 16 years of age; discharged for disability 20 June 1863; disowned at Oak Ridge. Died circa 1869; buried Oak Ridge.

Jones, Milfred. Born 22 April 1840; Oak Ridge, Grant County. Company C 12th Regiment; Sergeant; 22 years of age. Died at LaGrange, Tennessee, 13 January 1863.

Jones, Oliver H. Born 25 September 1841 of William D. and Fidelia Jones; Wabash, Wabash County. Company H 118th Regiment, 6 months; Sergeant; 21 years of age.

Jones, Reuben W. Born 12 April 1839 of Daniel and Elizabeth Jones; Mississinewa, Grant County. Company A 68th Regiment; 1st Lieutenant; 22 years of age; produced offering at Mississinewa. Died 1 September 1925; buried IOOF, Grant County.

Jones, Samuel. Honey Creek, Howard County. Company H 130th Regiment; Corporal; 43 years of age; produced offering at Honey Creek.

Jones, Thomas. Born 12 August 1833 of Lewis and Mary Jones; Back Creek, Grant County. Company A 71st Regiment, 6th Cavalry; 29 years of age; deserted 15 October 1862. Died circa 1875; buried Oak Ridge, Grant County.

Jones, Thomas Clarkson. Born 5 November 1840 of William Jones; Mississinewa, Grant County. Company C 89th Regiment; 21 years of age. Died at Memphis, Tennessee, 9 February 1863; buried Deer Creek, Grant County.

Jones, Wiley B. Born circa 1846. Company E 126th Regiment, 11th Cavalry; 18 years of age; disowned at Honey Creek, Howard County.

Jones, William P. Born 29 July 1842 of John and Sarah Jones; Honey Creek, Howard County. Company H 57th Regiment; 20 years of age. Died 8 December 1925; buried Albright Cemetery, Howard County.

Jordan, Andrew J. Born circa 1829; West Union, Morgan County. Company D 70th Regiment; 33 years of age. Died at Gallatin, Tennessee, 21 March 1863; buried West Union.

Joy, William. Born circa 1841. Back Creek, Grant County. Company H 8th Regiment; 20 years of age; discharged 26 December 1862. Buried Back Creek.

Kean (Keen), Jacob C. Born 25 April 1840 of Jacob B. and Edith Kean; Sand Creek, Bartholomew County. Company

E 26th Regiment; 21 years of age; discharged for disability 1 May 1862; disowned at Sand Creek.

Kelley, Moses T. Born 22 August 1839 of Samuel and Mary Kelley; Bloomfield, Parke County. Company I 31st Regiment; Corporal; 22 years of age; reenlisted Company A 85th Regiment; promoted Lieutenant in 116th Regiment, United States Colored Troops. Died 29 May 1913; buried Friends Cemetery, Parke County.

Kelley, William P. Born 8 December 1836 of Samuel and Mary Kelley; Bloomfield, Parke County. Company K 43rd Regiment; 24 years of age. Died 23 May 1862; buried Bloomfield.

Keltner, Jacob. Died 29 January 1867; buried Silver Creek Cemetery, Union County.

Kendall, Himelias. Born 3 July 1840 of James G. and Sally Kendall; Mill Creek, Hendricks County. Company B 117th Regiment, 6 months; Corporal; 22 years of age; disowned at Mill Creek.

Kendall, James. Born circa 1832; Maple Grove (Hicksite), Huntington County. Company H 130th Regiment; 32 years of age. Died at Nashville, Tennessee, 24 June 1864; buried Maple Grove.

Kendall, James Parnel. Born 4 October 1827 of James G. and Sally Kendall; Mill Creek, Hendricks County. Company G 99th Regiment; 34 years of age; disowned at Mill Creek.

Kennard, John. Born circa 1821 of Thomas and Elizabeth Kennard; Fall Creek (Hicksite), Madison County. Produced offering at Fall Creek. Died 17 March 1891.

Kenyon, Hoxie G. Born circa 1824. Company A 101st Regiment; Captain; 38 years of age; resigned 22 January 1863; disowned at Westfield, Hamilton County. Died circa 1886.

Kern, Amos J. Born circa 1844. Henry County. Company B 42nd Regiment; 20 years of age; drafted.

Kern, John A. Born circa 1841. Henry County. Company D 36th Regiment; Sergeant; 20 years of age; Killed at Kennesaw Mountain, Georgia, 23 June 1864.

Kern, Thomas C. Born circa 1844. Henry County. Company D 147th Regiment, 1 year; Commissary Sergeant; 21 years of age.

Kersey, Amos. Born 23 October 1842 of James C. and Elizabeth Kersey; Mill Creek, Hendricks County. Company I 27th Regiment; 18 years of age; produced offering at Mill Creek.

Kersey, Ezra. Born 14 November 1844 of James C. and Elizabeth Kersey; Mill Creek, Hendricks County. Company E 78th Regiment, 60 days; 17 years of age. Died 5 August 1863; buried Milliken's Bend, Louisiana.

Kersey, Isaac. Born 19 March 1838 of James C. and Elizabeth Kersey; Mill Creek, Hendricks County. Company D 70th Regiment; 24 years of age; discharged 21 November 1862; produced offering at Mill Creek.

Kersey, Jonathan. Born 11 September 1840 of James C. and Elizabeth Kersey; Mill Creek, Hendricks County. Company I 91st Regiment, 6 months; 22 years of age; disowned at Mill Creek.

King, James H. Born circa 1837. Company G 36th Regiment; Captain; 24 years of age. Killed at Stones River, Tennessee, 2 January 1863; buried Silver Creek Cemetery, Union County.

King, Levinas (Lavinus). Born circa 1840. From Wayne County. Company I 47th Regiment; 22 years of age. Died at Helena, Arkansas, 27 August 1862.

Kinley, Isaac. Born 19 May 1821; Milford (Hicksite), Wayne County. Company D 36th Regiment; Major; 39 years of age; wounded at Stones River, Tennessee; resigned his commission 20 May 1863; appointed Provost Marshal of the fifth congressional district; produced offering at Milford

(Hicksite). Died 18 April 1896; buried Spring Grove Cemetery, Cincinnati, Ohio.

Kivetts (Kivelts), Alfred A. Born 4 April 1844 of Margaret Kivetts; West Union, Morgan County. Company B 117th Regiment, 6 months; 19 years of age; produced offering at West Union.

Knight, Ira J. Born circa 1843 of John and Sarah Knight; Raysville, Henry County. Company H 8th Regiment; 18 years of age.

Lamar, Nathan S. Born 1 September 1843 of Samuel and Judith Lamar; Springfield, Wayne County. Company B 90th Regiment, 5th Cavalry; 20 years of age; taken prisoner in Stoneman's Raid and sent to Andersonville, Georgia. Died 11 June 1904; buried Earlham Cemetery.

Lamb, Absalom H. Born 2 November 1840 of Absalom and Frances Lamb; Honey Creek, Howard County. Company D 39th Regiment, 8th Cavalry; 22 years of age. Died 27 June 1900; buried IOOF, Howard County.

Lamb, George W. Born circa 1845 of Harvey Lamb; Springfield, Wayne County. Company K 124th Regiment; 19 years of age.

Lamb, Henry. Honey Creek, Howard County.

Lamb, Henry H. Born circa 1845 of Harvey Lamb; Springfield, Wayne County. Company K 124th Regiment; Corporal; 19 years of age.

Lamb, John. Born circa 1842 of Harvey Lamb; Springfield, Wayne County. Company C 57th Regiment; 19 years of age; wounded at Mission Ridge.

Lamb, John H. Born 21 February 1844 of Milo and Susan Lamb; Springfield, Wayne County. Company K 124th Regiment; 19 years of age.

Lamb, John S. Born circa 1841; Westfield, Hamilton County. Company D 75th Regiment; Musician; 21 years of age. Died 6 December 1913; buried Gray Friends, Hamilton County.

Lamb, Martin L. Born circa 1839 of Harvey Lamb; Springfield, Wayne County. Company C 57th Regiment; 22 years of age; taken prisoner at Franklin, exchanged, and on the way home he was killed in the explosion of the steamer *Sultana* 20 April 1865.

Lamb, William. Born 22 January 1846 of Bergis and Catharine Lamb; New Salem, Howard County. Company D 118th Regiment, 6 months; 17 years of age.

Lamb, William. Born circa 1838. Springfield, Wayne County. Company C 57th Regiment; 23 years of age; wounded at Kennesaw Mountain, Georgia.

Lamm, Joseph T. Born circa 1842. Company A 33rd Regiment; 19 years of age; produced offering at Mississinewa, Grant County.

Lamme, Jonathan. Born 27 February 1836 of Caleb and Sarah Lamme; Back Creek, Grant County. Company I 34th Regiment; 28 years of age. Died at New Orleans, Louisiana, 1 January 1865.

Lee, Benjamin F. Born circa 1844. Company I 123rd Regiment; 20 years of age. Died at Knoxville, Tennessee, 30 June 1864; buried Friends Cemetery, Howard County.

Lee, Chambers. Born 30 September 1837; Lick Creek, Orange County. Company I 112th Regiment, 8 days; 25 years of age. Died 22 May 1866; buried Newberry Cemetery, Orange County.

Lee, Hiram. Born 12 October 1833; Lick Creek, Orange County. Company F 131st Regiment, 13th Cavalry; 30 years of age. Died 19 February 1907; buried Lick Creek.

Lee, John M. Born 15 March 1844 of William Lee; Lick Creek, Orange County. Company F 131st Regiment, 13th Cavalry; 19 years of age. Killed at Murfreesboro, Tennessee, 15 December 1864.

Lee, William R. Born 13 May 1844 of John and Hannah Lee; Springfield, Wayne County. Company I 105th Regiment, 9 days; 19 years of age.

Leonard, Alfred. Born 8 January 1840 of Jonathan and Dorcas Leonard; Union, Howard County. Company I 38th Regiment; 21 years of age. Died 27 December 1921; buried Friends Cemetery, Howard County.

Leonard, Hiram. Born circa 1840 of Jesse and Belinda Leonard; Walnut Ridge, Rush County. Company C 79th Regiment; 22 years of age. Died at McMinnville, Tennessee, 25 July 1863.

Lester, Calvin A. Born circa 1844; Blue River, Washington County. 13th Light Artillery; 18 years of age. Died 11 August 1881; buried Blue River.

Leverton, John E. Born 19 November 1839 of Charles Leverton; Milford (Hicksite), Wayne County. 3rd Light Artillery; 22 years of age.

Lewelling, Henry Clayton. Born 18 December 1843 of Rachel Lewelling; Chester, Wayne County. Company A 133rd Regiment, 100 days; 20 years of age.

Lewis, Exum T. Born 25 July 1843 of Zimri and Peninah Lewis; Rocky Run, Parke County. Company B 115th Regiment, 6 months; Corporal; 20 years of age; disowned at Rocky Run.

Lewis, Jonathan. Born 24 September 1832 of John J. and Rebecca Lewis; Fall Creek (Hicksite), Madison County. Company I 110th Regiment, 5 days; 30 years of age. Died 24 February 1871; buried Fall Creek.

Lewis, Joseph. Born circa 1839; Camden (Hicksite), Jay County. Company F 75th Regiment; Captain; 25 years of age. Died circa 1895; buried Quaker Cemetery, Jay County.

Lewis, William H. Born 19 May 1840 of Jonah and Lavina Lewis; Bloomfield, Parke County. 2nd Light Artillery; 21 years of age.

Lindley, Calvin. Born 7 December 1829 of James and Ruth Lindley; Indianapolis, Marion County. 137th Regiment, 100 days; Quartermaster; 34 years of age. Died 1 December 1891; buried Crown Hill Cemetery, Marion County.

Lindley, Charles W. Born 5 September 1846 of Aaron and Julia Ann Lindley; Rush Creek, Parke County. Company C 116th Regiment, 6 months; 17 years of age; reenlisted Company G 133rd Regiment, 100 days.

Lindley, Elwood. Born 27 November 1845; Lick Creek, Orange County. Company M 131st Regiment, 13th Cavalry; 18 years of age. Died 18 August 1866; buried Lick Creek.

Lindley, George. Born circa 1835. Bloomfield, Parke County. Company C 116th Regiment, 6 months; 28 years of age.

Lindley, George T. Born 20 February 1846 of Alfred and Martha Jane Lindley; Lick Creek, Orange County. Company G 49th Regiment; Corporal; 15 years of age.

Lindley, J. Hiram. Born 17 July 1825 of James and Ruth Lindley; Indianapolis, Marion County. Company C 113th Regiment, 7 days; 37 years of age. Died 20 August 1876; buried Crown Hill Cemetery, Marion County.

Lindley, James G. Born circa 1826. White Lick, Morgan County. Company K 90th Regiment, 5th Cavalry; 36 years of age. Died at Indianapolis, Indiana, 19 December 1862; buried White Lick.

Lindley, James H. Born circa 1844 of Samuel and Anna B. Lindley; Lick Creek, Orange County. Company K 53rd Regiment; 17 years of age. Died 9 April 1863; buried Newberry Cemetery, Orange County.

Lindley, John T. Born circa 1841. Lick Creek, Orange County. Company D 66th Regiment; 21 years of age.

Lindley, Laban. Born circa 1843 of William and Anna Lindley; Lick Creek, Orange County. Company F 131st Regiment, 13th Cavalry; 1st Sergeant; 20 years of age. Died circa 1923; buried IOOF, Orange County.

Lindley, Thomas. Born circa 1837; Lick Creek, Orange County. Company B 24th Regiment; 24 years of age. Died 6 October 1863; buried Lick Creek.

Lindley, Thomas J. Born 7 October 1843; Westfield, Hamilton County. Company H 57th Regiment; Sergeant; 18

years of age; discharged for disability 3 August 1863; reenlisted Company D 136th Regiment, 100 days; reenlisted Company G 147th Regiment, 1 year; produced offering at Westfield. Died 19 September 1915, Hamilton County.

Lindley, William. Born 11 December 1835 of Thomas and Mary Lindley; Bloomfield, Parke County. Company C 116th Regiment, 6 months; 27 years of age. Died 18 June 1924; buried Rush Creek #2, Parke County.

Lindley, William R. Born circa 1834. Honey Creek, Howard County. Company E 126th Regiment, 11th Cavalry; 29 years of age. Died at Kokomo, Indiana, 3 May 1864; buried Lindley Cemetery, Howard County.

Lindley, William R. Born 6 January 1845; Lick Creek, Orange County. Company E 66th Regiment; 18 years of age; transferred to 59th Regiment 30 May 1865. Died 17 April 1910; buried Lick Creek.

Little, Alexander. Born 6 November 1839; Back Creek, Grant County. Company B 119th Regiment, 7th Cavalry; 24 years of age; transferred to Company D 7th Cavalry Reorganized; produced offering at Back Creek. Died 20 February 1924.

Little, Azel G. Born circa 1841; Back Creek, Grant County. Company H 12th Regiment, 1 year; 20 years of age. Died circa 1867; buried Back Creek.

Little, Joseph. Born 25 February 1835 of Nathan and Nancy Little; Back Creek, Grant County. Company C 89th Regiment; 27 years of age. Died circa 1909; buried Back Creek.

Little, Thomas. Born 9 December 1842; Back Creek, Grant County. Company B 119th Regiment, 7th Cavalry; 20 years of age; transferred to Company D 7th Cavalry Reorganized. Died circa 1904; buried Back Creek.

Long, James. Born 7 October 1847 of Henry Long; Oak Ridge, Grant County. Company I 151st Regiment, 1 year; 17 years of age. Died 6 June 1913; buried Veterans Facility, Grant County.

Lukens, Allen. Born 3 September 1821; Fall Creek (Hicksite), Madison County. Produced offering at Fall Creek. Died 28 June 1900.

Lukens, Richard M. Born circa 1827. Company C 107th Regiment, 10 days; Sergeant; 36 years of age; produced offering at Fall Creek (Hicksite), Madison County.

Lupton, Solomon. Born circa 1836. Camden (Hicksite), Jay County. Company C 39th Regiment, 8th Cavalry; Corporal; 25 years of age. Died 9 February 1876; buried Quaker Cemetery, Jay County.

MacPherson, Charles J. W. Company A 16th Regiment, United States Infantry. Died circa 1862 at Fort Halleck, Kentucky; buried Friends Cemetery, Wabash County.

McBride, John W. Born 1 March 1826 of Jeremiah and Elizabeth McBride; Lick Creek, Orange County. Buried Newberry Cemetery, Orange County.

McCoy, Isaac. Born 9 June 1841 of John and Elizabeth McCoy; Rush Creek, Parke County. 9th Light Artillery; 20 years of age; Bugler. Died near Corinth, Mississippi, 12 June 1862.

McCoy, Joseph Gilbert. Born 25 February 1825; Honey Creek, Howard County. Company B 87th Regiment; 39 years of age; discharged 11 February 1863. Died 13 October 1897; buried Friends Cemetery, Howard County.

McCracken, Elwood. Born circa 1841. 34th Regiment; 24 years of age; disowned at Pleasant Hill, Howard County.

McCune, Henry Will. Born circa 1838. Company G 84th Regiment; 24 years of age; transferred to Veteran Reserve Corps 28 May 1864.

McDaniels, John F. Born 27 July 1841; Blue River, Washington County. Company G 13th Regiment; 19 years of age; discharged for disability 9 April 1863. Died April 1863; buried Old Blue River.

McHattan, Samuel. Produced offering at Back Creek, Grant County.

McKinney, W. E. Company D 9th Regiment; drafted. Died of disease at Shield's Mills, Tennessee, 18 April 1865; buried Old Quaker (Hopewell) Cemetery, Jennings County.

Macy, Gamaliel B. Born circa 1844. 19th Light Artillery; 18 years of age; discharged for disability 17 May 1864. Buried Elm Grove Cemetery, Henry County.

Macy, Henry B. Born 14 February 1846 of Isaac and Eleanor Macy; Springfield, Wayne County. Company C 121st Regiment, 9th Cavalry; 17 years of age; wounded at battle of Franklin. Died 12 February 1865; buried West River Friends, Wayne County.

Macy, Horatio. Born circa 1841. Company F 52nd Regiment; 20 years of age. Died at home while absent with leave from City Hospital 28 December 1864; buried Friends Cemetery, Rush County.

Macy, Jethro. Born 25 June 1825 of Jonathan and Hannah Macy; Sparrow Creek, Randolph County. Company C 8th Regiment, 3 months; 35 years of age.

Macy, John. Born 8 May 1841 of Isaac and Eleanor Macy; Springfield, Wayne County. Company D 69th Regiment; Captain; 21 years of age; produced offering at Indianapolis for Springfield.

Macy, John C. Born 28 January 1840 of Thomas and Mary Macy; Back Creek, Grant County. Company F 34th Regiment; 24 years of age; produced offering at Back Creek.

Macy, John Lilburn. Born 27 September 1839 of Francis B. and Huldah Macy; Walnut Ridge, Rush County. Company G 16th Regiment; Sergeant; 22 years of age; disowned at Walnut Ridge.

Macy, John Winchester. Born 12 June 1843; Henry County. Company A 84th Regiment; 1st Sergeant; 19 years of age. Died 26 August 1912, Randolph County.

Macy, Sylvanus. Born 18 November 1843 of Isaac and Eleanor Macy; Springfield, Wayne County. Company D 69th Regiment; 18 years of age; taken prisoner at Richmond, Ken-

tucky, paroled, and exchanged; discharged for disability 19
June 1863; reported for military service at Springfield. Died
11 March 1911; buried West River Friends, Wayne County.

Marine, Jonathan F. Born 31 October 1816 of Jonathan and
Hannah Marine; New Garden, Wayne County. Company
I 124th Regiment; 47 years af age; Teamster; disowned at
New Garden. Died 9 September 1888.

Marine, Moorman. Born circa 1841 of Jonathan and Hannah
Marine; New Garden, Wayne County. Company C 57th
Regiment; Cook; 20 years of age; transferred to Veteran
Reserve Corps 30 September 1863; disowned at New
Garden.

Maris, Charles E. Honey Creek, Howard County. Company
L 126th Regiment, 11th Cavalry; produced offering at
Honey Creek. Buried Friends Cemetery, Howard County.

Maris, Enos Jones. Born 11 December 1845 of William and
Mary Maris; Bloomfield, Parke County. Company H 21st
Regiment; 18 years of age. Died on the steamer *Groesbeck*
18 September 1864.

Maris (Manis), George. Born 5 October 1834; Lick Creek,
Orange County. Company G 16th Regiment, 1 year; Corporal; 27 years of age. Buried Beech Grove Cemetery, Orange County.

Maris, George C. Born 15 January 1844; Rush Creek, Parke
County. Company A 85th Regiment; Corporal; 18 years
of age. Died 27 February 1929; buried Friends Cemetery,
Parke County.

Maris, Oliver. Born circa 1842; Orange County. Company
A 38th Regiment; 19 years of age. Died 18 January 1862;
buried Beech Grove Cemetery, Orange County.

Marsh, Elias. Born circa 1825. Walnut Ridge, Rush County.
Company G 90th Regiment, 5th Cavalry; 1st Sergeant; 37
years of age.

Marshall, Alonzo. Born 20 February 1840 of Thomas and
Cynthia Marshall; Springfield, Wayne County. Company

D 69th Regiment; 22 years of age; taken prisoner at Richmond, Kentucky, paroled, and exchanged; transferred to Veteran Reserve Corps 25 December 1863. Died 26 December 1920.

Marshall, Clayton. 23rd Regiment.

Marshall, Collin.

Marshall, Mahlon W. Born 14 October 1838 of Alfred and Hannah Marshall; Bloomfield, Parke County. Company A 85th Regiment; 23 years of age. Died 13 April 1926; buried Rockville, Parke County.

Marshall, Miles.

Marshall, Swain. Born 18 October 1839 of Thomas and Cynthia Marshall; Springfield, Wayne County. Company G 8th Regiment; 1st Lieutenant; 21 years of age. Died 16 March 1905; buried Springfield.

Marshall, Thomas. Born circa 1824. Company K 43rd Regiment; 37 years of age. Died Keokuk, Iowa, 1 October 1862; buried Rush Creek #2, Parke County.

Marshall, William. Born 27 April 1843 of William and Elizabeth Marshall; Rush Creek, Parke County. Company C 116th Regiment, 6 months; 20 years of age; reenlisted Company A 31st Regiment; disowned at Rush Creek.

Marshall, William. Born circa 1844. Jericho Friends, Randolph County. Company C 19th Regiment; 17 years of age. Died of disease at Indianapolis.

Marshall, William L. Born 23 November 1833; Honey Creek, Howard County. Company I 142nd Regiment, 1 year; 30 years of age. Died 9 September 1929; buried Friends Cemetery, Howard County.

Matthews, Benjamin F. Born 14 November 1841 of Joel and Hannah Matthews; Whitewater (Hicksite), Wayne County. Company F 69th Regiment; 20 years of age; captured at battle of Richmond, Kentucky, paroled, came home, taken sick. Died 25 September 1862.

Maudlin (Modlin), Nathan. Born circa 1819. Howard County. Company A 130th Regiment; 44 years of age. Died at Chattanooga, Tennessee, 4 June 1864.

Maxwell, James B. Born 10 September 1839 of David and Matilda Maxwell; Silver Creek-Salem, Union County. Company D 121st Regiment, 9th Cavalry; Sergeant; 23 years of age. Died 21 April 1867; buried Salem Cemetery, Union.

Maxwell, Milton. Born 18 January 1844 of Thomas and Jemima Maxwell; Silver Creek-Salem, Union County. Disowned at Salem.

Mendenhall, Caleb B. Born 14 June 1843 of Miles and Margaret Mendenhall; Mill Creek, Hendricks County. Company C 51st Regiment; 18 years of age. Died 21 April 1863.

Mendenhall, Caleb S. Born 8 May 1830 of Griffith and Elizabeth Mendenhall; Whitewater, Wayne County. Company I 84th Regiment; 1st Sergeant; 32 years of age; baggage-master on hospital train.

Mendenhall, Henry W. Son of John and Hannah Mendenhall; Whitewater, Wayne County. Disowned at Whitewater.

Mendenhall, Jesse H. Born 28 June 1840; Oak Ridge, Grant County. Disowned at Oak Ridge.

Mendenhall, John A. Born 21 October 1833 of Griffith and Elizabeth Mendenhall; Whitewater, Wayne County. Company I 41st Regiment, 2nd Cavalry; 27 years of age; captured in Stoneman's Raid and served as hospital steward while prisoner; transferred to 2nd Cavalry Reorganized; Hospital Steward. Died 10 February 1878; buried Earlham Cemetery.

Mendenhall, Jonathan C. Born 14 August 1836 of Thomas and Rebecca Mendenhall; Plainfield, Hendricks County. Company A 117th Regiment, 6 months; 26 years of age; produced offering at Plainfield.

Mendenhall, Joseph Coffin. Born 20 February 1845 of James and Millicent Mendenhall; Whitewater, Wayne County.

Company L 71st Regiment, 6th Cavalry; Corporal; 18 years of age; scout, guard, orderly.

Mendenhall, Kelita. Born circa 1842. Carthage Friends, Rush County. Company E 121st Regiment, 9th Cavalry; 21 years of age. Died at Cahawba Prison, Alabama, 26 March 1865.

Mendenhall, Nathan. Born 18 February 1823 of Aaron Mendenhall; Springfield, Wayne County. Company C 19th Regiment; 38 years of age.

Mendenhall, Samuel. Born 22 April 1848 of Nathan and Rhoda Mendenhall; Dover, Wayne County. Company F 124th Regiment; 15 years of age; discharged for physical disability 6 July 1864. Died 3 December 1892; buried Webster Cemetery, Wayne County.

Meredith, Henry Clay. Born 17 July 1843 of Solomon Meredith; Milford, Wayne County. Aide-de-camp to Solomon Meredith; Company K 108th Regiment; 2nd Lieutenant; 18 years of age. Died 5 July 1882 Wayne County.

Meredith, John M. Born 12 March 1843 of James and Mary M. Meredith; Whitewater (Hicksite), Wayne County. Company F 75th Regiment; 19 years of age. Died at Murfreesboro, Tennessee, 30 January 1863.

Meredith, Samuel H. Born circa 1839 of Solomon Meredith; Milford, Wayne County. Company A 19th Regiment; 22 years of age; Senior Aide to Brigadier General of the 19th Regiment; reenlisted same regiment; wounded at Gainesville, Virginia, and Gettysburg, Pennsylvania. Died from wounds 22 January 1864.

Meredith, Solomon. Born 29 May 1810; Milford, Wayne County. 19th Regiment; Brigadier General; 51 years of age; wounded at Gainesville, Virginia, and Gettysburg, Pennsylvania; commanded posts at Cairo, Illinois, and Paducah, Kentucky. Died 21 October 1875, Wayne County.

Middleton, Hudson. Born 3 July 1844 of Levi and Mary Middleton; Honey Creek, Howard County. Company G 57th Regiment; 20 years of age; dishonorable discharge for desertion; produced offering at Honey Creek. Died 11 September 1914; buried Friends Cemetery, Howard County.

Miller, Reuben R. Company H 8th Regiment. Buried Farmer's Institute, Tippecanoe County.

Miller, William Reuben. Company I 36th Regiment; discharged for physical disability 28 December 1863; disowned at Whitewater (Hicksite), Wayne County.

Millikan (Milikan), Eli F. Born 17 August 1843 of William Millikan; Springfield, Wayne County. Company C 36th Regiment; 17 years of age; produced offering at Springfield.

Milliner, Joseph H. Produced offering in Iowa for Back Creek, Grant County.

Mills, David H. Born 15 December 1846 of Dempsey and Sarah Ann Mills; Bloomfield, Parke County. Company B 115th Regiment, 6 months; 16 years of age. Died at Knoxville, Tennessee, 1 November 1863.

Mills, Elisha. Born circa 1827; Westfield, Hamilton County. Company D 75th Regiment; Sergeant Major; 35 years of age. Died 3 August 1915; buried Friends Cemetery, Wabash County.

Mills, Isaac. Born 28 November 1845 of Drura and Sarah Mills; Westfield, Hamilton County. Company E 57th Regiment; 15 years of age; discharged for disability 6 November 1862. Died 18 June 1880; buried Pleasant View Cemetery, Hamilton County.

Mills, James. Born 22 November 1818 of William and Dinah Mills; Bridgeport, Marion County. Company G 16th Regiment, 1 year; 45 years of age; transferred to 131st Regiment, 13th Cavalry. Died 27 July 1903; buried Friends Center Church, Marion County.

Mills, James S. Born circa 1836. Company A 9th Regiment; 28 years of age; drafted; produced offering at New Garden, Wayne County.

Mills, John. Born circa 1833. Springfield, Wayne County. Company D 69th Regiment; 29 years of age; Wagoner.

Mills, John H. Born 14 September 1843 of William C. and Rebecca Mills; White Lick, Morgan County. Company E 12th Regiment; Corporal; 18 years of age; produced offering at White Lick.

Mills, Nathan. Born 8 April 1843 of Aaron and Rebecca Mills; New Garden, Wayne County. Company K 3rd Regiment, Tennessee Volunteers; produced offering at New Garden.

Mills, William H. Born circa 1830. Sugar Plain, Boone County. Company B 72nd Regiment; 32 years of age. Died at New Albany, Indiana, 15 March 1863.

Milner, Jesse J. Born 22 August 1845 of George and Susannah Milner; Oak Ridge, Grant County. Reported for military service at Oak Ridge.

Modlin, Elias. Born circa 1846. Duck Creek, Henry County. Company A 19th Regiment; transferred to Company I 20th Regiment; 18 years of age. Buried Clear Spring Friends, Henry County.

Modlin, John H. Born 5 May 1841 of William and Elizabeth Ann Modlin; Duck Creek, Henry County. Company C 36th Regiment; Corporal; 20 years of age. Died at Nashville, Tennessee, 23 July 1864.

Modlin, Seth. Born 26 November 1843 of Elias Modlin; Duck Creek, Henry County. Company E 139th Regiment, 100 days; 20 years of age.

Montgomery, J. W. Born 17 April 1848; Lick Creek, Orange County. Company K 53rd Regiment; 13 years of age. Died 19 April 1904; buried IOOF, Orange County.

Moon, Benjamin F. Born 3 December 1839 of Jesse and Phebe Moon; New Salem, Howard County. Company C 26th Regiment; 22 years of age; discharged for disability 8 May 1862; reported for military service at New Salem.

Moon, James A. Born circa 1838. 16th Light Artillery; 23 years of age; disowned at Greenfield, Tippecanoe County. Died circa 1878; buried Farmer's Institute, Tippecanoe County.

Moon, Joseph B. Honey Creek, Howard County. Company C 26th Regiment; 19 years of age.

Moon, Thomas X. Born 5 June 1843 of Isaiah and Mary Moon; Mississinewa, Grant County. Company D 139th Regiment, 100 days; 21 years of age. Died 12 June 1929; buried IOOF, Grant County.

Moore, Charles H. C. Born 29 July 1832 of Charles and Anna Moore; Spiceland, Henry County. Company A 36th Regiment; 29 years of age.

Moore, Clarkson T. Son of Camm Moore; Whitewater (Hicksite), Wayne County. Disowned at Whitewater (Hicksite).

Moore, John L. Born circa 1843. Company D 136th Regiment, 100 days; 21 years of age; produced offering at Westfield, Hamilton County.

Moore, John O. Born 12 June 1842 of Joseph and Deborah Moore; Walnut Ridge, Rush County. Company A 38th Regiment; 22 years of age; drafted.

Moore, Joseph R. Born circa 1839; Lick Creek, Orange County. Company B 24th Regiment; 22 years of age; transferred to Company E 24th Regiment; Captain. Died circa 1928; buried IOOF, Orange County.

Moore, Josiah B. Born 7 May 1838 of William and Ann Moore; Spiceland, Henry County. Company A 36th Regiment; 25 years of age; transferred to Company H 30th Regiment; Corporal.

Moore, Marcus H. Born circa 1843. Company E 68th Regiment; 19 years of age; transferred to Veteran Reserve Corps 27 July 1863; disowned at Richland, Hamilton County.

Moore, Thomas C. Born 4 September 1840 of Joseph and Deborah Moore; Westfield, Hamilton County. Company A 101st Regiment; Corporal; 21 years of age; produced offering at Westfield.

Moore, William A. Born 28 October 1845 of Joseph and Deborah Moore; Westfield, Hamilton County. Company E 34th Regiment; 15 years of age; discharged for disability

21 October 1862; reenlisted Company G 147th Regiment, 1 year; produced offering at Westfield.

Morgan, Elihu. Born 29 February 1844 of Hezekiah and Eunice P. Morgan; White Lick, Morgan County. Produced offering at Fairfield, Hendricks County. Died circa 1935; buried Mooresville.

Morgan, Hezekiah. Born 11 October 1836 of Thomas Morgan; Plainfield, Hendricks County. Company G 148th Regiment, 1 year; 28 years of age; produced offering at Plainfield.

Morgan, John. Son of Nathan Morgan; Whitewater (Hicksite), Wayne County. Company C 90th Regiment, 5th Cavalry; Corporal; taken prisoner near Waynesboro, Georgia; disowned at Whitewater (Hicksite).

Morgan, John E. From Wayne County. Company G 5th Regiment, Ohio Volunteers.

Morgan, Nathan. Born 15 November 1823; Whitewater (Hicksite), Wayne County. Company C 41st Regiment, 2nd Cavalry; 37 years of age; produced offering at Whitewater (Hicksite). Died 11 February 1908; buried Ridge Cemetery, Wayne County.

Morical, Thomas. Born circa 1842. Mill Creek, Hendricks County. Company B 117th Regiment, 6 months; 21 years of age. Died at Camp Nelson, Kentucky, 6 October 1863; buried Mill Creek.

Morman (Moorman), Elijah L. Born 8 February 1840 of Lewis and Sarah Morman; Back Creek, Grant County. Company H 12th Regiment, 1 year; 21 years of age.

Morman (Moorman), Stephen. Born 19 June 1842 of Lewis and Sarah Morman; Back Creek, Grant County. Company K 130th Regiment; 21 years of age. Died in New York Harbor 25 May 1865.

Morman (Moorman), Zachariah. Born 24 May 1845 of Lewis and Sarah Morman; Back Creek, Grant County. Company D 54th Regiment, 1 year; 16 years of age.

Morris, Aaron. Born 23 November 1834; Milford (Hicksite), Wayne County. Company G 21st Regiment; Corporal; 26 years of age; produced offering at Milford (Hicksite). Died 15 February 1907.

Morris, Alfred. Born 28 May 1820 of Aaron and Sarah Morris; Blue River (Hicksite), Washington County. Company F 66th Regiment; Captain. Died 27 February 1895; buried Old Blue River.

Morris, Charles. Born 27 October 1843 of Samuel and Sarah Morris; Milford (Hicksite), Wayne County. Produced offering at Milford (Hicksite).

Morris, Charles C. Born 5 August 1849 of Exum and Eleanor Morris; Bloomfield, Parke County. Died 29 October 1920; buried Rockville.

Morris, Henry. Born 10 July 1842 of Jesse and Joanna Morris; Walnut Ridge, Rush County. Company K 134th Regiment, 100 days; 21 years of age; produced offering at Walnut Ridge.

Morris, John. Born 22 November 1821 of Aaron and Nanny Morris; New Garden, Wayne County. Company E 57th Regiment; 40 years of age. Died at Louisville, Kentucky, 28 July 1864.

Morris, Joseph. Born 22 September 1813 of Reuben and Miriam Morris; Indianapolis, Marion County. Company E 82nd Regiment; 1st Lieutenant; 51 years of age. Died 20 July 1899; buried Crown Hill Cemetery, Marion County.

Morris, Thomas A. Born 15 April 1844; Blue River (Hicksite), Washington County. Company D 38th Regiment; Corporal; 19 years of age. Died 29 July 1868; buried Old Blue River.

Morris, Thomas Elwood. Born 9 February 1847 of John T. and Rebecca Morris; Back Creek, Grant County. Company C 151st Regiment, 1 year; 18 years of age; produced offering at Back Creek.

Morris, William. Born 31 August 1821 of Aaron and Nanny Morris; New Garden, Wayne County. Company E 57th Regiment; 40 years of age. Died at Knoxville, Tennessee, 7 December 1863.

Mote, Thomas E. Born circa 1836. Company A 137th Regiment, 100 days; 28 years of age; disowned at Honey Creek, Howard County.

Moulder, William. Born 12 December 1842 of Archibald and Hannah Moulder; Kokomo, Howard County. Company F 131st Regiment, 13th Cavalry; Sergeant; 21 years of age. Died circa 1921; buried Friends Cemetery, Howard County.

Murphey, Miles. Born 14 November 1806. Governor's Military Staff, Colonel and Inspector General, 1861; 54 years of age. Died 17 February 1882, Henry County.

Murphy, John. Born 24 January 1817; Wabash, Wabash County. 14th Light Artillery; 45 years of age; veteran; disowned at Wabash.

Musgrove, John A. Bloomfield, Parke County. Company H 21st Regiment, 1st Heavy Artillery. Killed at Baton Rouge, Louisiana, 5 August 1862.

Myron, John. Born circa 1822; Jay County. Company B 126th Regiment, 11th Cavalry; 41 years of age. Died 25 April 1864; buried Quaker Cemetery, Jay County.

Neal, John. Springfield, Wayne County. First drafted into the Confederate Army; deserted; enlisted Company A 121st Regiment, 9th Cavalry.

Nelson, Jacob. Born 25 July 1814; Wabash County. Died 18 October 1865; buried Wabash County.

Newby, Daniel. Born 4 December 1838 of Thomas and Millicent Newby; Hopewell, Henry County. Company A 36th Regiment; Corporal; 22 years of age; discharged for disability 22 September 1862.

Newby, Henry F. Born 15 September 1834 of Frederick and Sarah Newby; Raysville, Henry County. Company F 84th

Regiment; Corporal; 27 years of age; produced offering at
Raysville. Died 2 June 1877; buried Raysville.

Newby, Isaac E. Born 4 August 1845 of Joshua and Sallie
Newby; Hinkles Creek, Hamilton County. Company M
39th Regiment, 8th Cavalry; 18 years of age. Died circa
1915; buried Hinkles Creek.

Newby, James. Born circa 1840. Milford, Wayne County.
Company I 36th Regiment; 21 years of age; Captain; disowned at Milford.

Newby, James Iven. Born circa 1835 of Thomas and Sarah
Newby; Henry County. Company D 36th Regiment; Corporal; 26 years of age.

Newby, John. Born 1 March 1843 of Axum and Rachel
Newby; Back Creek, Grant County. Company B 33rd
Regiment; 21 years of age; drafted; produced offering at
Back Creek.

Newby, John W. Born 11 April 1833 of Thomas and Sarah
Newby; Duck Creek, Henry County. Company D 36th
Regiment; Corporal; 28 years of age; discharged for dis-
ability 5 March 1862.

Newby, Joseph R. Born 8 December 1811 of Thomas and
Mary Newby; Driftwood, Jackson County. Company F
39th Regiment, 8th Cavalry; 51 years of age. Died at Seymour, Indiana, 20 May 1864; buried Friends Cemetery,
Jackson County.

Newby, Micajah. Born 12 December 1842 of Willis and Millicent Newby; Sand Creek, Bartholomew County. 15th
Light Artillery; 19 years of age; disowned at Sand Creek.

Newby, Nathan S. Born 8 May 1840 of John and Gulielma
Newby; Blue River, Washington County. Company D
38th Regiment; 21 years of age.

Newby, Samuel. Born 9 December 1844 of Axum and Rachel
Newby; Back Creek, Grant County. Company E 53rd
Regiment; Corporal; 17 years of age; produced offering at
Back Creek.

Newby, William. Born 1 November 1835 of Axum and Rachel Newby; Back Creek, Grant County. Company C 89th Regiment; Corporal; 26 years of age. Killed at Pleasant Hill, Louisiana, 9 April 1864.

Newby, William B. Born 13 April 1824 of Thomas and Sarah Newby; Spiceland, Henry County. Company D 36th Regiment; 37 years of age; discharged for disability 28 November 1862. Buried Old Quaker Church, Henry County.

Newlin, Henry. Born circa 1840. From Orange County. Company D 66th Regiment; 22 years of age. Died in Rebel prison at Richmond, Virginia, 14 January 1864.

Newlin, Henry H. Born circa 1842. Company I 63rd Regiment; 20 years of age; produced offering at White Lick, Morgan County.

Newlin, Henry H. Born 20 February 1842 of Nathan and Sarah Newlin; Bloomfield, Parke County. Company A 85th Regiment; 20 years of age; disowned at Bloomfield. Died 20 December 1879; buried Bethany Cemetery, Parke County.

Newlin, Joel. Born 7 October 1838 of Thomas and Martha J. Newlin; Lick Creek, Orange County. Company D 66th Regiment; 23 years of age. Died 9 May 1920; buried Concord Cemetery, Orange County.

Newlin, Samuel H. Born 1 March 1841 of Calvin and Rebecca Newlin; Bloomfield, Parke County. Company H 21st Regiment, 1st Heavy Artillery; 20 years of age; discharged for disability 19 August 1862.

Newsom, Charles. Produced offering at Sand Creek, Bartholomew County.

Newsom, David. Born 10 August 1839 of Isaac and Mary Newsom; Sand Creek, Bartholomew County. Company K 13th Regiment; 2nd Lieutenant; 21 years of age. Died circa 1884; buried Sand Creek.

Newsom, Eli. Born 28 September 1847 of Isaac and Mary Newsom; Sand Creek, Bartholomew County. Company A 120th Regiment; Corporal; 16 years of age.

Newsom, John Gurney. Born 2 September 1840 of Luke and Cynthia Newsom; Walnut Ridge, Rush County. Company D 67th Regiment; 21 years of age; disowned at Walnut Ridge.

Newsom, Jose. Born 11 December 1844 of Isaac and Mary Newsom; Sand Creek, Bartholomew County. Company A 53rd Regiment; 17 years of age; disowned at Sand Creek.

Newsom, Levi. Born 23 September 1839 of Micajah and Anna Newsom; Sand Creek, Bartholomew County. Company F 39th Regiment, 8th Cavalry; 21 years of age; discharged for disability 22 August 1862; produced offering at Sand Creek. Died circa 1896; buried Sand Creek.

Newsom, Robert. Born 20 August 1821 of David and Elizabeth Newsom; Sand Creek, Bartholomew County. Company F 39th Regiment, 8th Cavalry; 40 years of age; discharged for disability 29 August 1861. Died circa 1898; buried Sand Creek.

Nichols, Elijah. Born 31 July 1822 of Enoch and Rhoda Nichols; Cherry Grove, Randolph County. Company E 43rd Regiment; 39 years of age. Died of wounds at Mark's Mills, Arkansas, 30 January 1864.

Nichols, James. Born 8 October 1827 of Enoch and Rhoda Nichols; Cherry Grove, Randolph County. Company H 9th Regiment, 1 year; 37 years of age; Substitute. Died of disease 15 January 1865.

Nicholson, Elias Perry. Born 29 December 1840 of Samuel and Peninah Nicholson; Sand Creek, Bartholomew County. Company F 39th Regiment, 8th Cavalry; Sergeant; 20 years of age; disowned at Sand Creek. Died September 1920; buried Sand Creek.

Nicholson, Isaac P. Born 25 November 1838 of Samuel and Peninah Nicholson; Sand Creek, Bartholomew County. Company F 39th Regiment, 8th Cavalry; 22 years of age; discharged for disability 25 October 1862; produced offering at Sand Creek.

Nordyke, Edward Samuel. Born 7 October 1842 of David and Lydia Nordyke; Whitewater, Wayne County. Company I 8th Regiment, 3 months; 19 years of age; reenlisted in General John C. Fremont's Body Guard; reenlisted Company F 69th Regiment. Died on hospital boat near Helena, Arkansas, 14 February 1863.

Nordyke, Sylvanus Arthur. Born 11 January 1845 of David and Lydia Nordyke; Whitewater, Wayne County. Company A 133rd Regiment, 100 days; 19 years of age.

Ogborn, Allen W. Born circa 1840 of Edwin F. Ogborn; Henry County. Company B 19th Regiment; Sergeant; 21 years of age. Died of wounds received at battle of Gettysburg, Pennsylvania, 18 July 1863.

Ogborn, Edwin E. Born circa 1843. Company C 84th Regiment; taken sick and sent to hospital; served on detached duty; transferred to Veteran Reserve Corps 20 May 1864; 19 years of age; disowned at Whitewater (Hicksite), Wayne County.

Ogborn, James K. Produced offering at Chester, Wayne County.

Osborn, David. Born circa 1846 of Joseph Osborn; Mill Creek, Hendricks County. Company B 117th Regiment, 6 months; 17 years of age. Died at Danville, Indiana, 20 January 1864; buried Mill Creek.

Osborn, John H. Born 3 January 1840 of David and Abigail Osborn; Mill Creek, Hendricks County. Company C 25th Regiment, 1 year; 24 years of age; drafted. Buried Mill Creek.

Osborn, Samuel L. Born 11 August 1832 of William and Keziah Osborn; Back Creek, Grant County. Company I 12th Regiment, 1 year; 29 years of age.

Osborn, William T. Born circa 1845. Adopted son of Abram and Ruth Osborn; Lick Creek, Orange County. Company D 66th Regiment; 17 years of age.

Overman, Albert R. Born 14 May 1845 of Benjamin A. and
Mary Ann Overman; Blue River, Washington County.
Company C 112th Regiment, 8 days; 18 years of age. Died
21 October 1911; buried Blue River.

Overman, Curtis. Born 30 March 1844 of Silas Overman;
Mississinewa, Grant County. Company E 83rd Regiment;
20 years of age; drafted; produced offering at Mississinewa.

Overman, Cyrus Virgil. Born 31 August 1840 of Samuel
and Irene Overman; Blue River (Hicksite), Washington
County. Company E 90th Regiment, 5th Cavalry; 21 years
of age.

Overman, Eli H. Born 27 December 1837 of Stephen and
Polly Overman; Mississinewa, Grant County. Company A
75th Regiment; 26 years of age.

Overman, John Q. Born 28 July 1843 of Stephen and Polly
Overman; Mississinewa, Grant County. Company F 119th
Regiment, 7th Cavalry Reorganized; 19 years of age; pro-
duced offering at Mississinewa.

Overman, Joseph. Born 8 September 1841 of Jesse and Sarah
Overman; Mississinewa, Grant County. Company K 118th
Regiment, 6 months; Corporal; 21 years of age. Buried
IOOF, Grant County.

Overman, Milton. Born 22 August 1845 of Jesse and Sarah
Overman; Mississinewa, Grant County. Company D
153rd Regiment, 1 year; 19 years of age; disowned at Mississinewa. Died 5 June 1929; buried IOOF, Grant County.

Overman, William. Born 7 March 1842 of Stephen and Polly
Overman; Mississinewa, Grant County. Company A 75th
Regiment; 20 years of age. Buried IOOF, Grant County.

Overman, William. Born 28 July 1840 of John and Anna
Overman; Blue River (Hicksite), Washington County.
Company G 18th Regiment; 22 years of age; disowned at
Blue River (Hicksite). Died circa 1916; buried Old Blue
River.

Overman, William R. Born 20 March 1845 of Henry W. and Rebecca Overman; Bloomfield, Parke County. Company H 21st Regiment, 1st Heavy Artillery; 19 years of age. Died at New Orleans, Louisiana, 24 June 1865.

Owen (Owens), Elbert Colson. Born 7 April 1846 of Benjamin and Esther Owen; Plainfield, Hendricks County. Disowned at Plainfield. Died 3 June 1873; buried Sugar Grove, Hendricks County.

Owen, Elijah Gibson. Born 27 November 1840 of Benjamin and Esther Owen; Plainfield, Hendricks County. Killed in a battle in Tennessee 7 April 1862; buried 25 June 1862 Sugar Grove, Hendricks County.

Owen, John L. Born October 1843 of William and Mary Owen; Whitewater (Hicksite), Wayne County. Company F 69th Regiment; 18 years of age. Died 5 April 1925.

Owens, Peter H. Born 13 March 1838 of James and Susan Owens; Hinkles Creek, Hamilton County. Company C 130th Regiment; Corporal; 25 years of age.

Owens, William A. Born circa 1846. Company K 132nd Regiment, 100 days; 18 years of age; produced offering at Plainfield, Hendricks County.

Page, Preston. Born 17 June 1843; West Union, Morgan County. Company E 78th Regiment, 60 days; 19 years of age. Died 14 July 1917; buried West Union.

Parisho, James H. Born 6 March 1842 of John and Caroline Parisho; Sand Creek, Bartholomew County. Company K 24th Regiment; 20 years of age; disowned at Sand Creek.

Parker, A. George W. Hinkles Creek, Hamilton County. Company E 57th Regiment. Died at Nashville, Tennessee, 4 April 1862.

Parker, Charles. Born 24 December 1839 of Joshua D. and Anna Parker; Sand Creek, Bartholomew County. Company F 39th Regiment, 8th Cavalry; 21 years of age. Killed at Chickamauga, Georgia, 20 December 1863.

Parker, Edwin E. Born 11 December 1840 of Isaac and Mary Parker; Hopewell, Henry County. Company I 69th Regiment; Corporal; 21 years of age; discharged for disability 20 April 1863; disowned at Hopewell.

Parker, Ira C. Born 24 March 1841 of William and Mary Parker; Sand Creek, Bartholomew County. Company F 39th Regiment, 8th Cavalry; Musician; 20 years of age; disowned at Sand Creek. Died 23 December 1925; buried Seymour, Indiana.

Parker, Joshua D. Born 25 May 1819 of Benjamin and Asenath Parker; Blue River, Washington County. Company E 90th Regiment, 5th Cavalry; 43 years of age; discharged 25 April 1863. Died circa 1876; buried Blue River.

Parker, Nathan W. Born 29 July 1803; Raysville, Henry County. Company A 3rd West Virginia Cavalry; disowned at Raysville.

Parker, Robert. Company F 8th Wisconsin Infantry; wounded at Farmington, Mississippi, 9 May 1862; discharged for disability 20 October 1862; disowned at Raysville.

Parker, Willis. Born 11 November 1824 of William and Elizabeth Parker; Driftwood, Jackson County. Company G 6th Regiment, 3 months; 36 years of age.

Parnell, George. Born 20 November 1834 of James and Hannah Parnell; Fairfield, Hendricks County. Company K 79th Regiment; 27 years of age; transferred to Engineer Corps 20 July 1864.

Parry, Joseph W. Born 19 November 1840 of William and Mary Parry; Whitewater (Hicksite), Wayne County. Company K 78th Regiment, 60 days; Corporal; 21 years of age; guard; disowned at Whitewater (Hicksite).

Patten, Isaac. Born circa 1840. Company G 89th Regiment; 22 years of age; died in hospital at Fort Pickering, Tennessee, 15 January 1863. Buried Pleasant Hill, Howard County.

Patten, Lewis. Born circa 1840. Company G 89th Regiment; 22 years of age. Died in hospital at Memphis, Tennessee, 1 January 1864; buried Pleasant Hill, Howard County.

Patten, Martin. Born circa 1844. Company G 89th Regiment; 18 years of age; discharged for disability 3 September 1863. Buried Pleasant Hill, Howard County.

Patterson, Eli. Born 14 October 1830 of Hezekiah and Elizabeth Patterson; Spiceland, Henry County. Company G 147th Regiment, 1 year; 34 years of age; hospital duty; reported for military duty at Spiceland.

Patterson, Milton L. Born circa 1843. Company D 136th Regiment, 100 days; 21 years of age; produced offering at Westfield, Hamilton County.

Patterson, Monroe. Company I 11th Regiment; 19 years of age. Killed at battle of Winchester, Virginia, 19 September 1864; buried Silver Creek Cemetery, Union County.

Paxson, Thomas. Born circa 1845. Company C 39th Regiment, 8th Cavalry; 18 years of age; transferred to Veteran Reserve Corps. Died 4 April 1869; buried Quaker Cemetery, Jay County.

Peacock, Asahel S. Born circa 1842 of Jonah and Sarah Peacock; Jericho Friends, Randolph County. Company E 57th Regiment; 19 years of age. Died on board the steamer *Empress* 15 May 1862.

Peacock, Benjamin. Born circa 1826 of John and Ruth Peacock; Jericho Friends, Randolph County. Company I 105th Regiment, 8 days; 1st Lieutenant; 37 years of age. Discharged for disability 18 July 1863.

Peacock, Henry S. Born circa 1845. White River, Randolph County. Company B 119th Regiment, 7th Cavalry; 18 years of age; transferred to Company D 7th Cavalry Reorganized. Died at Humpstead, Texas, 12 September 1865.

Peacock, John Wiltse. Born 13 July 1846 of Elwood and Naomi Peacock; Honey Creek, Howard County. Company D

118th Regiment, 6 months; 17 years of age. Buried Friends Cemetery, Howard County.

Peacock, Jonah. Born circa 1816. Jericho Friends, Randolph County. Company E 57th Regiment; 45 years of age. Died at Camp Dennison, Ohio, 15 May 1862.

Peacock, Thomas. Born circa 1820. Jericho Friends, Randolph County. Company I 105th Regiment, Minute Men, 9 days; 43 years of age.

Peacock, William H. Born circa 1844. Jericho Friends, Randolph County. Company D 69th Regiment; 18 years of age; discharged for wounds 27 November 1862.

Pearson, Daniel. Born 16 June 1852 of Enoch and Rachel Pearson; Honey Creek, Howard County. Company H 140th Regiment, 1 year; 12 years of age. Died 6 December 1932; buried Russiaville.

Pearson, Enos. Born 30 September 1831 of Levi and Rachel Pearson; Duck Creek, Henry County. Company A 30th Regiment Reorganized; 33 years of age.

Peebles, Benjamin F. Born circa 1837 of John E. and Mary Peebles; Wabash, Wabash County. Company K 101st Regiment; 25 years of age; discharged 20 March 1863.

Peele, Isaac. Born 30 October 1831 of Jesse and Zilpha Peele; Sand Creek, Bartholomew County. Company F 39th Regiment, 8th Cavalry; 29 years of age; disowned at Sand Creek.

Peele, William S. Born 10 July 1844 of Fletcher and Asenath Peele; Sand Creek, Bartholomew County. Company F 39th Regiment, 8th Cavalry; 18 years of age. Died of wounds at Chattanooga, Tennessee, 19 September 1864.

Peele, Willis. Born 14 July 1837 of Jesse and Zilpha Peele; Sand Creek, Bartholomew County. Company F 39th Regiment, 8th Cavalry; 24 years of age.

Pegg, John A. Born 13 March 1844 of Valentine and Mary Ann Pegg; Cherry Grove, Randolph County. Company C

19th Regiment; 17 years of age; wounded at Gettysburg, Pennsylvania; transferred to Company A 20th Regiment.

Pemberton, Cyrus L. Born 13 November 1840 of John and Susannah Pemberton; Back Creek, Grant County. Company H 8th Regiment; 20 years of age. Died circa 1880.

Pemberton, Harmen (Harmon). Born 26 September 1841 of Jesse and Ruth Pemberton; Back Creek, Grant County. Produced offering at Back Creek.

Perkins, William T. Born 10 August 1837; New Salem, Howard County. Company C 130th Regiment; 26 years of age. Died 18 September 1911; buried Lamb Cemetery, Howard County.

Perry, Doctrine. Born 7 October 1848 of Thomas and Esther Perry. Company H 6th Regiment, 3 months; 12 years of age. Died 9 November 1862; buried Friends Cemetery, Jackson County.

Petty, James. Born circa 1847. Company C 148th Regiment, 1 year; 18 years of age; produced offering at Springfield, Wayne County.

Phens (Phenis), Peter A. Born circa 1831. Company D 12th Regiment, 1 year; 30 years of age. Died at Deming, Indiana, 24 January 1862; buried Hinkles Creek, Hamilton County.

Phillips, David. Born circa 1839. Company C 117th Regiment, 6 months; 24 years of age. Died circa 1895; buried West Union, Morgan County.

Phillips, Eli. Born 9 April 1838 of Eli and Margaret Phillips; Mill Creek, Hendricks County. Company C 51st Regiment; 23 years of age. Killed at Stones River Tennessee, 1 January 1863; buried Spring Friends, Hendricks County.

Phillips, Israel. Born 15 October 1840 of Eli and Margaret Phillips; Mill Creek, Hendricks County. Company E 78th Regiment, 60 days; 21 years of age. Died 18 October 1862; buried Spring Friends, Henry County.

Phillips, Josiah. Born 23 September 1839 of John and Mary
   Phillips; Mill Creek, Hendricks County. Company E 78th
   Regiment, 60 days; 23 years of age; disowned at Mill Creek.

Phillips, William. Born 3 January 1837 of Eli and Margaret
   Phillips; Mill Creek, Hendricks County. Company B 148th
   Regiment, 1 year; 28 years of age; disowned at Mill Creek.
   Died 12 December 1902; buried Spring Friends, Hendricks
   County.

Pickard, John S. Born 3 June 1830 of William and Mary
   Pickard; Bloomfield, Parke County. Company K 43rd
   Regiment; 31 years of age.

Pickard, William. Born 21 December 1817 of Henry and
   Eleanor Pickard; Bloomfield, Parke County. Company A
   14th Regiment; Corporal; 43 years of age.

Pickett, Alfred. Born circa 1833. Jericho Friends, Randolph
   County. Company A 84th Regiment; 29 years of age. Died
   at Chattanooga, Tennessee, 5 November 1863.

Pickett, George. Born 28 October 1841 of Aaron and Eunice
   Pickett; Bloomfield, Parke County. Company H 21st Reg-
   iment, 1st Heavy Artillery; 19 years of age. Died at New
   Orleans, Louisiana, 17 August 1862.

Pickett (Picket), John. Born circa 1833 of Simon and Rebecca
   Pickett; Spiceland, Henry County. Company I 69th Regiment; 28 years of age. Died 18 August 1874; buried Spiceland Township.

Pickett (Picket), Nathan. Born circa 1844. Sugar River,
   Montgomery County. Company B 72nd Regiment; 18
   years of age. Died at Bardstown, Kentucky, 16 November
   1862.

Pickrell (Picknell), William. Born circa 1841. Sugar River,
   Montgomery County. Company I 11th Regiment; Corporal; 20 years of age; veteran.

Pierson, Levi. Born 27 August 1832 of William and Anna
   Pierson; Cherry Grove, Randolph County. Company E

126th Regiment, 11th Cavalry; 31 years of age. Died 27 December 1908; buried Cherry Grove.

Pike, Stanford. Born circa 1830 of Wilson and Miriam Pike; Hopewell, Henry County. Company A 36th Regiment; 32 years of age. Died from wounds received at Chickamauga, Georgia, 13 October 1863.

Place, William A. Company F 75th Regiment; Wagoner. Died 21 November 1865; buried Quaker Cemetery, Jay County.

Pleas, Elwood. Born 5 April 1831 of Aaron and Lydia Pleas; Spiceland, Henry County. Company G 139th Regiment, 100 days; 32 years of age.

Pleas, Joseph H. Born 21 April 1846 of Aaron and Ann E. Pleas; Spiceland, Henry County. Company E 139th Regiment, 100 days; 18 years of age.

Polson, Charles W. Born 17 February 1838; Lick Creek, Orange County. Company D 66th Regiment; 24 years of age. Died 20 January 1867; buried Paoli Cemetery, Orange County.

Pool, Charles. Born 25 September 1840 of Charles and Elizabeth Pool; Blue River, Washington County. Company B 24th Regiment; Corporal; 21 years of age; discharged for disability 3 January 1862; disowned at Blue River.

Pool, Nathan. Born 29 April 1838 of Charles and Elizabeth Pool; Blue River, Washington County. Company I 50th Regiment; 23 years of age. Died of pneumonia and fever at Indianapolis, 11 December 1862; buried Whitewater 1 February 1864.

Poorman, George W. Born circa 1843. White River, Randolph County. Company E 84th Regiment; 19 years of age; discharged 14 June 1865.

Potter, Charles G. Born 7 December 1841 of Oliver H. Potter; Cherry Grove, Randolph County. Company B 90th Regiment, 5th Cavalry; 20 years of age; prisoner of war; paroled 27 February 1865.

Potts, Jesse N. Born circa 1840 of E. G. Potts; Whitewater (Hicksite), Wayne County. Company C 19th Regiment; Hospital Steward; 2nd Lieutenant; promoted Commissary of 1st Brigade, 2nd Division, Sheridan's Cavalry June 1865; 21 years of age; produced offering at Whitewater (Hicksite).

Potts, Lindley A. Son of E. G. Potts; Whitewater (Hicksite), Wayne County. 93rd Regiment, Ohio Volunteer Infantry; transferred to Pioneer Corps; discharged for disability December 1864.

Pounds, Anderson. Born circa 1845. 21st Regiment, 1st Heavy Artillery; 18 years of age; produced offering at Spring Creek, Iowa, for White Lick, Morgan County.

Powell, Elihu. Born 5 October 1836; Raysville, Henry County. Company F 6th Regiment, 3 months; 24 years of age.

Pray, Eli. Born 16 September 1846 of Joseph and Anna Jane Pray; White Lick, Morgan County. Company D 70th Regiment; 17 years of age; transferred to 33rd Regiment 8 June 1865.

Pressnall (Pressnel), Dempsey W. Born circa 1831. Duck Creek, Henry County. Company D 36th Regiment; 30 years of age; transferred to Veteran Reserve Corps 15 November 1863.

Pressnall, James S. Born 15 April 1839 of Jeremiah L. and Phebe Pressnall; Richland, Hamilton County. Company F 63rd Regiment; 1st Lieutenant; 23 years of age.

Preston, William F. Born circa 1838. Company A 69th Regiment; 24 years of age. Died at Newport, Indiana, 28 August 1863; buried Silver Creek Cemetery, Union County.

Pritchard, Charles. Born circa 1841 of Benjamin and Sarah Pritchard; Lick Creek, Orange County. Company B 24th Regiment; 23 years of age; transferred to Company A 24th Regiment 10 December 1864; Corporal.

Pritchard, Finley. Born circa 1836. White River, Randolph County. Company C 90th Regiment, 5th Cavalry; Corporal; 26 years of age.

Ptomy, John. Born 24 December 1832; Pipe Creek, Miami County. Company C 87th Regiment; 29 years of age; transferred to Veteran Reserve Corps; reported for military service at Pipe Creek.

Puckett, Samuel H. Born 2 October 1838 of Greenlee and Margaret Puckett; Back Creek, Grant County. Company F 45th Regiment, 3rd Cavalry; 22 years of age. Died at Washington, D.C., 9 July 1863.

Puckett, Zachariah. Son of Zachariah T. Puckett; Sparrow Creek, Randolph County. Company F 134th Regiment, 100 days; 19 years of age.

Puckett, Zachariah T. Sparrow Creek, Randolph County. Company F 134th Regiment, 100 days.

Purnell, Eli. Born 22 February 1844 of James and Hannah Purnell; Fairfield, Hendricks County. Company H 132nd Regiment, 100 days; 20 years of age.

Pursley, James M. Sparrow Creek, Randolph County. Company A 84th Regiment; discharged 11 July 1863.

Ratliff, Calvin. Born 25 October 1832 of Cornelius and Abigail Ratliff; Hopewell, Henry County. Company H 140th Regiment, 1 year; 31 years of age. Buried Clear Spring Friends, Henry County.

Ratliff, Eli. Born 23 April 1847; Wabash, Wabash County. Company H 130th Regiment; 16 years of age; disowned at Wabash.

Ratliff, Exum P. Born 16 May 1843 of Cornelius and Abigail Ratliff; Hopewell, Henry County. Company I 69th Regiment; 19 years of age.

Ratliff, Henry. Born 7 December 1838 of Jonathan and Sarah Ratliff; Hopewell, Henry County. Company I 69th Regiment; 23 years of age. Died at Memphis, Tennessee, December 1862.

Ratliff, Joseph Clayton. Born 6 July 1827; Wayne County. Civil War Enrolling Officer; 34 years of age. Died 16 October 1909, Wayne County.

Ratliff, Manoah. Born 18 January 1842. Company A 69th Regiment; 20 years of age; discharged 19 July 1863.

Ratliff, Nathan. Born 28 September 1832 of Nathan and Lydia Ratliff; Duck Creek, Henry County. Company K 36th Regiment; 31 years of age; transferred to Company H 30th Regiment Reorganized; Corporal.

Ratliff, Seth. Born 29 September 1834; Pipe Creek, Miami County. Produced offering at Pipe Creek. Died 26 May 1878.

Ratliff, Thomas R. Born 11 December 1843. Company A 69th Regiment; 18 years of age; prisoner of war. Died at Black River Bridge, Mississippi, 25 July 1863.

Rayl, Harmon. Born 4 October 1839 of Zadock and Delilah Rayl; Spiceland, Henry County. Company A 36th Regiment; 22 years of age. Died of brain fever at Whitesides, Tennessee, 18 December 1863; buried Spiceland.

Reagan, Jesse W. Born circa 1846; Fairfield, Hendricks County. Company A 11th Regiment; 18 years of age; produced free will offering at Fairfield. Died 18 March 1878; buried Old Quaker Church, West Newton.

Reagan, Joseph W. Born 29 August 1843 of Samuel and Ruth Reagan; White Lick, Morgan County. Company D 70th Regiment; 18 years of age; produced offering at White Lick.

Reams, John. Born circa 1824. Company F 27th Regiment; 37 years of age; discharged for disability 1864; disowned at West Union, Morgan County.

Reece, Joel. Disowned at Mississinewa, Grant County.

Reed, Albert Samuel. Born 4 August 1845 of Rowland T. and Drusilla A. Reed; Whitewater, Wayne County. Medical Cadet; 19 years of age; promoted to Assistant Surgeon of the Western Department.

Rees (Reese), Elvin. Born 10 February 1846 of Joel and Phoebe Rees; Hinkles Creek, Hamilton County. Company G 147th Regiment, 1 year; 19 years of age.

Rees (Reese), Elwood. Born 10 February 1846 of Joel and
Phoebe Rees; Hinkles Creek, Hamilton County. Company
G 147th Regiment, 1 year; 19 years of age.

Reeve, Jonathan F. Born 19 January 1843 of Charles and Mal-
inda Reeve; Fairfield, Hendricks County. Company A 77th
Regiment, 4th Cavalry; 20 years of age; produced free will
offering at Fairfield.

Reynard, Solomon. Born 14 April 1841 of Isaac and Lydia
Reynard; Sparrow Creek, Randolph County. Company E
57th Regiment; 21 years of age. Died in hospital at Nashville, Tennessee, 30 March 1863.

Reynard, Thomas C. Born 26 October 1848 of Jesse and Ann
Reynard; Sparrow Creek, Randolph County. Company C
121st Regiment, 9th Cavalry; 16 years of age.

Reynard, Timothy. Born 19 November 1842 of Isaac and Lydia Reynard; Sparrow Creek, Randolph County. Company
E 57th Regiment; 19 years of age. Died of disease at Nashville, Tennessee, 7 January 1863; buried Nashville National
Cemetery.

Reynolds, Daniel P. Born 1 September 1841 of Lewis and
Mary Reynolds; Westfield, Hamilton County. Company A
101st Regiment; Musician; 20 years of age; wounded; produced free will offering at Westfield.

Reynolds, David. Born 2 September 1840 of Mahlon and
Ruth Reynolds; Bloomfield, Parke County. Company K
43rd Regiment; 2nd Lieutenant; 21 years of age.

Reynolds, Henry. Born 13 July 1844 of Daniel and Margaret
Reynolds; Hopewell, Henry County. Company I 69th Regiment; 18 years of age. Died at Milliken's Bend, Louisiana,
4 August 1863.

Reynolds, Isaac. Born 22 March 1846 of Daniel and Margaret
Reynolds; Hopewell, Henry County. Company G 139th
Regiment, 100 days; 18 years of age; disowned at Hopewell.

Reynolds, Jeremiah. Born 24 September 1828 of Jeremiah and
Susannah Reynolds; Plainfield, Hendricks County. Com-

pany G 63rd Regiment; 33 years of age. Died in Confederate prison at Florence, South Carolina, 23 November 1864; buried Sugar Grove, Hendricks County.

Reynolds, John T. Born circa 1845. Company E 85th Regiment; 18 years of age; transferred to Company H 33rd Regiment; Corporal; disowned at Honey Creek (Hicksite), Vigo County.

Reynolds, Joseph Harper. Born 20 May 1840 of William and Abigail Reynolds; Bloomfield, Parke County. Company A 14th Regiment; 21 years of age.

Reynolds, Joseph W. Born circa 1843. Company E 85th Regiment; 20 years of age; transferred to Veteran Reserve Corps 5 April 1865; disowned at Honey Creek (Hicksite), Vigo County.

Reynolds, Lewis. Born 21 December 1843 of David and Jemima Reynolds; Pipe Creek, Miami County. Company F 16th Regiment; 18 years of age; discharged for disability 4 December 1862; disowned at Pipe Creek. Died 16 August 1917; buried IOOF, Grant County.

Reynolds, Milton. Born 1 November 1830 of Daniel and Margaret Reynolds; Milford, Wayne County. Company B 90th Regiment, 5th Cavalry; 33 years of age; sanitary agent.

Reynolds, William. Born 10 February 1838; Indianapolis, Marion County. Company G 113th Regiment, Minute Men; 25 years of age. Died 31 October 1913; buried Crown Hill Cemetery, Marion County.

Reynolds, William. Born 3 September 1841 of David and Jemima Reynolds; Pipe Creek, Miami County. Company F 16th Regiment; 20 years of age; produced offering at Pipe Creek.

Rich, Elam. Born 14 March 1840 of Aaron and Martha Rich; Cherry Grove, Randolph County. Company F 84th Regiment; 22 years of age. Died 24 February 1866.

Rich, Eli. Born 15 October 1836 of Aaron and Martha Rich; New Garden, Wayne County. Company C 19th Regiment; 24 years of age; discharged for wounds 3 May 1864.

Rich, Jordan Emery. Born circa 1843. Sugar River, Montgomery County. Company G 11th Regiment; 18 years of age. Died of wounds received at Champion's Hill, Mississippi, 28 May 1863.

Rich, Timothy J. Born 22 March 1841 of Peter and Amy Rich; Westfield, Hamilton County. Company H 57th Regiment; 20 years of age. Died 5 May 1862; buried Chester.

Ricks, James M. Born 19 March 1840 of John W. and Mary Ann Ricks; Honey Creek, Howard County. Company C 75th Regiment; 22 years of age; disowned at Honey Creek.

Ritter, John. Born circa 1841. Beech Grove, Marion County. Company A 149th Regiment, 1 year; 24 years of age. Died 4 March 1865; buried Crown Hill Cemetery, Marion County.

Ritz, Alexander. Soldier who died in 1864; 18 years of age; buried Sand Creek, Bartholomew County.

Robbins, George W. Born 3 May 1844 of Jacob and Lydia Robbins; Pipe Creek, Miami County. Company C 87th Regiment; 18 years of age; discharged 11 July 1864.

Robbins, William S. Born 19 June 1842 of Jacob and Lydia Robbins; Pipe Creek, Miami County. Company C 87th Regiment; 19 years of age; disowned at Pipe Creek.

Roberts, Charles. Born 2 December 1830 of Judah and Ruth Roberts; Westfield, Hamilton County. Company G 147th Regiment, 1 year; 34 years of age.

Roberts, Enoch W. Born 9 August 1841, grandson of Walter and Hannah Roberts; Dover, Wayne County. Company C 8th Regiment; Corporal; 20 years of age; disowned at Dover.

Roberts, William A. Company F 7th Regiment, 3 months. Died 8 July 1935; buried Quaker Cemetery, Jay County.

Roberts, William W. Son of Joshua and Hannah L. Roberts; Fall Creek (Hicksite), Madison County. 2nd Light Artillery; produced offering at Fall Creek.

Rogers, Addison E. Born circa 1847. Company C 148th Regiment, 1 year; 18 years of age; disowned at Mill Creek, Hendricks County.

Rogers, Benjamin F. Born 30 March 1843 of Jonathan J. and Hannah Rogers; Fall Creek (Hicksite), Madison County. Company D 34th Regiment; 18 years of age. Died 28 August 1873; buried Fall Creek.

Rogers, Charles. Produced offering at Fall Creek (Hicksite), Madison County.

Rogers, Joseph M. Born 23 April 1839 of Charles J. Rogers; Fall Creek (Hicksite), Madison County. Company B 89th Regiment; Sergeant; 23 years of age; produced offering at Fall Creek. Buried Fall Creek.

Rogers, Solon R. Born circa 1843. Company A 77th Regiment, 4th Cavalry; 20 years of age; disowned at Mill Creek, Hendricks County.

Ross, William S. Born 28 January 1845; Driftwood, Jackson County. Company K 39th Regiment, 8th Cavalry; 15 years of age. Died at Sand Town, Pennsylvania, 12 August 1864; buried Driftwood.

Roulet, David E. Born circa 1819. Company B 126th Regiment, 11th Cavalry; 44 years of age. Died 6 June 1868; buried Quaker Cemetery, Jay County.

Rowan, Jeremiah. Born 18 March 1847; White Lick, Morgan County. Company B 71st Regiment, 6th Cavalry; 16 years of age. Buried Crown Hill Cemetery, Marion County.

Ruble, Samuel M. Born 26 December 1814 of Owen and Rachel Ruble; White River, Randolph County. Company C 69th Regiment; 47 years of age.

Rubottom, Alphonso. Born 30 August 1846 of John M. and Laban Rubottom; Bloomfield, Parke County. Company G 133rd Regiment, 100 days; 17 years of age.

Rubottom, Caleb. Born 2 June 1842 of Ezekiel and Jane Rubottom; Bloomfield, Parke County. Company K 43rd Regiment; Corporal; 19 years of age.

Rubottom, Pleasant. Born 28 February 1846 of Zeno and Eleanor Rubottom; Bloomfield, Parke County. Company K 43rd Regiment; 18 years of age.

Rubottom, Zeno. Born 25 March 1815 of Simon and Elizabeth Rubottom; Bloomfield, Parke County. Company H 21st Regiment, 1st Heavy Artillery; 46 years of age.

Ruddick, Elwood. Born 25 September 1842 of Solomon and Mary Ruddick; Driftwood, Jackson County. Company G 67th Regiment; 19 years of age; disowned at Driftwood. Died 6 March 1882; buried Friends Cemetery, Jackson County.

Ruddick, Lindley. Born 20 October 1844 of Solomon and Mary Ruddick; Driftwood, Jackson County. Company G 67th Regiment; 17 years of age; disowned at Driftwood. Died 20 October 1914; buried Friends Cemetery, Jackson County.

Ruddick, William C. Born 28 October 1821 of William and Rachel Ruddick; Driftwood, Jackson County. Company E 31st Regiment; 42 years of age; drafted. Buried Friends Cemetery, Jackson County.

Rush, Iredell B. Born 8 June 1840 of Dugan and Elizabeth Rush; Back Creek, Grant County. Company F 34th Regiment; 2nd Lieutenant; 21 years of age.

Rush, Joseph N. Born circa 1824. Company D 139th Regiment, 100 days; Corporal; 40 years of age; disowned at Oak Ridge, Grant County.

Rushton, Caleb. Born 15 November 1844 of Joshua and Rachel Rushton; White Lick, Morgan County. Company E 12th Regiment; 17 years of age; mustered out as absent without leave; produced offering at White Lick. Buried Mooresville.

Rushton, Jesse Calvin. Born 30 November 1840 of Joshua and Rachel Rushton; White Lick, Morgan County. Company E 12th Regiment; Corporal; 21 years of age; produced offering at White Lick. Died 25 April 1877; buried Mooresville.

Rushton, Joshua. Born circa 1844. Plainfield, Hendricks County. Company A 117th Regiment, 6 months; 19 years of age.

Russell, Jesse J. Born 18 November 1843; Whitewater (Hicksite), Wayne County. Company F 75th Regiment; 18 years of age. Died at Murfreesboro, Tennessee, 28 February 1863.

Russell, John. Born 15 January 1849 of George and Clarissa Russell; Dover, Wayne County. Company B 156th Regiment, 1 year; 16 years of age; produced offering at Dover.

Saint, Abner P. Duck Creek, Henry County. Company C 71st Illinois Infantry. Died at Columbus, Kentucky, 22 July 1862.

Saint, Albert White. Born circa 1838. Duck Creek, Henry County. Company D 36th Regiment; 1st Lieutenant; 23 years of age; wounded at Stones River, Tennessee, 31 December 1862.

Saint, Henry H. Duck Creek, Henry County. Company C 71st Illinois Infantry; reenlisted 19th Light Artillery (Indiana).

Saint, William M. Born 6 March 1834 of Exum and Phebe Saint; Duck Creek, Henry County. Company B 59th Ohio Infantry; 1st Sergeant; 27 years of age; wounded at Chickamauga, Georgia, 20 September 1863; reenlisted 147th Regiment, 1 year (Indiana); Adjutant.

Sanders, James M. Born 2 March 1841; Westfield, Hamilton County. Company D 12th Regiment, 1 year; 20 years of age; Wagoner.

Schofield, David Brown. Born 30 September 1819 of Jonathan and Eleanor Schofield; Fall Creek (Hicksite), Madison County. Produced offering at Fall Creek.

Schofield, Joseph Fell. Born 7 June 1828 of Jonathan and Eleanor Schofield; Fall Creek (Hicksite), Madison County. Produced offering at Fall Creek. Died 30 March 1910.

Schooley, Cam. Born circa 1846. Company C 89th Regiment; 18 years of age; transferred to Company I 26th Regiment, 1 year, 10 July 1865; produced offering at Mississinewa, Grant County.

Schooley, Leander. Company K 28th Regiment, 1st Cavalry; disowned at Mississinewa, Grant County.

Schooley, William. Born 10 November 1845; Mississinewa, Grant County. Company D 139th Regiment, 100 days; 18 years of age.

Scott, Calvin. Born 8 October 1841 of James and Annice Scott; Back Creek, Grant County. Company C 12th Regiment; 20 years of age. Died 13 August 1874; buried Park Cemetery, Grant County.

Scott, Eli. Born 21 June 1842 of Stephen and Mahala Scott; Oak Ridge, Grant County. Produced offering at Oak Ridge.

Scott, Jesse A. Born 25 November 1847 of James and Annice Scott; Oak Ridge, Grant County. Company D 139th Regiment, 100 days; 16 years of age; reenlisted Company G 153rd Regiment, 1 year; produced offering at Oak Ridge. Died 19 January 1935.

Scott, John. Born 26 December 1843 of James and Annice Scott; Oak Ridge, Grant County. Company C 12th Regiment; 18 years of age. Died of wounds at Marietta, Georgia, 26 August 1864.

Scott, Levi. Born 21 January 1846 of Stephen and Mahala Scott; Oak Ridge, Grant County. Company H 118th Regiment, 6 months; 17 years of age; produced offering at Oak Ridge. Buried Park Cemetery, Grant County.

Sellars, Peter. Born 11 June 1834 of Jordan Sellars; White Lick, Morgan County. Company B 97th Regiment; 28 years of age. Died 24 February 1886; buried Mooresville.

Sharp, William. Born circa 1839. Company C 51st Regiment; 22 years of age; discharged 14 December 1864. Buried West Branch Friends, Hendricks County.

Shaw, Elijah J. Born 28 November 1842 of Aaron and Jane Shaw; West Union, Morgan County. Company D 70th Regiment; Corporal; 19 years of age; produced offering at West Union.

Shaw, Emsley. Born 3 March 1848 of Aaron and Jane Shaw; Plainfield, Hendricks County. 2nd Light Artillery; 16 years of age; produced offering at Plainfield.

Shinn, John M. Born circa 1844. Company K 75th Regiment; 18 years of age; discharged for disability 28 February 1863. Died 24 April 1863; buried Quaker Cemetery, Jay County.

Showan, Henry C. Disowned at Whitewater, Wayne County. Died March 1869.

Shugart, Charles A. Born circa 1842 of George Shugart; New Garden, Wayne County. Company A 69th Regiment; 20 years of age; discharged for disability 6 March 1863; disowned at New Garden.

Simons, Alfred. Produced offering at Greenwood, Hamilton County.

Small, Eli O. Born 5 March 1840 of Amos and Rachel Small; Mississinewa, Grant County. Company F 57th Regiment; 21 years of age; discharged for disability 1862; disowned at Mississinewa.

Small, Enoch P. Born 27 March 1836; Back Creek, Grant County. Produced offering at Back Creek.

Small, John. Company K 21st Regiment, 1st Heavy Artillery; 25 years of age; absent without leave from 10 October 1865; produced offering at Mississinewa, Grant County.

Small, Lemuel. Born 15 September 1844 of Amos and Rachel Small; Mississinewa, Grant County. Company A 139th Regiment, 100 days; 19 years of age. Died 27 January 1920.

Small, William. Born 6 June 1841 of Jesse and Millicent Small; Mississinewa, Grant County. Company I 11th Ohio Infantry. Died 30 December 1919; buried Park Cemetery, Grant County.

Smith, Amos D. Born 25 February 1822 of Benjamin and Tamer Smith; Milford, Wayne County. Company A 8th Regiment, 3 months; 39 years of age; reenlisted Company I 36th Regiment; 2nd Lieutenant.

Smith, Asa S. Born 9 January 1837 of Ezra Smith; Whitewater (Hicksite), Wayne County. Company C 41st Regiment, 2nd Cavalry; 24 years of age; transferred to 2nd Cavalry Reorganized; 1st Lieutenant. Died near Scottsville, Alabama, 2 April 1865.

Smith, Eli. Born 12 May 1844 of Ephraim and Rachel Smith; Mississinewa, Grant County. Company G 101st Regiment; 18 years of age; transferred to Veteran Reserve Corps 18 July 1864. Died 18 December 1928; buried Riverside Cemetery, Grant County.

Smith, Jackson. Born 13 December 1833; Springfield, Wayne County. Company H 140th Regiment, 1 year; Corporal; 30 years of age. Died 6 November 1895; buried Nettle Creek Friends, Wayne County.

Smith, Jacob. Born 4 May 1842 of Nathan and Rebecca Smith; Fall Creek (Hicksite), Madison County. Company E 101st Regiment; 20 years of age; transferred to Company E 58th Regiment; disowned at Fall Creek.

Smith, Jesse P. Born 28 July 1845 of Ephraim Smith; Wabash, Wabash County. Company H 118th Regiment, 6 months; Corporal; 17 years of age.

Smith, Joseph. Born 3 October 1837 of James and Sarah Smith; Milford, Wayne County. Company C 84th Regiment; 24 years of age; Nurse; Ambulance driver.

Spencer, David. Born 1 June 1839 of John and Elizabeth Spencer; Duck Creek, Henry County. Company D 36th Regiment; Sergeant; 22 years of age.

Spencer, David P. Born circa 1835. Milford (Hicksite), Wayne County. Company A 8th Regiment, 3 months; reenlisted

Company D 41st Regiment, 2nd Cavalry; 26 years of age. Died at Nashville, Tennessee, 18 December 1863.

Spencer, John A. Born 9 January 1842 of John and Elizabeth Spencer; Duck Creek, Henry County. Company D 36th Regiment; 19 years of age; wounded at Chickamauga, Georgia, 19 September 1863.

Spencer, Lindley H. Born 9 August 1835 of John and Elizabeth Spencer; Duck Creek, Henry County. Company I 69th Regiment; Sergeant; 27 years of age.

Spencer, Maurice L. Born 3 March 1843; Maple Grove (Hicksite), Huntington County. Died 28 June 1907; buried Mt. Hope, Huntington County.

Spohr, Harman. Born circa 1837 of John Spohr; Springfield, Wayne County. Company H 140th Regiment, 1 year; drafted; 23 years of age. Died at Murfreesboro, Tennessee, 19 December 1864; buried West River Friends, Wayne County.

Stacy, Edgar. Born 15 November 1839; West Union, Morgan County. Disowned at West Union.

Stafford, Matthew. Company C 117th Regiment, 6 months; Sergeant; 19 years of age; produced free will offering at Fairfield, Hendricks County.

Stafford, William H. Born 20 April 1844 of Daniel H. and Sarah G. Stafford; Hopewell, Henry County. Company I 69th Regiment; 18 years of age; produced offering at Hopewell. Died 12 February 1886; buried Rich Square Friends, Henry County.

Stanbrough, Joseph B. Born 29 March 1847 of John and Lydia Stanbrough; Westfield, Hamilton County. Company D 101st Regiment; 16 years of age; transferred to Company D 58th Regiment 22 June 1864.

Stanbrough, Levi. Born 27 May 1849 of Francis and Angeline Stanbrough; Westfield, Hamilton County. Company D 128th Regiment; 13 years of age. Buried Crownland Cemetery, Hamilton County.

Stanbrough, Nelson D. Born 6 July 1844 of John and Lydia Stanbrough; Westfield, Hamilton County. Company A 101st Regiment; 18 years of age.

Stanley, Harmon D. Born 3 October 1821 of John and Elizabeth Stanley; Hinkles Creek, Hamilton County. Company G 147th Regiment, 1 year; Corporal; 43 years of age. Died circa 1893; buried Hinkles Creek.

Stanley, John. Born 26 June 1845 of Wyatt and Mary Stanley; Walnut Ridge, Rush County. Company K 134th Regiment, 100 days; 18 years of age; disowned at Walnut Ridge.

Stanley, Mordica C. Born 8 March 1844 of Nathan and Sarah Stanley; Mill Creek, Hendricks County. Company F 126th Regiment, 11th Cavalry; Corporal; 19 years of age; produced offering at Mill Creek.

Stanley, Thomas E. Born 7 June 1846 of Jesse and Anna Stanley; Springfield, Wayne County. 20th Light Artillery; 16 years of age.

Stanley, William A. Born circa 1843 of Elwood and Martha Stanley; Spiceland, Henry County. Company F 6th Regiment, 3 months; 18 years of age.

Stansbury, James S. Born circa 1816. Company E 119th Regiment, 7th Cavalry; Sergeant; 47 years of age. Died at Camden, Indiana, 7 March 1864; buried Quaker Cemetery, Jay County.

Stanton, Isaac W. Born 25 March 1823 of Peter and Celia Stanton; Richland, Hamilton County. Company A 90th Regiment, 5th Cavalry; 2nd Lieutenant; 39 years of age.

Stanton, Thomas Franklin. Born 14 June 1830 of Samuel and Sarah Stanton; Silver Creek-Salem, Union County. Company C 84th Regiment; 32 years of age. Died 1 February 1917; buried Salem.

Starr, Benjamin. Son of Charles W. and Elizabeth Starr; Whitewater (Hicksite), Wayne County. Company C 41st Regiment, 2nd Cavalry; wounded in head at battle of Gallatin, Tennessee; discharged for physical disability 10 September 1862; produced offering at Whitewater (Hicksite). Died 24 August 1903.

Starr, Joseph W. Born circa 1841 of Charles W. and Elizabeth Starr; Whitewater (Hicksite), Wayne County. Company C 41st Regiment, 2nd Cavalry; Captain; 20 years of age; prisoner of war; produced offering at Whitewater (Hicksite). Died 29 March 1911.

Starr, William C. Born circa 1822 of Charles W. and Elizabeth Starr; Whitewater (Hicksite), Wayne County. 9th Regiment; Lieutenant Colonel; 39 years of age; confined in Libby Prison for three weeks; detailed as acting Provost Marshal General of the Department of West Virginia; promoted to Judge Advocate General of the Army of the Shenandoah; transferred to the staff of General Crook until expiration of commission, November 1864. Died 17 May 1897.

Stewart, William. Born 10 September 1833 of Samuel and Hannah Stewart; Hopewell, Henry County. Company A 36th Regiment; 28 years of age. Killed at Chickamauga, Georgia, 19 September 1863; buried at Chickamauga.

Stout, Jesse. Born 11 April 1843; Lick Creek, Orange County. Company H 131st Regiment, 13th Cavalry; 20 years of age. Died 20 June 1870; buried Lick Creek.

Stout, Thomas. Born 27 October 1832 of Ephraim and Ruth Stout; Westfield, Hamilton County. Company G 147th Regiment, 1 year; Sergeant; 32 years of age.

Stout, Thomas. Born circa 1846. Company D 135th Regiment, 100 days; 18 years of age; produced offering at Honey Creek, Howard County.

Stout, William. Born 18 August 1835; Lick Creek, Orange County. Company B 24th Regiment; 28 years of age. Died 13 July 1919; buried Lick Creek.

Strattan (Stratton), Joseph H. Born 13 March 1838 of Benjamin and Emily Strattan; Whitewater (Hicksite), Wayne County. Company I 84th Regiment; Corporal; 24 years of age.

Strattan (Stratton), Joseph I. Born circa 1840 of Zimri and Hannah Strattan; Whitewater, Wayne County. Company E 57th Regiment; Corporal; 21 years of age. Died of typhoid pneumonia at Shiloh, Tennessee, 8 May 1862.

Stratton, Benjamin F. Born 13 November 1842 of Benjamin and Anna Stratton; Hopewell, Henry County. Company E 139th Regiment, 100 days; 21 years of age. Died 29 November 1869.

Stratton, Joseph M. Born 8 December 1846 of Joseph P. and Martha W. Stratton; Milford (Hicksite), Wayne County. Company A 133rd Regiment, 100 days; 17 years of age.

Straughan, Daniel W. Born circa 1844. Company G 89th Regiment; 18 years of age. Died 18 September 1863; buried South Union, Howard County.

Strawbridge, William T. Born 21 July 1843 of Thomas C. and Susan Strawbridge; Chester, Wayne County. Company E 69th Regiment; 19 years of age; discharged for physical disability 20 November 1862; disowned at Chester.

Stubbs, Allen. Born circa 1835. Company A 69th Regiment; 27 years of age. Died of chronic diarrhea at Memphis, Tennessee, 17 August 1863.

Sturdevant, Henry A. Born 15 December 1841 of Benjamin and Rhoda Sturdevant; Hinkles Creek, Hamilton County. Company I 153rd Regiment, 1 year; Sergeant; 23 years of age. Died 17 February 1923; buried Hinkles Creek.

Sullivan, John. Born circa 1827. Wabash, Wabash County. Company F 153rd Regiment, 1 year; 38 years of age.

Sumner, Cassell (Cashwell) (Caswal) B. Born 23 November 1841 of Eli J. and Jane Sumner; White Lick, Morgan County. Company E 12th Regiment; Corporal; 20 years of age. Died 3 February 1867; buried West White Lick.

Sumner, James M. Born circa 1839 of Martin Sumner; Hinkles Creek, Hamilton County. Company I 39th Regiment, 8th Cavalry; 22 years of age. Died circa 1922; buried Hinkles Creek.

Sumner, William Bowater. Hinkles Creek, Hamilton County. Company A 90th Regiment, 5th Cavalry; Commissary Sergeant. Buried Hinkles Creek.

Swafford, Christian L. Born 7 January 1823; Back Creek, Grant County. Company D 153rd Regiment, 1 year; 42 years of age. Died 28 April 1913; buried Back Creek.

Swafford, William H. H. Born circa 1841. Company G 47th Regiment; 21 years of age. Died 18 July 1863; buried Friends Cemetery, Wabash County.

Swain, Cyrus. Born circa 1839. Company C 84th Regiment; 23 years of age; transferred to Veteran Reserve Corps 20 May 1864; disowned at Milford, Wayne County.

Swain, Job. Born 12 August 1834 of Elihu and Mary Swain; Springfield, Wayne County. Company I 39th Regiment, 8th Cavalry; Sergeant; 27 years of age.

Swain (Swaim), Jonathan I. Born circa 1848 of David and Ann Swain; Bloomfield, Parke County. Company A 85th Regiment; 14 years of age. Died 14 September 1897; buried Friends, Parke County.

Swain, Lorenzo D. Born 10 June 1840 of Elihu and Mary Swain; Springfield, Wayne County. Company E 54th Regiment, 1 year; 22 years of age.

Swain, Remus. Born 17 January 1839 of Jonathan and Eunice Swain; Salem, Union County. Disowned at Salem.

Swain, Thomas M. Born 26 January 1834 of Howland and Phoebe Swain; Duck Creek, Henry County. Company E 139th Regiment, 100 days; 1st Lieutenant; 30 years of age.

Swain (Swaim), William B. Born 10 January 1847; Rush Creek, Parke County. Company I 137th Regiment, 100 days; 17 years of age. Died 14 September 1917; buried Rush Creek #2.

Swain, William B. Born circa 1844. Company B 117th Regiment, 6 months; 19 years of age; produced offering at Plainfield, Hendricks County.

Swallow, John C. Born circa 1837. Company C 39th Regiment, 8th Cavalry; 24 years of age. Died at home 15 January 1862; buried Quaker Cemetery, Jay County.

Sweet, Eli M. Born 29 May 1833 of Solomon and Catherine Sweet; Spiceland, Henry County. Company D 36th Regiment; Corporal; 28 years of age; discharged for disability 25 July 1862.

Symonds, Samuel. Born 12 November 1832 of Thomas and Abigail Symonds; Milford, Wayne County. Company C 84th Regiment; 29 years of age; discharged 13 August 1863; produced offering at Milford.

Symons, Benjamin Franklin. Born 28 August 1842 of John and Rebekah Symons; Hopewell, Henry County. 54th Regiment, 1 year; 20 years of age. Died at Memphis, Tennessee, 17 March 1863.

Talbert, Asa. Son of Job and Amanda Talbert; Westfield, Hamilton County.

Talbert (Talbott), Harrison. Born 19 April 1842 of Jesse and Hannah Talbert; Walnut Ridge, Rush County. 3rd Light Artillery; 19 years of age; disowned at Walnut Ridge.

Talbert, James Marshall. Born 7 April 1843 of Sylvanus and Phoebe Talbert; Salem, Union County. Company G 36th Regiment; 22 years of age; transferred to Veteran Reserve Corps; disowned at Salem.

Talbert, Nathan. Born 17 September 1844 of Elijah and Mary Talbert; Westfield, Hamilton County. Company C 130th Regiment; 19 years of age; disowned at Westfield.

Talbert, William. Born 30 August 1842 of Elijah and Mary Talbert; Westfield, Hamilton County. Company A 101st Regiment; Corporal; 19 years of age; disowned at Westfield.

Talbert, William H. Born 21 April 1846 of Sylvanus G. and Phebe Talbert; Plainfield, Hendricks County. Company A 29th Regiment; 17 years of age; substitute. Died at Chattanooga, Tennessee, 12 January 1865; buried Chattanooga.

Taylor, George. Born 7 July 1820 of George and Elizabeth Taylor; Silver Creek-Salem, Union County. Company H 36th Regiment; Sergeant; 40 years of age; deserted 28 August 1863.

Taylor, Henry. Born circa 1847 of James and Elizabeth Taylor; Springfield, Wayne County. 19th Light Artillery; 17 years of age. Died 11 April 1914; buried Nettle Creek Friends, Wayne County.

Taylor, Israel B. Born circa 1825 of Jesse and Deborah Taylor; Indianapolis, Marion County. Company G 107th Regiment, Minute Men; 38 years of age. Died 17 October 1896; buried Crown Hill Cemetery, Marion County.

Taylor, Joseph. Born circa 1825. Union, Howard County. Company D 89th Regiment; Corporal; 37 years of age; discharged for disability 27 January 1863.

Taylor, Thomas Elwood. Born circa 1845. 54th Regiment, 1 year; reenlisted Company B 21st Regiment, 1st Heavy Artillery; 18 years of age; reported for military service at Springfield, Wayne County.

Taylor, Wilson. Born 24 April 1838 of John and Mareb Taylor; Springfield, Wayne County. Company I 84th Regiment; 24 years of age; transferred to 57th Regiment.

Tharp, Jonathan. Born circa 1842 of Jeremiah Tharp; Wayne County. Company E 69th Regiment; 20 years of age; wounded and taken prisoner at Richmond, Kentucky; discharged for disability. Died 19 March 1863; buried Center Friends Cemetery, Wayne County.

Thistlethwaite, William, Jr. Born circa 1833. Company A (or I) 8th Regiment, 3 months; 28 years of age; disowned at Whitewater (Hicksite).

Thomas, Aaron. Born 4 March 1842 of Snead and Miriam Thomas, Honey Creek, Howard County. Disowned at Honey Creek.

Thomas, Clark D. Born 3 February 1844 of Snead and Miriam Thomas; Honey Creek, Howard County. Company C 137th Regiment, 100 days; 20 years of age; produced offering at West Union, Morgan County, for Honey Creek. Died 23 February 1876; buried Honey Creek.

Thomas, Henly. Born circa 1842. Company A 119th Regiment, 7th Cavalry; 21 years of age; disowned at Pipe Creek, Miami County.

Thomas, Henry. Born circa 1843. Company G 130th Regiment; 21 years of age; discharged 6 June 1864 Washington, D.C.; produced offering at Pipe Creek, Miami County.

Thomas, Isaiah. Born 4 October 1844 of Elijah and Lavina Thomas; Back Creek, Grant County. Company F 34th Regiment; 19 years of age; produced offering at Back Creek.

Thomas, Lewis W. Born circa 1814; Fall Creek (Hicksite), Madison County. Company C 140th Regiment, 1 year; 49 years of age. Died circa 1864; buried Fall Creek.

Thomas, Lindley L. Born 25 November 1847 of Snead and Miriam Thomas; Honey Creek, Howard County. Company E 126th Regiment, 11th Cavalry; 16 years of age; disowned at Honey Creek. Died 16 October 1938.

Thomas, Luke. Born 9 May 1846 of Snead and Miriam Thomas; Honey Creek, Howard County. Company G 131st Regiment, 13th Cavalry; 17 years of age; produced offering at Honey Creek.

Thomas, Marquis L. Born 22 May 1840 of Elijah and Naomi Thomas; New Garden, Wayne County. Company F 5th Ohio Cavalry; Sergeant; 21 years of age; captured near Rienzi, Mississippi; eventually taken to Beele Isle where he remained for seven months; paroled 20 March 1864.

Thompson, Henry. Born 18 October 1835; Lick Creek, Orange County. Company D 66th Regiment; Corporal; 26 years of age. Died 17 October 1884; buried Lick Creek.

Thompson, Jesse H. Born 2 April 1846 of Owen and Rachel Thompson; Bloomfield, Parke County. Company D 66th Regiment; 16 years of age. Died at Corinth, Mississippi, 8 January 1863.

Thompson, Nathan D. Born 7 August 1842 of Jonathan and Sarah Thompson; Lick Creek, Orange County. Company D 66th Regiment; 20 years of age.

Thornburg, George C. Born 15 September 1831 of Walter and Rebecca Thornburg; Dover, Wayne County. 19th Light Artillery; Quartermaster Sergeant; 30 years of age; Wagoner.

Thornburg, Henry H. Born 25 September 1837 of John and Elizabeth Thornburg; Springfield, Wayne County. Company D 39th Regiment, 8th Cavalry; 23 years of age. Died at Hubbard's Cove 31 August 1862.

Thornburg, Isaac T. Born 27 August 1824 of Nathan and Rebecca Thornburg; Cherry Grove, Randolph County. Company H 84th Regiment; 37 years of age; discharged 20 June 1863.

Thornburg (Thornburgh), John C. Born circa 1840. Walnut Ridge, Rush County. Company E 12th Regiment; 22 years of age. Died of typhoid fever at Mooresville, Indiana, 5 October 1862; buried Walnut Ridge.

Thornburg, John R. Born circa 1840 of William Thornburg; Springfield, Wayne County. Company B 69th Regiment; Corporal; 21 years of age. Died after a protracted illness in a hospital 6 December 1861.

Thornburg, John W. Born 25 June 1845 of Isaac and Rhoda Thornburg; Sparrow Creek, Randolph County. Company K 84th Regiment; Sergeant; 17 years of age.

Thornburg, Walter. Born 18 May 1830 of Dempsey and Jane Thornburg; Springfield, Wayne County. Company B 90th Regiment, 5th Cavalry; 33 years of age; transferred to Company H 71st Regiment, 6th Cavalry; captured during Stoneman's Raid; taken to Andersonville, Georgia, then to Florence, South Carolina. Died in prison 12 November 1864.

Thornburg (Thornburgh), William. Born 3 March 1842 of Walter and Rebecca Thornburg; Dover, Wayne County. Produced offering at Dover.

Thorne, Samuel A. Born circa 1845 of Benjamin and Selina Thorne; Wayne County. Company B 36th Regiment; 17 years of age. Died at Camp Wickliffe, Kentucky, 5 June 1862; buried Fairfield Friends, Wayne County.

Tincher, William H. Born 17 January 1844 of Harden and Cathrine Tincher; Back Creek, Grant County. Company B 117th Regiment, 6 months; 19 years of age. Died 20 September 1903; buried Riverside Cemetery, Grant County.

Tomlinson, Joseph H. Born 4 April 1846 of Andrew and Ruth Tomlinson; Bloomfield, Parke County. 9th Light Artillery; 15 years of age; discharged 1862. Died 4 March 1863; buried Friends Cemetery, Parke County.

Towel (Towell), Jonathan. Born 15 August 1840 of George and Mary Towel; Rush Creek, Parke County. Company H 21st Regiment, 1st Heavy Artillery; 23 years of age; discharged for disability 22 November 1864; disowned at Rush Creek. Died 21 August 1924; buried Rush Creek #2.

Towell, William Henry. Born 21 June 1844 of Isaac and Sarah Towell; Bloomfield, Rush County. Company H 21st Regiment, 1st Heavy Artillery; 19 years of age. Died at Fort Gaines, Georgia, 17 October 1865.

Townsend, Hiram. Born April 1840 of Eli and Rachel Townsend; Sparrow Creek, Randolph County. Company A 84th Regiment; 22 years of age.

Trueblood, Alva. Born 30 January 1838 of Joshua and Zelpha Trueblood; Blue River (Hicksite), Washington County. Company G 13th Regiment; 1st Lieutenant; 23 years of age.

Trueblood, Francis Marion. Born 8 July 1842 of Milton and Rebecca Trueblood; Blue River, Washington County. Company E 90th Regiment, 5th Cavalry; 20 years of age; disowned at Blue River.

Trueblood, John. Born circa 1815 of James and Betsey Trueblood; Lick Creek, Orange County. Company D 66th Regiment; 47 years of age.

Trueblood, Joseph. Born circa 1826. Company D 38th Regiment; 38 years of age; discharged Louisville, Kentucky, 28 June 1865. Buried Highland Friends, Washington County.

Trueblood, Joshua G. Born circa 1829. Company E 53rd Regiment; 32 years of age. Died 23 May 1906; buried Highland Friends, Washington County.

Trueblood, Lindley M. Born 4 August 1833 of William and Ruth Ellen Trueblood; Lick Creek, Orange County. Company E 112th Regiment, Minute Men; 29 years of age.

Trueblood, Oliver Q. Born 20 March 1832 of Nathan and Mary Trueblood; Blue River, Washington County. Company E 53rd Regiment; Corporal; 29 years of age. Died 8 May 1862; buried in Tennessee.

Trueblood, Samuel J. Born circa 1846. Company A 144th Regiment, 1 year; 19 years of age. Died 8 February 1904; buried Hicksite Friends, Washington County.

Trueblood, Thomas. Born circa 1823. Company G 18th Regiment; 38 years of age. Buried Hicksite Friends, Washington County.

[Unknown]. Jose. Son of Rachel [Unknown].

Unthank, Charles R. Born 22 November 1846 of Pleasant and Sarah Ann Unthank; Dover, Wayne County. Company I 84th Regiment; 17 years of age; prisoner of war; paroled 26 November 1864.

Venable, Jesse E. Born circa 1844 of William and Sarah Venable; Westfield, Hamilton County. Company G 147th Regiment, 1 year; 20 years of age. Buried Crownland Cemetery, Hamilton County.

Vestal, Hiram. 2nd Light Artillery; 19 years of age; disowned at Plainfield, Hendricks County.

Vestal, John N. Company A 7th Regiment, 3 months; reenlisted Company A 77th Regiment, 4th Cavalry; Sergeant; disowned at Plainfield, Hendricks County.

Walthall, Thomas E. Born 2 August 1845 of William and Sarah Walthall; Vermilion, Illinois. Company E 115th Regiment, 6 months; 18 years of age. Died 13 October 1912; buried Hopewell Friends, Vermillion County, Indiana.

Walton, Jesse. Born circa 1836. Company G 16th Regiment; 26 years of age. Died of congestive fever 31 July 1863; buried Friends Cemetery, Rush County.

Ward, Evan Morris. Born circa 1842. Company B 34th Regiment; 19 years of age; Principal Musician; reported for military service at Camden (Hicksite), Jay County. Buried IOOF, Jay County.

Ward, Iram H. Born 5 April 1842; West Union, Morgan County. Company C 117th Regiment, 6 months; Corporal; 21 years of age. Died 3 March 1927; buried West Union.

Wasson, Thomas J. Born 14 February 1843 of John Macamy and Ann Wasson; Whitewater (Hicksite), Wayne County. Company B 19th Regiment; Corporal; 18 years of age. Killed at battle of Gettysburg 1 July 1863; buried Gettysburg Cemetery.

Wasson, William H. Son of John Macamy Wasson; Whitewater (Hicksite), Wayne County. Company D 121st Regiment, 9th Cavalry; Carpenter, Nurse.

Webb, Benjamin. Born circa 1830. Company I 139th Regiment, 100 days; Captain; 34 years of age; disowned at Whitewater, Wayne County.

Weeks, John W. Born 12 December 1835 of James and Cassandra Weeks; Chester, Wayne County. Company F 156th Regiment, Ohio National Guard, 100 days; 2nd Lieutenant of Patrol Guards; 28 years of age.

Wees (Wee), James. Born circa 1832. Company A 101st Regiment; Corporal; 30 years of age. Died of disease at Louisville, Kentucky, 9 July 1863; buried Old Friends Westfield, Hamilton County.

Welch, Amos. Born 10 April 1838; Tippecanoe County. Company A 108th Regiment, Minute Men; 25 years of age.

West, Edward. Born 3 January 1843; Whitewater (Hicksite), Wayne County. Company F 75th Regiment; 19 years of age. Died at Murfreesboro, Tennessee, 27 January 1863.

West, Henry. Born circa 1839. Whitewater (Hicksite), Wayne County. Company F 75th Regiment; Corporal, 23 years of age.

Wetherald, Edgar K. Born circa 1838 of Henry L. and Ann Wetherald; Milford (Hicksite), Wayne County. Company A 102nd Regiment, 7 days; 1st Lieutenant; 25 years of age.

Wetherald, Henry L., Jr. Born circa 1842 of Henry L. and Ann Wetherald; Milford (Hicksite), Wayne County. Company K 40th Regiment; reenlisted same regiment; 19 years of age. Killed at Kennesaw Mountain, Georgia, 18 June 1864.

Wetherald, Oscar C. Born circa 1846 of Henry L. and Ann Wetherald; Milford (Hicksite), Wayne County. Company K 40th Regiment; 18 years of age. Died of typhoid fever at Nashville, Tennessee, 14 December 1864.

Whinery, Mark. Born 6 May 1812. Civil War Paymaster; 49 years of age. Died 21 February 1879, Marion County, Indiana.

White, Carter B. Born circa 1813; Lick Creek, Orange County. Company F 131st Regiment, 13th Cavalry; 50 years of age; Wagoner. Died 13 June 1901; buried Beech Grove Cemetery, Orange County.

White, Elijah. Born 22 September 1821 of Henry and Mary White; Walnut Ridge, Rush County. Company I 148th Regiment, 1 year; 43 years of age.

White, Isaac. Born circa 1840 of Isaac and Louisa White; Westfield, Hamilton County. Company D 12th Regiment, 1 year; 21 years of age; disowned at Westfield.

White, Jacob. Born circa 1843; Driftwood, Jackson County. Company B 22nd Regiment; 18 years of age. Killed in battle at Perryville, Kentucky, 8 October 1862.

White, John. Company D 101st Regiment; produced offering at Greenwood, Hamilton County.

White, John M. Born 21 December 1823 of Isaac and Mahala White; Walnut Ridge, Rush County. Company C 9th Regiment; 41 years of age; drafted.

White, John Miles. Born 23 April 1843 of Maxmilian and Martha White; Hendricks County. Company B 7th Regiment; Corporal; 18 years of age.

White, Jonathan. Born 9 April 1850 of Joel and Cynthia Ann White; White Lick, Morgan County. Company H 148th Regiment, 1 year; 14 years of age.

White, Lewis W. Born 13 October 1832 of Maxmilian and Ruth White; Blue River, Washington County. Company G 18th Regiment; Corporal; 28 years of age; discharged for disability 9 August 1862.

White, Mordecai. Born 20 July 1828 of Isaac and Louisa White; Westfield, Hamilton County. Company G 147th Regiment, 1 year; Sergeant; 36 years of age.

White, Sylvanus. Born circa 1835. White River, Randolph County. Company C 8th Regiment, 3 months; Corporal; 26 years of age; reenlisted Company G 8th Regiment.

White, Thomas C. Born circa 1845. 9th Light Artillery; 19 years of age. Died at Memphis, Tennessee, 18 October 1864; buried Rush Creek #2, Parke County.

White, William O. Born circa 1836 of David K. and Mary M. White; Hamilton County. Company G 147th Regiment, 1 year; 28 years of age. Died 5 August 1868; buried Old Friends Westfield, Hamilton County.

Whitson, Newton. Born 17 February 1843 of John and Sinah Whitson; Dover, Wayne County. Company K 124th Regiment; Sergeant; 20 years of age.

Whitson, Willis. Born 27 July 1844 of Amos and Rebecca Whitson; Mississinewa, Grant County. Company C 89th Regiment; 18 years of age. Died at Memphis, Tennessee, 28 February 1863.

Wickersham (Wickeshen), Nathan P. Born circa 1828. Company G 89th Regiment; Sergeant; 34 years of age. Died at home 1 August 1863; buried New London Friends, Howard County.

Wilcutts, J. Calvin. Born 13 September 1841 of Thomas and Mary W. Wilcutts; Mississinewa, Grant County. Company

C 89th Regiment; 20 years of age. Died at Fort Pickering, Tennessee, 27 March 1863.

Wiles, William Davis. Born 4 February 1828 of Luke and Rhoda Wiles; Hopewell, Henry County. Company A 36th Regiment; Captain; 33 years of age; disowned at Hopewell.

Wilkey, William H. Born 2 October 1840 of Willis and Mary Wilkey; Rush Creek, Parke County. Company H 21st Regiment, 1st Heavy Artillery; Sergeant; 20 years of age. Died 31 October 1921; buried Rush Creek #2.

Willhite, Willis H. Born 1 March 1824 of Israel and Jane Willhite; Plainfield, Hendricks County. Company D 70th Regiment; 36 years of age; wounded; produced offering at Plainfield.

Williams, Allen G. Company N 119th Regiment, 7th Cavalry; 17 years of age. Died at Indianapolis; buried Quakerdom Cemetery, Porter County.

Williams, Elias H. Born circa 1835. Company H 39th Regiment, 8th Cavalry; 26 years of age; discharged for disability 2 May 1862. Buried Pleasant Hill, Howard County.

Williams, Henry C. Born 2 September 1840 of Henry and Nancy Williams; Springfield, Wayne County. Company B 90th Regiment, 5th Cavalry; 21 years of age; disowned at Springfield.

Williams, Jesse D. Born 3 July 1849; Pleasant Hill, Howard County. Company E 154th Regiment, 1 year; 15 years of age; produced offering at Pleasant Hill. Died 18 September 1906; buried Friends Cemetery, Howard County.

Williams, John. Born circa 1837; Washington County. Company B 49th Regiment; 23 years of age. Died at London, Kentucky, May 1862; buried Hicksite Friends, Washington County.

Williams, John D. Born circa 1835 of Isaac and Sibby (Libby) Williams; White Lick, Morgan County. Company E 12th Regiment; 27 years of age. Killed at Richmond, Kentucky, 30 August 1862; buried West White Lick.

Williams, John P. Born circa 1845. Company F 124th Regiment; Corporal; 19 years of age; disowned at Pleasant Hill, Howard County.

Williams, John R. Born 8 June 1839 of Robert and Mary Williams; Lick Creek, Orange County. Company D 40th Iowa Regiment. Died at Columbus, Kentucky, 1 April 1863; buried Beech Grove Cemetery, Orange County.

Williams, Philip P. Born circa 1845. Company I 153rd Regiment, 1 year; 20 years of age; produced offering at Westfield, Hamilton County.

Williams, Thomas B. Born 20 August 1828; Mississinewa, Grant County. Company A 40th Ohio Regiment. Died 17 October 1913; buried Veterans Facility, Grant County.

Williams, Thomas E. Born 28 October 1838; White Lick, Morgan County. Company E 12th Regiment; 23 years of age; produced offering at White Lick. Died circa 1912; buried Mooresville, Indiana.

Williams, William. Born circa 1839; Washington County. Company F 66th Regiment; 23 years of age. Died at Marietta, Georgia, 26 August 1864; buried Hicksite Friends, Washington County.

Williams, William. Born 22 November 1843 of Jason and Abigail Williams; Duck Creek, Henry County. Company G 139th Regiment, 100 days; 20 years of age. Died at Munfordville, Kentucky, 20 July 1864.

Williamson, Clement A. Born 15 November 1835; Bloomfield, Parke County. Company A 85th Regiment; Corporal; 26 years of age. Died 7 February 1886; buried Friends Cemetery, Parke County.

Willis, Jeremiah. Born 19 August 1843 of Benjamin and Rebecca Willis; Sparrow Creek, Randolph County. Company I 105th Regiment, Minute Men; 19 years of age.

Wilson, Daniel T. Born 15 August 1843 of Jesse and Hannah Wilson; Wabash, Wabash County. Company K 118th Reg-

iment, 6 months; 20 years of age. Died circa 1904; buried
Friends Cemetery, Wabash County.

Wilson, Henry E. Born 12 April 1850 of Nathan and Mary
Wilson; Back Creek, Grant County. Company K 13th Reg-
iment Reorganized; 14 years of age; deserted 24 May 1865.
Died 11 June 1935; buried Maple Grove Cemetery, Grant
County.

Wilson, Henry H. Born circa 1844. Sugar River, Montgomery County. Company B 72nd Regiment; 18 years of age.

Wilson, John. Born 15 October 1806 of Samuel and Christian
Wilson; Lick Creek, Orange County. Company D 28th
Regiment, United States Colored Troops; Corporal; 57
years of age. Died 30 April 1900; buried Newberry Cemetery, Orange County.

Wilson, Joseph. Born 11 February 1840; Back Creek, Grant
County. Produced offering at Back Creek.

Wilson, Lindsey. Born 19 December 1832 of John and Mary
Wilson; Back Creek, Grant County. Company I 33rd Reg-
iment; 31 years of age; drafted; produced offering at Back
Creek. Died 20 May 1906; buried Park Cemetery, Grant
County.

Wilson, Nathan. Born 2 February 1843 of Joseph G. and
Hope Wilson; Raysville, Henry County. Produced offering
at Raysville.

Wilson, Thomas. Born 3 May 1841 of Jesse and Hannah Wilson; Back Creek, Grant County. Company C 89th Regiment; 21 years of age. Died at Memphis, Tennessee, 14
November 1863; buried Back Creek.

Wilson, William A. Born 20 February 1822 of Payton and
Hannah Wilson; Lick Creek, Orange County. Company I
112th Regiment, Minute Men; Sergeant; 41 years of age.

Wilson, William S. Born 29 July 1835 of John and Mary
Wilson; Lick Creek, Orange County. Company G 49th
Regiment; 25 years of age; discharged 9 January 1864. Died
11 June 1865; buried Newberry Cemetery, Orange County.

Wiltse, David. Born 29 December 1836 of Simeon and Elizabeth Wiltse; Wabash, Wabash County. Company F 41st Regiment, 2nd Cavalry; 24 years of age. Died 28 December 1919.

Wiltse, Josiah. Born 6 July 1838 of Simeon and Elizabeth Wiltse; Honey Creek, Howard County. Produced offering at Honey Creek.

Winslow, Allen. Born 2 January 1834 of Daniel and Rebecca Winslow; Back Creek, Grant County. Company M 127th Regiment, 12th Cavalry; 30 years of age; produced offering at Back Creek.

Winslow, Benjamin W. Born 18 February 1843 of John and Ann Jane Winslow; Sand Creek, Bartholomew County. Company F 39th Regiment, 8th Cavalry; 19 years of age. Died of wounds at Nashville, Tennessee, 22 January 1863; buried Dayton.

Winslow, Cyrus. Born 14 September 1843 of Jesse and Penina Winslow; Back Creek, Grant County. Company D 33rd Regiment; 21 years of age; drafted; produced offering at Back Creek.

Winslow, Henry. Born 26 January 1829 of John and Elizabeth Winslow; Back Creek, Grant County. Company D 139th Regiment, 100 days; 35 years of age; produced offering at Back Creek. Died 18 March 1901; buried Park Cemetery, Grant County.

Winslow, John. Born 4 July 1833 of Thomas and Martha Winslow; Back Creek, Grant County. Company I 33rd Regiment; 31 years of age; drafted; produced offering at Back Creek.

Winslow, John. Born circa 1833; Blue River (Hicksite), Washington County. Company E 53rd Regiment; 31 years of age; drafted. Buried Old Blue River.

Winslow, John M. Born circa 1839. Company B 16th Regiment, 1 year; Corporal; 22 years of age; disowned at Whitewater, Wayne County.

Winslow, Jonathan. Born 26 August 1841 of Henry and Anna Winslow; Back Creek, Grant County. Company C 89th Regiment; Corporal; 21 years of age; produced offering at Back Creek. Died 17 November 1907; buried Park Cemetery, Grant County.

Wise, John Milton. Born 18 October 1845 of John S. and Elizabeth C. Wise; Back Creek, Grant County. 21st Regiment, 1st Heavy Artillery; 17 years of age; produced offering at Back Creek.

Wolfington, William Alonzo. Born circa 1839; Lick Creek, Orange County. Company B 24th Regiment; Sergeant; 22 years of age; reenlisted Company F 131st Regiment, 13th Cavalry; discharged 8 December 1864. Died circa 1865; buried Beech Grove Cemetery, Orange County.

Woodard, Alpheus L. Born 14 December 1846 of Thomas C. and Mary Woodard; Raysville, Henry County. Company I 69th Regiment; 15 years of age; produced offering at Raysville.

Woodard, John E. Born 27 November 1834 of Isaac N. and Lucy A. Woodard; Bloomfield, Parke County. Company F 126th Regiment; 11th Cavalry; 2nd Lieutenant; 30 years of age; resigned as 2nd Lieutenant 4 February 1865; produced free will offering at Bloomfield. Died 25 August 1916; buried Friends Cemetery, Parke County.

Woodruff, William C. Born 14 February 1848 of Israel and Mary Woodruff; New Garden, Wayne County. Company A 133rd Regiment, 100 days; 16 years of age.

Woodward, Joshua Hadley. Born 1 January 1841 of Pryor and Susannah Woodward; Mill Creek, Hendricks County. Company E 12th Regiment; Corporal; 21 years of age. Killed at Missionary Ridge near Chattanooga, Tennessee, 25 November 1863; buried Mill Creek Friends.

Woody, Allison Gray. Born 26 May 1845 of Hugh and Elizabeth Woody; Springfield, Wayne County. Company G 25th Regiment; 19 years of age; drafted. Died 26 November 1914; buried Nettle Creek Friends, Wayne County.

Woody, Lewis. Born 20 August 1844 of Levi and Gulielma Woody; Blue River, Washington County. Company D 38th Regiment; 17 years of age; produced offering at Blue River.

Wooten, Joel. Born circa 1823 of Lewis Wooten; White River, Randolph County. Company A 147th Regiment, 1 year; 42 years of age.

Wooton, Daniel P. Born circa 1838. New Garden, Wayne County. Company C 41st Regiment, 2nd Cavalry; reenlisted same regiment; 2nd Lieutenant; 23 years of age; detailed as Commissary of 2nd Brigade of Cavalry. Died October 1891; buried Albuquerque, New Mexico.

Wooton, James H. Company L 21st Regiment, 1st Heavy Artillery.

Wright, Benjamin C. Born 7 November 1844 of Jacob T. and Matilda Wright; Indianapolis, Marion County. Company A 132nd Regiment, 100 days; 19 years of age. Died 29 January 1905; buried Crown Hill Cemetery, Marion County.

Wright, Benjamin F. Born 11 January 1833 of Cyrus and Miriam Wright; Whitewater, Wayne County. Company I 84th Regiment; Sergeant; 29 years of age; wounded in arm at Lovejoy Station.

Wright, Charles. Born 13 July 1837 of Cyrus and Miriam Wright; Whitewater, Wayne County. Company D 72nd Regiment; 25 years of age. Died 10 February 1879.

Wright, Francis M. Born 1 July 1837 of Charles D. and Mary Wright; Blue River, Washington County. Company E 90th Regiment, 5th Cavalry; 25 years of age; produced offering at Blue River. Died 28 September 1865; buried Old Blue River.

Wright, William. Born 25 March 1843 of Cyrus and Miriam Wright; Whitewater, Wayne County. Company I 84th Regiment; 19 years of age. Killed at Tunnel Hill, Georgia, 9 May 1864.

Wright, Zenas J. Born 5 June 1843 of John and Joanna W. Wright; Oak Ridge, Grant County. Company K 130th

Regiment; Corporal; 20 years of age; produced offering at
Oak Ridge.

Yates, Enoch Henry. Born 31 August 1846 of Enoch and Sarah
A. Yates; Mississinewa, Grant County. Company M 90th
Regiment, 5th Cavalry; 15 years of age; discharged 15 No-
vember 1862.

Yonkmar, Jacob H. Born circa 1839. Maple Grove (Hicksite),
Huntington County. Company B 153rd Regiment, 1 year;
26 years of age.

York, Eli. Born 7 July 1830; Rush Creek, Parke County.
Company A 85th Regiment; 32 years of age. Died of
wounds at Columbia, Tennessee, 22 March 1863.

Yost, John W. Sparrow Creek, Randolph County. Company
C 8th Regiment, 3 months.

# Appendix D

## Soldiers Buried in Quaker Cemeteries

The following list of names is a compilation of soldiers who are buried in Indiana Quaker cemeteries, but because the names of these men were found neither in Heiss' *Abstracts* nor birth and death records of the Quaker churches, the author was unable to determine whether or not these soldiers were members of the Society of Friends at the time of the Civil War. Therefore, their names do not appear and are not counted among the 1,212 documented cases of Quaker military service listed in Appendix C. The names of these individuals were culled primarily from the Veterans Graves Registration found in the Commission on Public Records, State Archives Division. Helpful, too, were local cemetery records discussed in Appendix C and Terrell's *Report of the Adjutant General of the State of Indiana*. Whenever possible, the same type of information is included in the following brief portraits as was given in the biographies of Quaker soldiers found in Appendix C.

Adams, James L. Born 14 May 1830. Company A 131st Regiment, 13th Cavalry; 33 years of age. Died 16 June 1907; buried Friends Cemetery, Wabash County.

Alexander, Cyrus H. Born circa 1834. Company F 84th Regiment; Corporal; 28 years of age; discharged 16 June 1863 at Nashville, Tennessee. Buried Old Knightstown Cemetery, Henry County.

Anthony, David (Daniel) F. Born circa 1838. Company B 57th Regiment; discharged 5 May 1862. Buried Cherry Grove, Randolph County, 5 February 1912; 73 years of age.

Armstrong, Milton. Company A 18th United States Infantry. Buried in Hamilton County.

Atcheson, Ransom. Born 10 March 1843; Bloomingdale, Parke County. Company I 137th Regiment, 100 days; 21 years of age. Died 24 February 1932; buried Friends Cemetery, Parke County.

Baker, Peter D. Born circa 1842. Company A 101st Regiment; 22 years of age; transferred to Veteran Reserve Corps 15 June 1864. Buried Old Friends Westfield, Hamilton County.

Bales, Hiram. Company I 40th Regiment; drafted; 1 year. Died 16 January 1895; buried Rush Creek #2, Parke County.

Ballenger, John. Company B 57th Regiment. Buried Ridge Cemetery, Wayne County.

Ballenger, Nathan. Born circa 1842 of Jonathan Ballenger. 124th Regiment. Died circa 1921; buried Ridge Cemetery, Wayne County.

Bannon, Samuel P. Born 25 December 1847. Company B 120th Regiment. Died 18 February 1931; buried Friends Cemetery, Parke County.

Barker, Michael W. Born circa 1840. Company K 40th Regiment; Sergeant; 23 years of age. Died 15 April 1917; buried Sugar Plain, Boone County.

Basye, Thomas. Born circa 1825. 36th Regiment; Hospital Steward; appointed surgeon; resigned for disability 25 March 1863. Buried Old Quaker Cemetery, Henry County.

Beard, Albert E. Born circa 1846. Company F 126th Regiment, 11th Cavalry; 17 years of age. Died 29 May 1901; buried Friends Cemetery, Parke County.

Beeson, Newton. Buried Westland Friends, Hancock County.

Bennett, Matthew F. Born circa 1836. Company D 129th Regiment; 27 years of age. Died 14 December 1881; buried Friends Cemetery, Wabash County.

Bennett, Tarlton. Born circa 1842. 17th Light Artillery; 20 years of age; discharged 1 October 1862. Buried Old Quaker Church, Marion County.

Black, William H. Born 13 May 1840. Company F 36th Regiment; 21 years of age. Died 25 February 1904; buried Webster, Wayne County.

Boswell (Roswell), George W. Born circa 1835. Company B 78th Regiment, 60 days; 26 years of age. Died 29 September 1900; buried Friends Cemetery, Parke County.

Bosworth, Jacob. Born 28 September 1845. Company H 100th Regiment; 16 years of age; discharged 22 March 1863; reenlisted Company I 139th Regiment, 100 days; Sergeant. Died 16 November 1915; buried Quaker Cemetery, Jay County.

Bowman, John. Died 26 January 1898; buried Quaker Cemetery, Jay County.

Bradley, Charles F. Born circa 1827. Company F 103rd Ohio Regiment. Died 8 March 1910; buried Friends Cemetery, Howard County.

Brain, Conrad. Born 17 February 1838. Died 10 August 1897; buried Bridgeport, Marion County.

Brown, Joseph H. Born circa 1837. Company H 21st Regiment; 27 years of age; deserted 21 May 1864. Died 16 April 1922; buried Friends Cemetery, Parke County.

Brown, William D. Born circa 1837. Company D 13th Regiment; captured at Allegheny 13 December 1861. Died 17 December 1924; buried Jericho Friends, Randolph County.

Bryant, Richard B. Born 16 October 1835. Company B 59th Regiment; Musician; 26 years of age. Died 26 February 1902; buried West Branch Friends, Hendricks County.

Burnett, Archibald. Born circa 1848. Company D 28th Regiment; 15 years of age. Died 23 December 1871; buried Newberry Cemetery, Orange County.

Busing, John. Born circa 1834. Died circa 1878; buried Park Cemetery, Grant County.

Cain, William. Born 28 October 1811. Company A 69th Regiment. Died 20 July 1876; buried Ridge Cemetery, Wayne County.

Canan, George W. Born 18 February 1843. Company B 115th Regiment, 6 months; Corporal; 20 years of age. Died 19 February 1915; buried Rush Creek #2, Parke County.

Carmer, James C. Born circa 1820. Company A 53rd Regiment; 42 years of age. Buried Sand Creek Friends, Bartholomew County.

Carter, James A. Born 29 February 1836. Company H 21st Regiment, 1st Heavy Artillery; 28 years of age. Died 10 October 1909; buried Friends, Parke County.

Cartwright, William J. Born circa 1836. Company B 16th Regiment; 26 years of age; discharged for wounds received at Richmond, Kentucky, 22 November 1863. Buried Hicksite Friends, Washington County.

Chapman, John W. Born 25 May 1838. 9th Light Artillery; 23 years of age. Died 13 August 1881; buried Friends Cemetery, Parke County.

Chavis, Henry. Born 16 July 1843; Orange County. Company F 28th Regiment, United States Colored Troops; 20 years of age. Died 24 September 1930; buried Friends Cemetery, Parke County.

Cheeseman, William H. Born circa 1846. Company G 147th Regiment, 1 year; Corporal; 19 years of age. Buried Hinkles Creek, Hamilton County.

Childers, Gideon T. Born 15 August 1843 of Isaac and Hannah Childers; Orange County. Company E 125th Regiment,

10th Cavalry; 19 years of age. Died 18 July 1929; buried IOOF, Orange County.

Churchman, Elijah. Born circa 1837. Company D 53rd Regiment; 24 years of age. Died circa 1928; buried Blue River, Washington County.

Clarke, Jesse J. Born 22 September 1840. Company I 31st Regiment; 21 years of age; discharged for wounds 9 June 1865. Died 15 January 1922; buried Friends Cemetery, Parke County.

Clover, Nathan. Born circa 1844. Company E 52nd Regiment; 17 years of age; transferred to Company I 52nd Regiment Reorganized. Died circa 1929; buried Hinkles Creek, Hamilton County.

Coats, William F. Company B 71st Regiment, Ohio Volunteers. Died 30 May 1903; buried White River, Randolph County; 79 years of age.

Coffin, Maben D. Born circa 1839. Company C 144th Regiment; 26 years of age. Buried Highland Friends, Washington County.

Comer, James. Born 14 November 1820. Company G 106th Regiment, 6 days; 42 years of age. Died 4 June 1904; buried New London Friends, Howard County.

Conaroe, Samuel. Born circa 1821. Company I 7th Regiment; 41 years of age; discharged for disability 18 December 1863. Died circa 1896; buried Bridgeport, Marion County.

Conklin, Anthony M. Born 29 October 1841. Company D 75th Regiment; 1st Lieutenant; 23 years of age. Killed in Mexico 24 December 1880; buried Westfield Anti-Slavery Friends, Hamilton County.

Conklin, John S. Born 6 July 1812. Company D 136th Regiment, 100 days; 51 years of age. Died 23 July 1881; buried Westfield Anti-Slavery Friends, Hamilton County.

Conner, William S. Born circa 1826. Company B 124th Regiment; 37 years of age. Died circa 1909; buried Ridge Cemetery, Wayne County.

Cooper, John. Died 1 October 1880; buried Friends Cemetery, Wabash County.

Copeland, John. Born 17 March 1846. Company D 78th Regiment, 60 days; 16 years of age. Died 26 June 1928; buried Friends Cemetery, Parke County.

Cox, John W. Born 23 December 1820. Company G 133rd Regiment, 100 days; 43 years of age. Died 27 March 1912; buried Friends Cemetery, Parke County.

Craft, John W. Born January 1846. Company A 85th Regiment; 18 years of age; transferred to 33rd Regiment 1 June 1865. Died 27 November 1919; buried Friends Cemetery, Parke County.

Crone, Michael M. Born 6 July 1839 of David and Huldah Crone; Bridgeport, Marion County. Company C 81st Regiment; 22 years of age; discharged 18 April 1863. Died circa 1915; buried Bridgeport.

Dafey (Dailey), Michael. 13th Indiana Battery. Buried Friends Cemetery, Miami County.

Dannetell, A. K. Born circa 1846. Company H 31st Regiment; Substitute. Died circa 1905; buried Friends Cemetery, Jackson County.

Davis, Charles. Born circa 1843. Company E 109th Regiment, Minute Men, 8 days; 20 years of age. Died 27 December 1871; buried Westfield Anti-Slavery Friends, Hamilton County.

Davis, John E. Born 25 October 1845. Company B 115th Regiment, 6 months; 17 years of age. Buried Friends Cemetery, Parke County.

Davis, Simeon H. Born circa 1844 of Hezekiah Davis. Company C 121st Regiment, 9th Cavalry; 19 years of age. Died 18 September 1916; buried Webster, Wayne County.

Dawson, John. Died 12 March 1877; buried Quaker Cemetery, Jay County.

Dean, David. Born 14 February 1838. 19th Light Artillery. Died 23 November 1894; buried Fairfield Friends, Wayne County.

Dean, John. Born circa 1812. 29th Regiment; 51 years of age. Died circa 1890; buried Back Creek, Grant County.

Dean, Leroy M. Born 15 September 1844. 19th Light Artillery; 19 years of age. Died 15 May 1880; buried Fairfield Friends, Wayne County.

Dean, William F. Born circa 1832. Company B 11th Regiment, 3 months; 29 years of age; Drummer. Died circa 1907; buried Fairfield Friends, Wayne County.

Demint, James G. Born circa 1840. Company C 69th Regiment; 22 years of age. Died 9 May 1911; buried White River, Randolph County.

Demory, Robert. Born circa 1826. 14th Regiment, United States Colored Troops; 38 years of age. Died 8 January 1895; buried Poplar Run, Randolph County.

Dempsy, James. Born circa 1842. Company E 28th Regiment, United States Colored Troops; 22 years of age. Buried Westfield Anti-Slavery Friends, Hamilton County.

Derman, Jefferson. Born 22 February 1847. Company F 39th Regiment, 8th Cavalry; 17 years of age. Died 19 January 1893; buried Friends Cemetery, Parke County.

DeWees, Benjamin L. Born circa 1845. Company I 139th Regiment, 100 days; 19 years of age. Died 15 February 1930; buried Quaker Cemetery, Jay County.

Dillon, Alphaus. Born 9 August 1844. Company A 59th Regiment; Musician; 17 years of age. Died 11 February 1939; buried West Union, Morgan County.

Dillon, Jonathan P. Born circa 1822. Company E 139th Regiment, 100 days; 41 years of age. Died 21 October 1904; buried Friends Cemetery, Howard County.

Downs, William. Born 9 April 1835. Company D 147th Regiment, 1 year; 29 years of age. Died circa 1910; buried Hopewell Friends, Vermillion County.

Duggard, Samuel. Born circa 1842. 28th Regiment, United States Colored Troops; 23 years of age. Died circa 1870; buried Friends Cemetery, Howard County.

Eaton, James R. Born circa 1836. Company I 6th Regiment, 3 months; 25 years of age. Buried Hinkles Creek, Hamilton County.

Ellis, Jonathan. Born 3 December 1841 of Levi and Mary Ellis. Company C 73rd Illinois Regiment; Corporal. Died 1 October 1921; buried Hopewell Friends, Vermillion County.

Engle, Valentine. Died 23 November 1874; buried Quaker Cemetery, Jay County.

Ensler, Lewis. Buried Friends Cemetery, Howard County.

Ephlin, Josiah M. Born 4 May 1840. Company A 85th Regiment; 22 years of age. Died 14 July 1924; buried Friends Cemetery, Parke County.

Farmer, George. Born circa 1847. Company K 11th Regiment; 18 years of age. Buried West White Lick, Morgan County.

Finney, Robert J. Born 10 December 1845. Company E 149th Regiment; Corporal; 19 years of age. Died 11 December 1912; buried Friends Cemetery, Parke County.

Flinn, William A. Born 13 November 1836. Company E 23rd Regiment; 24 years of age. Died 22 January 1912; buried Highland Friends, Washington County.

Forsha, David R. Born 25 June 1845. Company E 70th Regiment; 17 years of age. Died 25 January 1928; buried Old Quaker Church, Marion County.

Francis, William H. Born circa 1838. Company F 79th Regiment; 24 years of age. Buried Bridgeport, Marion County.

Franklin, Ruben C. Born circa 1828. Company C 70th Regiment; 34 years of age. Died circa 1902; buried West Union, Morgan County.

Frazier, Martin L. Born circa 1845 of James Frazier. Company L 71st Regiment, 6th Cavalry; 18 years of age; discharged 10 November 1863; reenlisted Company C 121st Regiment, 9th Cavalry. Buried Fairfield Friends, Wayne County.

Freeman, William. Born 26 April 1809. 52nd Regiment; Surgeon; resigned 29 August 1863; reentered 119th Regiment, 7th Cavalry; Surgeon; dismissed 10 May 1864. Died 17 April 1883; buried Quaker Cemetery, Jay County.

Fridly, Peter. Born circa 1832. Company C 11th Ohio Infantry. Died circa 1885; buried Quaker Cemetery, Jay County.

Frost, Isaac. Born circa 1827. Company A 90th Regiment, 5th Cavalry; 36 years of age. Buried Westfield Anti-Slavery Friends, Hamilton County.

Fryar, David H. Ohio Volunteers. Died 25 February 1904; buried Cherry Grove, Randolph County.

Gardner, Beecher M. Born circa 1844. Company G 67th Regiment; 18 years of age. Buried Driftwood, Jackson County.

Gaylor, John A. Company D 110th Ohio Regiment. Died 4 January 1903; buried White River, Randolph County.

George, Enos. Born circa 1842. Company I 109th Regiment, Minute Men; 21 years of age. Died circa 1926; buried West Grove Friends, Hamilton County.

Gibbons, John M. Born 12 February 1844. Company B 49th Regiment; 16 years of age. Died 1 April 1926; buried Blue River, Washington County.

Gibson, James P. Born circa 1833. Company B 34th Regiment; Corporal; 28 years of age. Buried Quaker Cemetery, Jay County.

Gilbert, John Thomas. Died 10 June 1928; buried Jericho Friends, Randolph County.

Glover, William E. Born circa 1832. Company H 9th Regiment; drafted. Died 17 February 1898; buried Cherry Grove, Randolph County.

Goldsberry, John A. Born 11 July 1835. 21st Regiment, 1st Heavy Artillery; Assistant Surgeon; resigned 11 July 1865. Died 7 March 1901; buried Friends Cemetery, Parke County.

Goldsberry, Owen. Buried Quaker Cemetery, Jay County.

Good, Jacob. Company E 101st Ohio Regiment. Buried Quaker Cemetery, Jay County.

Gray, [no first name given]. Buried Old Quaker Church, Marion County.

Grisell, Theodore E. Company H 138th Regiment, 100 days; Corporal. Died 26 April 1916; buried Quaker Cemetery, Jay County.

Hall, J. P. Company C 18th Regiment; Musician. Buried Driftwood, Jackson County.

Hansing, Anthony F. Born circa 1837. Company I 148th Regiment, 1 year; 27 years of age. Died 30 April 1900; buried Bridgeport, Marion County.

Harlan, Jonathan. Born circa 1845. Company D 84th Regiment; Captain; 18 years of age. Died circa 1915; buried Salem, Union County.

Harper, William. Born circa 1834. Company A 47th Regiment; Sergeant; 27 years of age. Buried Quaker Cemetery, Jay County.

Hart, John T. Born 7 November 1843. Company A 85th Regiment; 18 years of age. Died 29 November 1931; buried Friends Cemetery, Parke County.

Hatfield, Allen A. Born circa 1818. Company A 49th Regiment; Corporal; 43 years of age. Died 13 June 1896; buried Old Quaker Church, Marion County.

Heath, Josiah. Born 4 February 1842. Company A 85th Regiment; 20 years of age; discharged 27 December 1862. Died 28 November 1920; buried Rush Creek #2, Parke County.

Heaton, Daniel M. Born circa 1839. Company D 89th Regiment; 23 years of age. Died circa 1895; buried Friends Cemetery, Howard County.

Hedrick, Benjamin F. Born circa 1846. Company D 77th Regiment, 4th Cavalry; 17 years of age. Died circa 1928; buried Blue River, Washington County.

Hefner, Nicholas. Company B 34th Regiment. Buried Dunkirk Friends, Randolph County.

Hess, Calvin. Born circa 1843. Company D 75th Regiment; 19 years of age. Buried Westfield Anti-Slavery Friends, Hamilton County.

Hiatt, Samuel. Born circa 1838. Company B 126th Regiment, 11th Cavalry; 2nd Lieutenant; 25 years of age. Buried Quaker Cemetery, Jay County.

Hilligoss, Joseph. Company C 8th Regiment, United States Colored Troops. Buried Webster, Wayne County.

Hindman, Samuel. Born 22 February 1839 of Andrew and Margaret Hindman. Company B 19th Regiment; 1st Lieutenant; 24 years of age; wounded severely in leg; resigned 14 March 1863. Died 28 December 1895; buried Ridge Cemetery, Wayne County.

Hobson, Jesse B. Born 4 April 1840. Company G 108th Regiment, 7 days; 22 years of age. Died 8 April 1924; buried Rush Creek #2, Parke County.

Hope, W. S. Company C 75th Regiment; 23 years of age; discharged for disability 5 December 1863. Buried New London Friends, Howard County.

Houser, Eli. Died 15 November 1909; buried Quaker Cemetery, Lynn, Indiana.

Hubbard, John W. Born 21 July 1850. Company C 22nd Regiment; 12 years of age; discharged for disability 18 March 1863. Died 22 May 1921; buried Friends Cemetery, Howard County.

Hubbard, William. Born circa 1839. Died circa 1919; buried West Union, Morgan County.

Hunt, Elijah. Born circa 1845. Company C 148th Regiment, 1 year; 20 years of age. Buried Westland Friends, Hancock County.

Hunt, Jasper. Born 15 September 1826. Company B 85th Regiment; Corporal; 35 years of age. Died 20 April 1907; buried Friends Cemetery, Parke County.

Hyde, William S. Born circa 1819. Company B 126th Regiment, 11th Cavalry; 44 years of age. Buried Quaker Cemetery, Jay County.

Irby, Columbus. Born circa 1845. Company I 118th Regiment, 6 months; 18 years of age. Buried Friends Cemetery, Howard County.

Ireland, William A. Born 22 December 1836. Company A 14th Regiment; transferred to Company B 20th Indiana Volunteers. Died 22 October 1897; buried Rush Creek #2, Parke County.

Jackson, James A. Born 5 March 1842. Company E 26th Regiment; 19 years of age; discharged for disability 21 March 1863. Died 17 January 1904; buried Fairfield, Hendricks County.

Jackson, John W. Born 26 March 1839. Company I 31st Regiment; 22 years of age. Died 13 June 1920; buried Rush Creek #2, Parke County.

Jackson, William. Born 26 March 1842. Company F 16th Regiment; 20 years of age. Died 2 September 1882; buried Old Quaker Church (West Newton), Marion County.

Jester, Jacob. Born 4 August 1802. Company A 86th Regiment; 60 years of age. Died 20 April 1881; buried Westfield Anti-Slavery Friends, Hamilton County.

Johnson, Jeptha J. Born 17 August 1842. Company B 60th Ohio Regiment; 19 years of age. Died 9 August 1922; buried West Union, Morgan County.

Johnson, Samuel. Born circa 1819. Company C 57th Ohio Regiment. Died 20 March 1888; buried Quaker Cemetery, Jay County.

Johnson, Sanford. Born circa 1846. Company E 78th Regiment, 60 days; 16 years of age. Died 13 March 1888; buried West Union, Morgan County.

Jones, George. Born circa 1826. Company G 124th Regiment; 37 years of age. Died 20 September 1915; buried White River, Randolph County.

Journigan, Eli. Born circa 1837. Company K 11th Regiment; Corporal; 24 years of age. Died 17 April 1907; buried Webster, Wayne County.

Kearns, William. Buried Westland Friends, Hancock County.

Keever, Abraham. Born circa 1843. Company A 9th Regiment; 21 years of age; drafted. Died circa 1929; buried West River, Wayne County.

Kelly, Francis M. Born circa 1841. Company E 89th Regiment; 21 years of age. Died 6 April 1870; buried Quaker Cemetery, Jay County.

Kershner, Benjamin F. Born 13 April 1842. Died 26 September 1902; buried Friends Cemetery, Wabash County.

Kidder, Bradley E. Born circa 1840. Company H 34th Regiment; 21 years of age. Died 25 December 1889; buried North Union, Howard County.

Kidder, James E. Born circa 1835. Company C 75th Regiment; discharged 19 January 1864. Died 2 May 1887; buried North Union, Howard County.

Kirkman, Jonathan. Company I 36th Regiment; transferred to Veteran Reserve Corps. Buried Webster, Wayne County.

Kitchel, John W. Born 14 March 1847. Company I 131st Regiment, 13th Cavalry; 17 years of age. Died 7 November 1914; buried Friends Cemetery, Parke County.

Kitterman, Ennias. Born circa 1845. 19th Light Artillery; 17 years of age; taken prisoner at Bentonville, North Carolina, March 1865. Died circa 1924; buried West Grove, Wayne County.

Kriner, Andrew. Company G 71st Ohio Regiment. Buried Raysville, Henry County.

Lamb, Job. Born circa 1844. Company G 121st Regiment, 9th Cavalry; 20 years of age. Buried Bridgeport, Marion County.

Landers, Louis C. Born 29 January 1846. Company B 116th Regiment, 6 months; 17 years of age; reenlisted Company C 150th Regiment, 1 year. Died 21 February 1910; buried Old Quaker Church (West Newton), Marion County.

Leamon, John. Company B 144th Regiment, 1 year. Buried Driftwood, Jackson County.

Lehman, Fred. Born 2 January 1844. Died 12 November 1913; buried Friends Cemetery, Howard County.

Lemmons, Robert. Born circa 1836. Company C 50th Regiment; 25 years of age; discharged for disability 11 December 1863. Buried Driftwood, Jackson County.

Lewis, John B. Born 16 August 1842. Died 12 March 1915; buried Friends Cemetery, Parke County.

Lewis, John S. D. Born circa 1844. Company H 12th Regiment; 17 years of age. Died circa 1877; buried Back Creek, Grant County.

Linson, George. Born circa 1838. Company A 145th Regiment, 1 year; 27 years of age. Died 6 January 1881; buried South Union, Howard County.

Little, W. C. Buried Friends Cemetery, Parke County.

Lybrook, David. Born circa 1834. Company G 89th Regiment; 1st Sergeant; 28 years of age. Died 4 August 1893; buried South Union, Howard County.

McCool, Mark. Born circa 1826. Company C 26th Regiment; 35 years of age; reenlisted Company I 31st Regiment; transferred to Veteran Reserve Corps 30 September 1863. Buried Friends Cemetery, Parke County.

McCoy, Jacob. Born circa 1818. Company D 33rd Regiment; 43 years of age; drafted. Died circa 1877; buried Back Creek, Grant County.

McCoy, William F. Born circa 1834. Company D 75th Regiment; 28 years of age; transferred to Veteran Reserve Corps 1 July 1863. Died 13 February 1877; buried Westfield Anti-Slavery Friends, Hamilton County.

McCoy, William Harrison. Born circa 1838. Company G 89th Regiment; 24 years of age. Died 2 February 1875; buried Friends Cemetery, Howard County.

McCracken, William P. Born circa 1839. Company D 70th Regiment; 2nd Lieutenant; 23 years of age. Died 13 September 1901; buried West Union, Morgan County.

McDaniel, Lewis. Born circa 1844. Company H 99th Regiment; 18 years of age; discharged 13 March 1865. Died 30 September 1890; buried Mill Creek, Hendricks County.

McKinley, Patrick. Born circa 1847. Company A 148th Regiment, 1 year; 18 years of age. Buried Ridge Cemetery, Wayne County.

Markle, Jacob. Born circa 1845 of Gideon Markle. Company I 57th Regiment; Corporal; 16 years of age. Died circa 1923; buried Webster, Wayne County.

Martin, Morgan. Born 7 July 1825. Died 19 October 1900; buried Blue River, Washington County.

Massena, John H. Died 19 January 1880; buried Friends Cemetery, Howard County.

Mays, William L. Born circa 1832. Company C 110th Regiment, 5 days; Musician; 30 years of age. Died 25 May 1922; buried Friends Cemetery, Parke County.

Merrell, Benjamin. Born circa 1833. Home Guards. Died circa 1879; buried North Union, Howard County.

Miller, William H. Born circa 1844. Company G 89th Regiment; 18 years of age. Died 3 February 1883; buried South Union, Howard County.

Milton, George. Born circa 1844. Company E 28th Regiment, United States Colored Troops; 21 years of age; detailed on guard duty at Indianapolis. Buried Webster, Wayne County.

Montague, Lafayette. Company G 12th Ohio Cavalry. Died 22 May 1900; buried West Union, Morgan County.

Montgomery, David. Born circa 1828. Company K 83rd Regiment; 34 years of age. Died circa 1902; buried Salem, Union County.

Moody, Pierce. Born circa 1844. 69th Regiment; 18 years of age; reenlisted 15th Light Artillery. Died 23 November 1893; buried Quaker Cemetery, Lynn, Indiana.

Moore, John E. Born circa 1843. Company D 136th Regiment, 100 days. Died 9 March 1909; buried West Grove, Hamilton County.

Moore, William H. Born circa 1842. Company G 144th Illinois Infantry; Musician. Died 24 April 1913; buried Nettle Creek Friends, Wayne County.

Moore, Willis P. Born circa 1839. Company A 38th Regiment; 22 years of age. Died circa 1923; buried Rush Creek #2, Parke County.

Moorman, Robert F. Born circa 1833. 10th Light Artillery; 28 years of age. Died circa 1896; buried Webster, Wayne County.

Morgan, A. James. Company E 149th Regiment. Died 9 January 1922; buried Friends Cemetery, Parke County.

Morgan, Jonathan. Born circa 1790. Died circa 1874; buried Quaker Cemetery, Jay County.

Morgan, William H. Born circa 1835. Company E 75th Regiment; 27 years of age; transferred to Veteran Reserve Corps 29 July 1864. Buried White River, Randolph County.

Morrett, Hiram W. Born circa 1844. Died circa 1920; buried Salem, Union County.

Morris, Thomas McGuire. Born circa 1826. Company H 153rd Regiment, 1 year; Sergeant. Died 17 February 1907; buried Friends Cemetery, Wabash County.

Morris, Thomas N. Born 29 December 1837. Company G 117th Regiment, 6 months; 25 years of age. Died 28 May 1885; buried Hicksite Friends, Washington County.

Morrison, Daniel. Born circa 1828. Company G 89th Regiment; 34 years of age. Died 21 February 1879; buried Friends Cemetery, Howard County.

Murray, Martin. Born circa 1834. 19th Light Artillery; 28 years of age. Buried Fairfield, Wayne County.

Newby, Stephen. Born circa 1836. Company D 12th Regiment, 1 year; 25 years of age. Buried Hinkles Creek, Hamilton County.

Newman, Joel A. Born circa 1831. Company C 19th Regiment; 1st Lieutenant; 30 years of age; resigned 9 February 1863. Died 1 February 1912; buried Cherry Grove, Randolph County.

Nicholas, Joshua. Born circa 1832. Company B 34th Regiment; 30 years of age. Buried Quaker Cemetery, Jay County.

Nicholson, F. Company F 39th Regiment, 8th Cavalry. Buried Sand Creek, Bartholomew County.

Norris, Joseph M. Born circa 1845. Company F 123rd Regiment; 18 years of age. Buried Old Quaker Church (West Newton), Marion County.

Northan, Daniel. Born circa 1845. Company C 130th Regiment; 18 years of age. Buried Old Friends Westfield, Hamilton County.

Oliver, Samuel. Born 28 October 1834. Company I 27th Regiment; 26 years of age. Died 11 October 1903; buried West Branch Friends, Hendricks County.

Owens, James. Born circa 1833. Company F 124th Regiment; 31 years of age. Died 10 December 1872; buried West Grove, Wayne County.

Owens, William E. Born circa 1823. Company G 147th Regiment, 1 year. Died 14 February 1899; buried Hinkles Creek, Hamilton County.

Parker, John Burley. Born circa 1845. Died 6 December 1920; buried Friends Cemetery, Wabash County.

Patten, Frank C. Born circa 1846. Company B 90th Regiment, 5th Cavalry; 18 years of age; transferred to Company H 71st Regiment, 6th Cavalry. Buried Gray Friends, Hamilton County.

Pickard, Alexander. Born circa 1835. Company K 16th Regiment; 27 years of age; paroled prisoner; absent on sick leave. Died circa 1885; buried Back Creek, Grant County.

Pitkman (Pittman), Samuel S. Born circa 1844. Company A 101st Regiment; Corporal; 18 years of age. Buried Westfield Anti-Slavery Friends, Hamilton County.

Poland, W. F. M. Born circa 1836. Company D 67th Regiment; 25 years of age; transferred to Company K 24th Regiment. Died circa 1930; buried Sand Creek, Bartholomew County.

Porter, Daniel A. Born circa 1829. Company F 126th Regiment, 11th Cavalry; Captain; 34 years of age; discharged 15 October 1864. Died circa 1900; buried Friends Cemetery, Parke County.

Porter, Elias A. Born circa 1827. Company H 100th Regiment; 35 years of age. Buried Quaker Cemetery, Jay County.

Potter, Mathias. Born circa 1837. Company A 38th Regiment; 27 years of age; transferred to Veteran Reserve Corps. Buried South Union, Howard County.

Pratt, Jeremiah. Born 19 January 1841. Company H 41st Regiment, 2nd Cavalry; 22 years of age; transferred to Company H 2nd Cavalry Reorganized; Corporal. Died 27 February 1915; buried Friends Cemetery, Wabash County.

Pritchard, Finley. Died 1 January 1902; buried White River, Randolph County.

Pritchard, Joseph A. Born 1 April 1844. Company A 86th Regiment; 18 years of age. Died 10 November 1902; buried Friends Cemetery, Howard County.

Ratliff, Henry C. Born circa 1844. Company K 79th Regiment; 18 years of age; Corporal. Died circa 1918; buried Sugar Grove, Hendricks County.

Reynolds, Albert. Died 28 June 1904; buried Quaker Cemetery, Miami County.

Rice, Henry. Buried Friends Cemetery, Howard County.

Richards, James B. Born circa 1844. 14th Light Artillery; 19 years of age. Died 2 June 1915; buried Friends Cemetery, Wabash County.

Ridgeway, David R. Born 3 October 1828 of Joseph and Margaret Ridgeway; Wabash, Wabash County. Died 27 August 1907; buried Friends Cemetery, Wabash County.

Rigby, Eli. Born circa 1841. Company H 30th Regiment; 20 years of age. Died circa 1872; buried Quaker Cemetery, Jay County.

Rigsby, Zikariah (Zimri). Born circa 1837. Company G 52nd Regiment; 24 years of age; discharged for disability 26 October 1862. Buried Friends Cemetery, Rush County.

Rile, James M. Born circa 1828. Company I 45th Regiment, 3rd Cavalry. Died circa 1931; buried Salem, Union County.

Riley, John H. Born circa 1843. Company A 69th Regiment; 19 years of age. Died 27 August 1913; buried Crown Hill Cemetery, Marion County.

Roberts, Alexander. Born circa 1838. Company K 36th Regiment; Corporal; 23 years of age. Died circa 1870; buried Friends Cemetery, Howard County.

Roberts, David F. Born circa 1841. Company D 26th Regiment; 21 years of age; discharged for disability 6 January 1864. Died 13 February 1901; buried Quaker Cemetery, Jay County.

Roberts, John. Died 2 August 1869; buried Friends Cemetery, Howard County.

Roberts, Uriah. Born circa 1847. Company F 28th Regiment, United States Colored Troops; 18 years of age. Died 3 April 1871; buried Friends Cemetery, Howard County.

Robertson, W. F. Born circa 1843. Company A 39th Regiment, 8th Cavalry; 19 years of age. Buried North Union, Howard County.

Robins, Albert. Born circa 1844. Company K 50th Regiment; 20 years of age; transferred to 52nd Regiment. Died circa 1923; buried Friends Cemetery, Jackson County.

Rogers, John T. Born 14 June 1833. Company G 16th Regiment, 1 year; 27 years of age. Died 16 May 1914; buried Fall Creek (Hicksite), Madison County.

Rushton, George. Born 13 September 1846. 53rd Regiment; Substitute; 19 years of age. Died 7 April 1912; buried West Union, Morgan County.

Russell, Hugh F. Born circa 1830. Died circa 1909; buried Rush Creek #2, Parke County.

Savage, Charles. Born circa 1835. Company K 8th Regiment; 26 years of age. Buried Friends Cemetery, Jackson County.

Shafer, Joseph. Company D 119th Regiment, 7th Cavalry. Died 18 September 1897; buried Cherry Grove, Randolph County.

Shaw, Orlando. Born circa 1834. Company I 28th Regiment, 1st Cavalry; Corporal; 27 years of age. Buried Westfield Anti-Slavery Friends, Hamilton County.

Sheaffer, Isaac A. Born circa 1844. Company C 35th Ohio Regiment. Died circa 1929; buried Gray Friends, Hamilton County.

Shelley, Samuel. Company D 117th Regiment, 6 months. Buried Old Quaker Church, Marion County.

Shields, David M. Born 8 May 1846. Company G 59th Regiment; 17 years of age. Died 11 October 1889; buried Blue River, Washington County.

Shields, Jesse. Born 15 September 1840. Company B 49th Regiment; Corporal; 21 years of age; discharged 29 November 1864. Died 7 February 1870; buried Hicksite Friends, Washington County.

Shipp, Sanford C. Born circa 1837. Company B 17th Regiment; 24 years of age. Died 5 November 1890; buried Crown Hill Cemetery, Marion County.

Sholty, Samuel. Born circa 1844. Died 1 June 1916; buried Friends Cemetery, Wabash County.

Simpson, Joseph R. Born circa 1842. Company A 121st Regiment, 9th Cavalry; 21 years of age. Died 25 July 1892; buried Bridgeport, Marion County.

Slay, Anthony M. Born circa 1825. Company B 34th Regiment; Corporal; 36 years of age. Buried Friends Cemetery, Wabash County.

Smith, James S. Born circa 1840. Company D 101st Regiment; 22 years of age. Buried Westfield Anti-Slavery Friends, Hamilton County.

Smithson, Jonathan. Born circa 1841. Died 1873; buried Back Creek, Grant County.

Snyder, Henry. Born 9 January 1836. Company I 31st Regiment; 25 years of age; reenlisted same regiment; transferred to 1st United States Engineers 20 July 1864. Died 29 September 1924; buried Friends Cemetery, Parke County.

Somer, Samuel. Born circa 1835. Company G 153rd Regiment, 1 year; 30 years of age. Buried Quaker Cemetery, Jay County.

Souders, Henry. Born circa 1830. Died circa 1871; buried Quaker Cemetery, Jay County.

Spurgeon, William. Buried Hicksite Friends, Washington County.

Stanfield, John G. Buried Driftwood, Jackson County.

Stanfield, S. W. Company A 137th Regiment, 100 days. Buried Driftwood, Jackson County.

Stetson, Thomas H. Died 1884; buried Cedar Friends, Randolph County.

Stevens, W. H. Born circa 1827. Company I 36th Regiment; 34 years of age. Died circa 1918; buried Silver Creek, Union County.

Stout, Martin M. Born circa 1832. Company F 50th Regiment; 29 years of age. Died 23 January 1869; buried Rush Creek #2, Parke County.

Stout, William A. Born circa 1845. Company K 21st Regiment, 1st Heavy Artillery; 18 years of age. Died circa 1926; buried West Union, Morgan County.

Strayhorn, John W. Born circa 1843. Company G 16th Regiment; 19 years of age. Died 5 August 1872; buried Friends Cemetery, Rush County.

Swaim, Newton. Born 9 August 1820. Company C 78th Regiment, 60 days; 41 years of age. Died 5 June 1908; buried Friends Cemetery, Parke County.

Taylor, Enoch. Born circa 1837. Company B 12th Regiment, 1 year; 24 years of age. Died 11 March 1884; buried Friends Cemetery, Howard County.

Taylor, Henry. Born circa 1847. 19th Light Artillery; 16 years of age. Died circa 1914; buried Nettle Creek Friends, Wayne County.

Teeguarden, William R. Born 16 February 1843. Died 20 November 1907; buried Salem, Union County.

Thatcher, Alexander. Born 2 February 1824. Company C 101st Regiment; 38 years of age; discharged 17 March 1863. Died 22 February 1896; buried Friends Cemetery, Howard County.

Thomas, Richard D. Born circa 1836. Company D 21st Regiment, 1st Heavy Artillery; 27 years of age. Died circa 1877; buried West Union, Morgan County.

Thompson, Albert. Born 14 March 1837. Company K 97th Regiment; 25 years of age. Died 22 January 1933; buried Poplar Grove, Parke County.

Thompson, Isaac E. Born circa 1847. Company H 154th Regiment, 1 year; 18 years of age. Died 28 February 1879; buried Friends Cemetery, Howard County.

Thompson, James W. Born 21 September 1836. Company G 18th Regiment; 24 years of age. Died 6 January 1921; buried Hicksite Friends, Washington County.

Thompson, John M. Born circa 1821. Company F 124th Regiment; 43 years of age. Buried Webster, Wayne County.

Thomson, J. E. Born circa 1834. Company B 126th Regiment, 11th Cavalry; 29 years of age. Buried Quaker Cemetery, Jay County.

Thornbrough, George E. Born 23 September 1840. Company H 13th Regiment; 20 years of age. Buried Bridgeport, Marion County.

Thornbrough, Henry. Born circa 1834. Company A 103rd Regiment, 8 days; 28 years of age. Died circa 1920; buried Bridgeport, Marion County.

Thornbrough, Isaac. Born circa 1840. Company B 13th Regiment Reorganized; 22 years of age; transferred to Company D 13th Regiment; wounded at Rich Mountain and

Cold Harbor; reenlisted Company H 13th Regiment. Died 31 January 1899; buried Bridgeport, Marion County.

Tompkins, James. Buried Salem, Union County.

Underwood, Theodore W. Born circa 1846. Company H 138th Regiment, 100 days; 18 years of age. Buried Quaker Cemetery, Jay County.

Van Meter, Joseph. Born 4 May 1837. Company C 109th Regiment, 8 days; 26 years of age. Died 28 January 1925; buried Hicksite Friends, Washington County.

Walling, Henry V. Born circa 1842. Company F 75th Regiment; Sergeant; 20 years of age. Died 12 September 1875; buried Quaker Cemetery, Jay County.

Ward, George. Born 29 August 1841. Company F 15th Regiment. Died 10 February 1915; buried Fairfield Friends, Wayne County.

Ward, Rufus H. Born 8 February 1838. Company D 70th Regiment; 24 years of age. Died 1 May 1885; buried West Union, Morgan County.

Warren, Zimri. Born circa 1824. Company H 11th Regiment; 41 years of age. Buried West Branch Friends, Hendricks County.

Watson, Allen H. Born circa 1836. 22nd Light Artillery; 26 years of age. Buried Friends Cemetery, Rush County.

Watson, Martin J. Born 23 November 1836. Company K 70th Regiment; Corporal; 25 years of age. Died 5 May 1907; buried Bridgeport, Marion County.

Wilcoxen, Josiah Thomas. Born circa 1845 of John Wilcoxen. Company K 124th Regiment; 18 years of age. Died 5 March 1904; buried Fairfield Friends, Wayne County.

Williams, Joel. Born 23 March 1838. Company G 45th Regiment, 3rd Cavalry; 23 years of age. Died 6 September 1899; buried West Union, Morgan County.

Williams, William T. Born circa 1846. Company E 47th Regiment; 18 years of age. Buried Friends Cemetery, Wabash County.

Wilson, Charles. Born 14 November 1848 of Joseph and Elizabeth Wilson. Company A 47th Regiment; Sergeant. Buried Quaker Cemetery, Jay County.

Wilson, Edward. Died 28 March 1893; buried Quaker Cemetery, Jay County.

Wood, Samuel J. Born circa 1836. Company L 126th Regiment, 11th Cavalry; 27 years of age. Died circa 1898; buried Friends Cemetery, Wabash County.

Woods, Robert. Company A 38th Regiment; Corporal. Buried Lick Creek, Orange County.

Wrenn, Joseph T. Born 3 May 1840. Company D 75th Regiment; Corporal; 22 years of age. Died 19 September 1877; buried Westfield, Hamilton County.

# Appendix E

## Ages of Quaker Soldiers[1]

| Ages | Number of Men |
|:---:|:---:|
| 12-15 | 27 |
| 16 | 23 |
| 17 | 53 |
| 18 | 137 |
| 19 | 105 |
| 20 | 91 |
| 21 | 91 |
| 22 | 73 |
| 23 | 44 |
| 24 | 46 |
| 25 | 33 |
| 26 | 26 |
| 27 | 20 |
| 28 | 24 |
| 29 | 26 |
| 30 | 18 |
| 31-35 | 68 |
| 36-40 | 54 |
| 41-45 | 37 |
| 46-50 | 10 |
| 51 and over | 10 |
| | |
| Total Reported | 1016 |

[1]Age is that on the date of muster.

# Notes

## Preface

1. The Quaker population in 1860 is estimated to have been between 16,000 and 20,000 out of a total of 1,350,428 persons who resided in Indiana. In 1988 approximately 13,100 Quakers lived in Indiana. The total population, according to the 1980 Federal Census, was 5,490,000.

## Introduction

1. Howard K. Beale, "What Historians Have Said about the Causes of the Civil War," in *Theory and Practice in Historical Study: A Report of the Committee on Historiography*, Social Science Research Council, Bulletin 54 (1946), 55, quoted in Gerald N. Grob and George Athan Billias, eds., *Interpretations of American History: Patterns and Perspectives*, 3d ed., 2 vols. (New York: Free Press, 1978), 1:363-64.

2. The author confined the geographic area of examination to the following counties: Bartholomew, Boone, Grant, Hamilton, Hancock, Hendricks, Henry, Howard, Huntington, Jackson, Jay, Madison, Marion, Miami, Montgomery, Morgan, Orange, Parke, Randolph, Rush, Tippecanoe, Union, Vermillion, Vigo, Wabash, Washington, and Wayne. From most of the foregoing twenty-seven counties, the author read monthly meeting records for both men and women of forty-five Quaker meetings for the years 1861-69 inclusive. The names of the meetings and respective counties are: Sand Creek of Bartholomew County; Mississinewa and Back Creek of Grant County; Poplar Ridge (1866-69 only), Westfield, and Greenwood of Hamilton County; Fairfield, Plainfield, and Mill Creek of Hendricks County; Duck Creek, Spiceland, Hopewell, and Raysville of Henry County; Honey Creek, New Salem, and Pleasant Hill of Howard County; Driftwood of Jackson County; Fall Creek (Hicksite—women only) of Madison County; Bridgeport and Beech Grove (1863-69) of Marion County; Pipe Creek of Miami County; West Union and White Lick of Morgan County; Lick Creek (women only) of Orange County; Rocky Run (1864-69, men only), Rush

Creek, and Bloomfield of Parke County; Cherry Grove, White River, and
Sparrow Creek of Randolph County; Walnut Ridge of Rush County; Greenfield of Tippecanoe County; Silver Creek-Salem of Union County; Wabash
of Wabash County; Blue River and Blue River (Hicksite) of Washington
County; and West Grove, Milford, Milford (Hicksite), Whitewater, Whitewater (Hicksite), New Garden, Springfield, Dover, and Chester of Wayne
County.

3. The following ten meetings were researched in this manner: Sugar Plain
in Boone County; Oak Ridge in Grant County; Hinkles Creek and Richland
in Hamilton County; Maple Grove (Hicksite) in Huntington County; Camden (Hicksite) in Jay County; Indianapolis in Marion County; Sugar River in
Montgomery County; Carthage in Rush County; and Honey Creek (Hicksite) in Vigo County.

4. See Appendix C for a full discussion of the research methods employed.

CHAPTER 1

1. Rufus M. Jones, *The Faith and Practice of the Quakers* (London: Methuen
& Co., 1927; reprint, Philadelphia: Book and Publications Committee, Phil-
adelphia Yearly Meeting of the Religious Society of Friends, 1958), 25; Harry
Emerson Wildes, *Voice of the Lord: A Biography of George Fox* (Philadelphia:
University of Pennsylvania Press, 1965), 71-75; Thomas Clarkson, *A Portrai-
ture of Quakerism* (Indianapolis: Merrill & Field, 1870), viii; James Bowden,
*The History of the Society of Friends in America*, 2 vols. (London: Charles Gil-
pin, 1850; reprint, New York: Arno Press, 1972), 1:29-30.

2. Rufus M. Jones, *The Quakers in the American Colonies* (New York: Russell & Russell, 1962), 3-4, 54-376 passim.

3. Stephen B. Weeks, *Southern Quakers and Slavery: A Study in Institutional
History* (Baltimore: The Johns Hopkins Press, 1896), 1, 284-85; Bernhard
Knollenberg, *Pioneer Sketches of the Upper Whitewater Valley: Quaker Stronghold
of the West* (Indianapolis: Indiana Historical Society *Publications*, Vol. 15,
No. 1, 1945), 18.

4. Errol T. Elliott, *Quakers on the American Frontier: A History of the West-
ward Migrations, Settlements, and Developments of Friends on the American Conti-
nent* (Richmond, Ind.: Friends United Press, 1969), 60-83. The Whitewater
Monthly Meeting was the first meeting in Indiana to receive Quakers from
North Carolina; the first certificate of removal was granted in 1811. Weeks,
*Southern Quakers*, 265.

5. John D. Barnhart, *Valley of Democracy: The Frontier Versus the Plantation in
the Ohio Valley, 1775-1818* (Bloomington: Indiana University Press, 1953),
164-65.

6. Knollenberg, *Pioneer Sketches*, 53-54. Meanwhile, sufficient numbers of
Friends had settled in Ohio to establish the Ohio Yearly Meeting in 1813.
Elliott, *Quakers on the American Frontier*, 63; Margaret H. Bacon, *The Quiet
Rebels: The Story of the Quakers in America* (New York: Basic Books, 1969),
79. In 1858 at the time of the creation of the western meeting, the Indiana
Yearly Meeting included Friends in southern and western Ohio, Indiana, Illi-
nois, and Iowa. The Iowa Yearly Meeting was established in 1863, and the

Kansas Yearly Meeting was created in 1872. The Friends of southwestern Ohio remained part of the Indiana Yearly Meeting until 1892 when the Wilmington (Ohio) Yearly Meeting was established. Willard Heiss, ed., *Abstracts of the Records of the Society of Friends in Indiana*, 7 vols. (Indianapolis: Indiana Historical Society, 1962-77), 1:x-xii.

7. Weeks, *Southern Quakers*, 1-2, 271-72.

8. Emma Lou Thornbrough, *Indiana in the Civil War Era 1850-1880* (Indianapolis: Indiana Historical Bureau and Indiana Historical Society, 1965), 609-10. See p. 3 for names of counties where Quakers resided. U.S. Department of Interior, *Statistics of the United States in 1860; Compiled from the Original Returns and Being the Final Exhibit of the English Census* (Washington, D.C.: U.S. Government Printing Office, 1866), 382. It is virtually impossible to determine an accurate count of the number of Quakers who lived in Indiana on the eve of the Civil War. See Jacquelyn S. Nelson, "The Military Response of the Society of Friends in Indiana to the Civil War," *Indiana Magazine of History* 81 (June 1985): 128-30 for a more detailed explanation.

9. Thornbrough, *Indiana in the Civil War Era*, 20-24; Louis Thomas Jones, *The Quakers of Iowa* (Iowa City: The State Historical Society of Iowa, 1914), 134.

10. Thornbrough, *Indiana in the Civil War Era*, 24; Jones, *Quakers of Iowa*, 135-36; Heiss, *Abstracts*, 1:xxvii. Quakers initiated the Free Produce Movement as a method to weaken slavery by refusing to buy or use products made by slaves. Union County Friends organized the Western Free Produce Association in 1842, and several local organizations were formed in Indiana. Levi Coffin, the famous abolitionist, was prominent in this movement as he opened a Free Produce Store in Cincinnati. Thornbrough, *Indiana in the Civil War Era*, 20n.

11. Minutes of the Indiana Yearly Meeting of Anti-Slavery Friends held at Newport, Wayne County, Indiana, 1850.

12. Ibid., 1853, 1854. The amount of goods not made by free labor that had been purchased by members from 1851 to 1856 were: 1851, $386.03; 1852, $552.37; 1853, $704.45; 1854, $798.00; 1855, $428.25, not all meetings reported; 1856, $267.00, not all meetings reported.

13. Jones, *Quakers of Iowa*, 144-45.

14. Thornbrough, *Indiana in the Civil War Era*, 15.

15. Ibid., 486.

16. Ibid., 486-517.

17. John William Buys, "Quakers in Indiana in the Nineteenth Century" (Ph.D. diss., University of Florida, 1973), 17-23. Losing one's membership was called disownment.

18. This information can be found in virtually all of the monthly meeting minutes the author reviewed for the years 1861-69.

19. Clarkson, *Portraiture of Quakerism*, 89-95; Minutes of the Indiana Yearly Meeting of Friends held at Richmond, Wayne County, Indiana, 1861-65.

20. Indiana Quakers also split over the teachings of Elias Hicks, an eastern Quaker who stressed that entry into the heavenly kingdom depended upon obedience to the Inner Light only, not the authority of Elders or even the Scriptures. The Hicksite separation created little havoc in Indiana as most of

the yearly meetings there remained Orthodox (beliefs based on scriptural doctrine). For a more detailed account of this and other divisive issues see Caroline N. Jacob, *Builders of the Quaker Road, 1652-1952* (Chicago: H. Regnery Co., 1953); Elliott, *Quakers on the American Frontier;* and Bacon, *Quiet Rebels.*

CHAPTER 2

1. John L. Nickalls, ed., *The Journal of George Fox* (Cambridge, England: University Press, 1952), 65, 399-404.
2. Daniel J. Boorstin, *The Americans: The Colonial Experience* (New York: Random House, 1958), 48. The quotation is the answer to the sixth query on the religious health of the monthly meetings and can be found in all the monthly meeting minutes that the author reviewed for the years 1861-69.
3. Isa. 2:4; Mic. 4:3; Matt. 5:21; Thomas Clarkson, *A Portraiture of Quakerism* (Indianapolis: Merrill & Field, 1870), 345; Matt. 5:38-39, 43-48.
4. James 4:1; Rom. 8:9; Clarkson, *Portraiture of Quakerism,* 345.
5. Peter Brock, *Pacifism in the United States from the Colonial Era to the First World War* (Princeton, N.J.: Princeton University Press, 1968), 713-14; *The Discipline of the Society of Friends, of the Indiana Yearly Meeting* (Richmond, Ind.: E. Morgan & Sons, 1964), 44. The quotation is credited to Saint Martin to Julian the Apostate, Roman Emperor and nephew of Constantine I, circa 300 A.D.
6. Brock, *Pacifism,* 334-35.
7. Ibid., 183-85.
8. For further information on Quakers in the Revolution, see ibid., 183-258 and Arthur J. Mekeel, *The Relation of the Quakers to the American Revolution* (Washington, D.C.: University Press of America, 1979).
9. Epistle of Counsel and Caution from the Meeting for Sufferings of the Indiana Yearly Meeting, quoted in Minutes of the Cherry Grove Monthly Meeting of Men Friends held at Lynn, Randolph County, Indiana, 7th month 13th 1861.
10. Epistle from the Meeting for Sufferings of the Western Yearly Meeting, quoted in Minutes of the Fairfield Monthly Meeting of Men Friends held at Fairfield, Hendricks County, Indiana, 5th month 9th 1861.
11. Copies of the messages were sent to each Orthodox yearly meeting in the United States, quoted in Minutes of the Fairfield Monthly Meeting of Men Friends, 7th month 11th 1861.
12. Minutes of the Indiana Yearly Meeting of Friends, 1860, pp. 14-15; 1862, pp. 14-15; 1863, p. 19; 1864, pp. 9-10; *Minutes of Western Yearly Meeting of Friends Held at Plainfield, Hendricks County, Indiana, 1865,* pp. 15-16.
13. Margaret H. Bacon, *The Quiet Rebels: The Story of the Quakers in America* (New York: Basic Books, 1969), 116; Margaret E. Hirst, *The Quakers in Peace and War: An Account of Their Peace Principles and Practice* (London: Swarthmore Press, 1923), 424.
14. Chester Forrester Dunham, *The Attitude of the Northern Clergy toward the South, 1860-1865* (Toledo, Ohio: Gray Co., 1942), 117; Emma Lou Thornbrough, *Indiana in the Civil War Era 1850-1880* (Indianapolis: Indiana Historical Bureau and Indiana Historical Society, 1965), 627; Stephen B. Weeks, *South-*

*ern Quakers and Slavery: A Study in Institutional History* (Baltimore: The Johns Hopkins Press, 1896), 303; Rufus M. Jones, *The Later Periods of Quakerism*, 2 vols. (London: Macmillan & Co., 1921), 2:729, 737, 738; Elbert Russell, *The History of Quakerism* (New York: Macmillan Co., 1942), 410; Brock, *Pacifism*, 727.

15. Brock, *Pacifism*, 727; Jones, *Later Periods*, 2:729. The author found one historian who noted that many Quakers enrolled for military duty. See Bernhard Knollenberg, *Pioneer Sketches of the Upper Whitewater Valley: Quaker Stronghold of the West* (Indianapolis: Indiana Historical Society *Publications*, Vol. 15, No. 1, 1945), 119. See also Kenneth Alan Radbill, "Socioeconomic Backgrounds of Nonpacifist Quakers during the American Revolution" (Ph.D. diss., University of Arizona, 1971). For works concerning Quakers and pacifism see the following: Edward Needles Wright, *Conscientious Objectors in the Civil War* (New York: A. S. Barnes, 1931); Lillian Schlissel, ed., *Conscience in America: A Documentary History of Conscientious Objection in America, 1757-1967* (New York: E. P. Dutton & Co., 1968); Brock, *Pacifism*; and Peter Brock, "Colonel Washington and the Quaker Conscientious Objectors," *Quaker History* 53 (Spring 1964): 12-26.

16. R. C. Brumfield and Willard Heiss, *Jericho Friend's Meeting and Its Community, Randolph County, Indiana, 1818 to 1958* (Ann Arbor, Mich.: Edwards Brothers, 1958), 53-54; "Brief History of Carthage Friends Meeting" (typed manuscript, 1939, Rushville Public Library, Rushville, Ind.), 12; J. B. Freeman, "History of New Salem Church," taken from a Kokomo newspaper, circa 1932, and microfilmed with the Minutes of the New Salem Monthly Meeting (Indiana Historical Society Library); Ludovic Fields and Clayton Fields, "History of Westfield Monthly Meeting of Friends" (typed manuscript, n.d., Noblesville Public Library, Noblesville, Ind.); Ethyl Clark Horney and George W. Moore, "The Hinkle Creek Friends" (typed manuscript, 1966, Noblesville Public Library).

17. George W. Julian to Stephen Weeks, 18 September 1895, quoted in Weeks, *Southern Quakers*, 306n; Willard Heiss, ed., *Abstracts of the Records of the Society of Friends in Indiana*, 7 vols. (Indianapolis: Indiana Historical Society, 1962-77), 1:xix; Lydia Stanton to Miriam W. Green, 22 January 1865, Miriam W. Green Papers, Indiana Historical Society. The "Springboro" referred to in this letter is probably Springborough in Warren County, Ohio, giving evidence to the fact that many Ohio Quakers had close ties with their counterparts in Indiana. Letter written by William Stubbs Elliott, quoted in James O. Bond, "He Carried Three Packs: A Biography of Elisha Mills" (typed manuscript, n.d., Noblesville Public Library, Noblesville, Ind.), 6. This is obviously an exaggeration but does reflect the belief that there was much war sentiment among young Quaker men.

18. Minutes of the Back Creek Monthly Meeting of Men Friends held at Back Creek, Grant County, Indiana, 9th month 18th 1862; Minutes of the Hopewell Monthly Meeting of Men Friends held at Hopewell, Henry County, Indiana, 8th month 16th 1862.

19. *Discipline of the Society of Friends*, 45.

20. Minutes of the Raysville Monthly Meeting of Men Friends held at Raysville, Henry County, Indiana, 9th month 23rd 1865. Many Quaker writings contain flagrantly misspelled words and are characterized by im-

proper use of grammar and punctuation, or lack thereof. In order to preserve
the exact statements, the author chose neither to correct these errors, nor
place *sic* after each misspelled word. The reader should assume that all quota-
tions have been kept intact.

21. Minutes of the Milford Monthly Meeting of Men Friends held at Milford, Wayne County, Indiana, 6th month 24th 1865. See Appendix A for the
complete statement.

22. Rachel [last name unknown] to Ann [last name unknown], 1 January
1866, Susan Unthank Collection, Indiana Division, Indiana State Library.

23. Joseph Moore to John Hodgkin, 3 June 1862, Joseph Moore Papers,
Lilly Library, Earlham College, Richmond, Indiana. Moore taught geology
and botany at Earlham. The number of Quakers who produced offerings
was reached after a close examination of all monthly meeting minutes
available.

24. Minutes of the Raysville Monthly Meeting of Men Friends, 7th month
28th 1866.

25. See Appendix C. Simple addition totals 1,214. Two men, however,
were disowned and later died in the war. Hence the total is 1,212.

26. W. H. H. Terrell, *Report of the Adjutant General of the State of Indiana*,
8 vols. (Indianapolis: State Printer, 1865-69), *Statistics and Documents* (a separately paginated part of *Report of the Adjutant General*), 1:5. The exact number
is 208,367. The 62 percent was computed by dividing 208,367 by 334,310,
the total number of males aged 15-49 in Indiana as reported by the federal
census of 1860. The 21-27 percent was reached by the following mathemati-
cal computations. According to the Yearly Meeting Minutes of 1857, 1,800
Friends (male and female) from the ages 15 through 19 resided in Indiana.
This age group was chosen because the Quakers kept accurate records of
young people via their yearly Education Report while infrequently reporting
their total population, and this unit coincides with the age categories of the
federal census. The percentage of this group in the entire state of Indiana,
according to the federal census of 1860, is 11.41 percent, computed by dividing 1,350,428, the total population of Indiana, into 154,085, the total number of persons in the 15-19 age bracket in Indiana. Dividing 1,800 by .1141
yields 15,776, the approximate number of Quakers in Indiana circa 1860. For
convenience sake this figure has been rounded up to 16,000. Emma Lou
Thornbrough, author of *Indiana in the Civil War Era*, suggested the Quaker
population to be 15,000 in 1850. Margaret E. Hirst, author of *The Quakers in
Peace and War*, asserted that the number of Friends could be as high as 20,000
by the time of the Civil War. For purposes of this book, and to allow for
error, the resident Quaker population has been determined to lie between
16,000 and 20,000. According to the federal census of 1860, the percentage of
males of the total Indiana population in the 15-19 age bracket was 24.8 percent, computed by dividing 334,310, the total male population 15-49, by
1,350,428. Multiplying 16,000 and 20,000 by 24.8 percent yields, approximately, 4,000 (3,968) to 5,000 (4,960) Quaker males between the ages 15 and
49. The above percentages were computed by dividing 1,093, the number of
Quaker males belonging to the Indiana Yearly Meeting or the Western Yearly
Meeting who enrolled for military duty, by 4,000 and 5,000. The remaining
119 soldiers were Hicksite Quakers for whom the author has no population

figures. An analysis of seventeen Indiana monthly meetings that included membership statistics in their minutes in 1865 reveals that approximately 24 percent of their men aged 15-49 participated in military service during the Civil War. This statistic supports and adds credence to the percentages found for Quakers in the entire state of Indiana. The 6 to 7.5 percent was calculated by dividing 300, the top estimate, by 4,000 and 5,000.

27. Terrell, *Report of the Adjutant General*, 1:40-43; *Statistics and Documents*, 1:187-88. The author examined registration records housed in the Indiana Commission on Public Records, State Archives Division, and determined the number of conscientious objectors in the Quaker counties designated for this survey to be 2,486, excluding Jennings County. This number includes persons who were not Quakers, such as Dunkers, but who also lived in those counties where Quakers lived. The number of Quakers who identified themselves as conscientiously opposed to bearing arms was 2,170 and includes Jennings County. General Order Number 64, *General Orders*, State of Indiana Adjutant General's Office, Indianapolis, 1 August 1862 (unidentified photocopy, Lilly Library, Earlham College). Other counties: (Union), 12 "conscientious," 14 soldiers; (Vermillion), no "conscientious," 3 soldiers; (Vigo), no "conscientious," 2 soldiers; (Washington), 35 "conscientious," 39 soldiers.

28. Terrell, *Report of the Adjutant General, Statistics and Documents*, 1:187-88. Huntington County enrollment records list forty-seven conscientious objectors, and only five Quakers became soldiers.

29. Thomas E. Drake, *Quakers and Slavery in America* (New Haven, Conn.: Yale University Press, 1950), 197. Civil War regiments numbered from the 6th through the 156th, plus twenty-six batteries of Light Artillery. At least twenty Quakers served in out-of-state regiments or the regular army. *Indianapolis Daily Journal*, 23 April 1861; Terrell, *Report of the Adjutant General*, 2:4, 6; 4:8-9; *Statistics and Documents*, 1:6.

30. *Rushville Weekly Republican*, 13 November 1891; Heiss, *Abstracts*, 4:25, 416. Company A had a total of 116 men; Company D, 107. Terrell, *Report of the Adjutant General*, 2:361-62; 3:98-101; *Statistics and Documents*, 1:14. *Howard Tribune* (Kokomo), 14 August 1862. In the above examples of mass enlistment, only those Quakers who could be documented by Heiss' *Abstracts* were included in the total number of 1,212 Quaker soldiers, numbering 49 out of the total of 393 reported by the newspapers. Since the *Abstracts* are far from complete, it is very likely that the remaining 344 men were Quakers, but the author chose not to include nonrecorded Friends. The author also found 276 soldiers buried in Quaker cemeteries but could not document them with Heiss' *Abstracts*. Had the above soldiers plus the 276 buried in Quaker cemeteries been enumerated, the total number of Quaker soldiers would soar to 1,832; the percentages would then increase from the limits of 21-27 percent to 36-45 percent.

31. The information was based upon the war records, determined from Terrell's *Report of the Adjutant General* and the official records kept in the Indiana Commission on Public Records, State Archives Division, of 1,117 out of 1,212 Quakers.

32. This information was based upon reading the monthly meeting minutes for the years 1861-70.

33. Heiss, *Abstracts*, 1:xix; Drake, *Quakers and Slavery*, 197; "Brief History
of Carthage Friends Meeting," 12; Brumfield and Heiss, *Jericho Friend's
Meeting*, 54. The information that fourteen meetings refused to disown
soldiers was based upon reading the monthly meeting minutes for the years
1861-70. Written apologies obviated the need for disciplinary action in some
of these meetings. Not all veterans who belonged to these meetings,
however, produced acknowledgments. Those who did not were not
disowned.

34. Boorstin, *The Americans*, 1:41.

35. John William Buys, "Quakers in Indiana in the Nineteenth Century"
(Ph.D. diss., University of Florida, 1973), 300; Russell, *History of Quakerism*,
408. Russell noted that the Society's relief work during the war forced
Quakers out of isolation.

36. Jones, *Later Periods*, 2:728.

<h3 style="text-align:center">CHAPTER 3</h3>

1. Solomon Meredith to Anna Meredith, 23 May 1863, Solomon Meredith
Papers, Indiana Historical Society.

2. Daniel Wooton to Miriam W. Green, 1 May, 11 July 1861; 31 August
1863, Miriam W. Green Papers, Indiana Historical Society.

3. John E. Morgan to his sister, 25 May, 10 October 1863, John Edward
Morgan Collection, Indiana Historical Society; Swain Marshall to his par-
ents, 8 January, 19 August 1863, Marshall Correspondence, ibid.; Alonzo
Marshall to Elvira Marshall, undated letter that was in the possession of the
late Cecil Charles in 1981; Manoah Ratliff to Sarah Ratliff, 15 August 1862,
Civil War Collections-Ratliff, microfilm, ibid.

4. Minutes of the White Lick Monthly Meeting of Men Friends held at
White Lick, Morgan County, Indiana, 1st month 27th 1866.

5. Minutes of the Milford Monthly Meeting of Men Friends held at Milford, Wayne County, Indiana, 6th month 24th 1865. See Appendix A for the
complete statement.

6. Anna Starr to William Starr, 31 May 1863, William Starr Collection,
Indiana Historical Society. Clinton later found a way to serve his country as a
tax collector for the federal government. See Chapter 5, pp. 67-68.

7. Alonzo Marshall to Elvira Marshall, undated letter that was in the possession of the late Cecil Charles in 1981; Swain Marshall to his parents,
7 September 1864, ibid. Swain's older brother, Clayton, joined the armed
forces, and Alonzo was one of Swain's younger brothers. Orlando Swain
(Bub) had just turned seventeen when Swain wrote the letter; he did not volunteer for military duty after all.

8. Daniel Wooton to Miriam W. Green, 23 September, 17 November 1862,
Miriam W. Green Papers.

9. The percentage was calculated by dividing 61 by 1,117, the total number of known military records of Quakers. See Appendix C for a full discussion of the methods used to determine the military records of Quakers. For
the state of Indiana as a whole, 11,718 men reenlisted for military service.

Dividing this number by 208,367, the total number of troops furnished by Indiana, the percentage computes to be 5.6. W. H. H. Terrell, *Report of the Adjutant General of the State of Indiana*, 8 vols. (Indianapolis: State Printer, 1865-69), *Statistics and Documents* (a separately paginated part of *Report of the Adjutant General*), 1:5.

10. Swain Marshall to his father, 18 February, 27 August 1864, Marshall Correspondence; Swain Marshall to his parents, 27 August 1864, ibid.

11. Daniel Wooton to Miriam W. Green, 31 August 1863, Miriam W. Green Papers.

12. The statistics were based upon the known ages of 1,016 out of 1,212 Quakers in uniform on the date of muster. Eighteen-year-olds also composed the largest group for the state of Indiana as a whole. Terrell, *Report of the Adjutant General, Statistics and Documents*, 1:110.

13. This information was derived from Heiss' birth and death records. Names of the parents of soldiers were checked to determine the familial relationship.

14. Sarah Spray Diary, 23 August 1862, Indiana Historical Society; Dan King to Walter Carpenter, 8 July 1862, letters written by and about Earlham College students, 1861-65, Archives, Lilly Library, Earlham College, Richmond, Indiana; Terrell, *Report of the Adjutant General*, 5:445. See Appendix C for King's military record.

15. Bell Irvin Wiley, *The Life of Billy Yank: The Common Soldier of the Union* (Indianapolis: Bobbs-Merrill Co., 1951), 37-38.

16. Daniel Wooton to Miriam W. Green, 11 July 1861, Miriam W. Green Papers.

17. Minutes of the Spiceland Monthly Meeting of Men Friends held at Spiceland, Henry County, Indiana, 5th month 5th 1866.

18. This figure is the number of military personnel in those positions and, thus, does not include any civilian Friends who may have worked in army hospitals. This information was found primarily in Terrell's *Report of the Adjutant General*. Providing for the possibility of error in his compilation, the twenty Quakers most likely represent the minimum number; an accurate calculation is virtually impossible to determine. In addition, the Society of Friends did not usually send ministers to war. In one case, however, a Quaker entered the service as a combat soldier and was promoted to chaplain. In another instance a Quaker was disowned prior to the outbreak of hostilities but was reinstated as a member of the Friends after the fighting had ceased.

19. Terrell, *Report of the Adjutant General*, 1:166-97, 3:189. Morgan's Raid, if successful, was to relieve the pressure on the flank and rear of the Confederate army in the West under Generals Braxton Bragg and Simon Bolivar Buckner, which was in a perilous position in 1863. Morgan ignored direct orders to operate only in Kentucky and crossed the Ohio River into Indiana. Morgan was finally hemmed in near Salineville, Ohio, and surrendered 26 July 1863. See also Lorine Letcher Butler, *John Morgan and His Men* (Philadelphia: Dorrance & Co., 1960); Cecil Fletcher Holland, *Morgan and His Raiders: A Biography of the Confederate General* (New York: Macmillan Co., 1942); and

Basil Wilson Duke, *History of Morgan's Cavalry* (Cincinnati: Miami Printing and Publishing Co., 1867). See also Appendix C for a complete discussion on how the military regiments of Quakers were determined.

20. Thomas R. Ratliff to Sarah Ratliff, 5 August 1862, Civil War Collections–Ratliff, microfilm; Wiley, *Life of Billy Yank*, 38; Terrell, *Report of the Adjutant General*, 1:50-53. See Chapter 6, pp. 89-94 for a discussion of the draft law of 1864. The former percentage is based on dividing 22 by 1,117, the number of known military records of Quakers. The latter percentage was calculated by dividing 17,903 draftees by 208,367. See Appendix C for a complete discussion of how the military records were determined.

21. Letter written by William Stubbs Elliott, quoted in James O. Bond, "He Carried Three Packs: A Biography of Elisha Mills" (typed manuscript, n.d., Noblesville Public Library, Noblesville, Ind.), 8; ibid., 6; Richard P. Ratcliff, *The Quakers of Spiceland, Henry County, Indiana: A History of Spiceland Friends Meeting 1828-1968* (New Castle, Ind.: Community Printing Co., 1968), 62; Thomas E. Drake, *Quakers and Slavery in America* (New Haven, Conn.: Yale University Press, 1950), 197.

22. Swain Marshall to his parents, 6 March, 22 April 1863, Marshall Correspondence.

23. Swain Marshall to his parents, 6 March 1862, ibid.; R. Gordon to [no name], 15 January 1862, Susan Unthank Collection, Indiana Division, Indiana State Library; Alonzo Marshall to his parents, 22 August 1862, Marshall Correspondence.

24. John E. Morgan to home, 13 March 1864, John Edward Morgan Collection; Joseph H. Plase to his mother, 12 August 1864; 16 March 1865, Susan Unthank Collection.

25. Terrell, *Report of the Adjutant General, Statistics and Documents*, 1:114. The latter percentage was computed by dividing 8,927 deserters by 208,367. See also Appendix C for a discussion of how military records of Quakers were determined.

26. R. Gordon to [no name], 15 January 1862, Susan Unthank Collection; Rachel [last name unknown] to Ann [last name unknown], 1 January 1866, ibid.; Swain Marshall to his parents, 27 August 1864, Marshall Correspondence.

27. Daniel Wooton to Miriam W. Green, 29 December 1861; 17 November 1862; 31 August 1863, Miriam W. Green Papers.

28. Wiley, *Life of Billy Yank*, 37-44.

CHAPTER 4

1. Thomas R. Ratliff to Sarah Ratliff, 15 August 1862, Civil War Collections-Ratliff, microfilm, Indiana Historical Society; Isaac Barker to Josephine Barker, 5 March 1865, Isaac Barker Papers, ibid.; William S. Elliott Diary, 25 March 1864, repeated on 16 April 1864, ibid.; H. Will McCune to Maggie Wright, 7 September 1862, Marshall Correspondence, ibid.

2. Joseph H. Plase to his mother, 17 March 1864, Susan Unthank Collection, Indiana Division, Indiana State Library; Alonzo Marshall to his parents, 22 August, 21 October 1862, Marshall Correspondence; Daniel Wooton to

Miriam W. Green, 2 October 1861, Miriam W. Green Papers, Indiana Historical Society; Swain Marshall to his father, 18 February 1864, Marshall Correspondence.

3. Swain Marshall to his parents, 27 August 1864, Marshall Correspondence; Daniel Wooton to Miriam W. Green, 30 October 1863, Miriam W. Green Papers.

4. R. Gordon to [no name], 15 January 1862, Susan Unthank Collection; Daniel Wooton to Miriam W. Green, 2 October, 10 December 1861, Miriam W. Green Papers; Isaac Barker to Josephine Barker, 29 May 1865, Isaac Barker Papers.

5. Daniel Wooton to Miriam W. Green, 3 June 1863, Miriam W. Green Papers; Swain Marshall to his parents, 2 August 1864, Marshall Correspondence.

6. John Goodnoe to J. T. Unthank, 1 January 1862, Susan Unthank Collection; Martha Talbert White Diary, 24 December 1862, Indiana Historical Society; John E. Morgan to his sister, 25 May 1863, John Edward Morgan Collection, ibid.

7. Swain Marshall to his parents, 6 March 1862, Marshall Correspondence.

8. Daniel Wooton to Miriam W. Green, 22 May 1862; 30 October 1863, Miriam W. Green Papers.

9. Swain Marshall to Rhoda Neal, 8 June 1863, Marshall Correspondence; Swain Marshall to his parents, 7 September, 22 July 1864, ibid.; John E. Morgan to his sister, 28 November 1863, John Edward Morgan Collection.

10. Eli Ratliff to Sarah Ratliff, 11 March 1865, Civil War Collections-Ratliff, microfilm; Swain Marshall to his parents, 29 May 1863; 7 September 1864, Marshall Correspondence; Swain Marshall to Rhoda Neal, 8 June 1863, ibid.

11. John E. Morgan to his sister, 20 September, 25 May 1863, John Edward Morgan Collection.

12. Isaac Barker to Josephine Barker, 14 May 1865, Isaac Barker Papers; Swain Marshall to his parents, 24 July 1865, Marshall Correspondence.

13. Daniel Wooton to Miriam W. Green, 2 October, 10 December, 1861, Miriam W. Green Papers.

14. Manoah Ratliff to Sarah Ratliff, 10 January 1863, Civil War Collections-Ratliff, microfilm; Swain Marshall to his parents, 22 February 1863, Marshall Correspondence; Swain Marshall to his father, 18 February 1864, ibid.

15. John E. Morgan to his sister, 25 May 1863, John Edward Morgan Collection.

16. Isaac Barker to Josephine Barker, 4 June 1865, Isaac Barker Papers; Swain Marshall to his parents, 19 August, 22 April 1863, Marshall Correspondence; William S. Elliott Diary, 6 February 1864.

17. See Jacquelyn S. Nelson, "Civil War Letters of Daniel Wooton: The Metamorphosis of a Quaker Soldier," *Indiana Magazine of History* 85 (March 1989): 50-57.

18. Daniel Wooton to Miriam W. Green, 1 May 1861, Miriam W. Green Papers. John E. Morgan is an illustration of a similar, although more ex-

treme, case. That his decision to fight in the war may have defied the teachings of his parents is revealed in a letter received by the Indiana Historical
Society from Donald S. Morgan, dated 23 November 1969. In part it reads:
"Although John Morgan may have written letters to his parents, it is interesting to note that none of his letters [deposited in the Historical Society Li-
brary] mentions his father or mother, nor enquires for their health. Since he
defied their wishes and the tenets of the Quaker faith, it seems possible that
there was an estrangement accounting for this."

    19. Daniel Wooton to Miriam W. Green, 14 February 1862; 14 March
1863, Miriam W. Green Papers.

    20. Ibid., 31 August 1863.

    21. Bell Irvin Wiley, *The Life of Billy Yank: The Common Soldier of the Union*
(Indianapolis: Bobbs-Merrill Co., 1951), 27-28.

    22. Ibid., 28, 36, 54.

    23. Ibid., 190.

    24. Ibid., 79.

    25. Ibid., 83.

    26. Ibid., 247.

    27. Ibid., 247, 248.

    28. Ibid., 235-36.

## CHAPTER 5

    1. Margaret E. Hirst, *The Quakers in Peace and War: An Account of Their
Peace Principles and Practice* (London: Swarthmore Press, 1923), 427; Samuel T.
Pickard, *Life and Letters of John Greenleaf Whittier*, 2 vols. (Cambridge, Mass.:
Riverside Press, 1894), 2:441.

    2. U.S. Department of War, *The War of the Rebellion: A Compilation of the
Official Records of the Union and Confederate Armies* (Washington, D.C.: U.S.
Government Printing Office, 1900), series 3, 4:1269-70. The number of enlistments was 2,778,304; W. H. H. Terrell, *Report of the Adjutant General of the
State of Indiana*, 8 vols. (Indianapolis: State Printer, 1865-69), 1:431-36; *Statistics and Documents* (a separately paginated part of *Report of the Adjutant General*), 1:314-18; Emma Lou Thornbrough, *Indiana in the Civil War Era
1850-1880* (Indianapolis: Indiana Historical Bureau and Indiana Historical
Society, 1965), 164-66.

    3. Terrell, *Report of the Adjutant General*, 1:6; Coffin Family Papers, assem-
bled by Percival Brooks Coffin, 1917, Lilly Library, Earlham College, Richmond, Indiana. This story was told by Colonel Oran Perry, soldier from
Wayne County, and published in the *Indianapolis News* in 1890.

    4. *Randolph County Journal*, 25 April 1861. Later in the war newspapers
would list contributors along with either amounts of money or types of articles given. In response to Governor Oliver P. Morton's appeal in April 1861,
the *Randolph County Journal* was the only newspaper that the author read that
listed donors. Nevertheless, it seems reasonable to conclude that Quakers in
other counties also contributed supplies.

    5. Thornbrough, *Indiana in the Civil War Era*, 167.

    6. Terrell, *Report of the Adjutant General*, 1:315-19. For a complete discus-
sion of the problems and solutions to equipping Indiana's troops see Robert

W. Ceder, "The Raising and Equipping of Armies in Indiana 1860-1865" (Ed.D. diss., Ball State University, 1968).

7. Terrell, *Report of the Adjutant General*, 1:315, 324. The United States Sanitary Commission, begun by private initiative, was a civilian auxiliary to the War Department's medical bureau. Commonly regarded as the forerunner of the Red Cross, this mammoth organization tended to the needs of sick and wounded soldiers, both Union and Confederate. Two of the women who performed distinguished service in caring for wounded men were Clara Barton and Dorothea Dix. J. G. Randall and David Donald, *The Civil War and Reconstruction*, 2d ed. (Boston: D. C. Heath & Co., 1961), 488-89; Thornbrough, *Indiana in the Civil War Era*, 170-71.

8. Terrell, *Report of the Adjutant General*, 1:327. Out of this amount Indiana citizens gave $16,049.50 to the United States Sanitary Commission.

9. The only possible exception to unorganized benevolence that the author uncovered was recorded in the *Richmond Palladium* of 1 June 1864. Dr. William Hannaman, president of the Indiana Sanitary Commission, reported that $165 was contributed by Friends from the White Lick Quarterly Meeting, Morgan County. The information on voluntary contributors was found in newspapers published in Wayne, Rush, Henry, Howard, and Parke counties. The names of the contributors were cross-checked with Heiss' *Abstracts* and the Militia Enrollment of 1862 to identify those who were Quakers. A complete list of newspapers can be found in the bibliography. It proved impossible to survey every county in which Quakers lived at the time of the Civil War. Efforts to do so were hampered by an absence of Quaker birth and death records in a specific county or counties, a lack of newspapers from which to find the contributors, or too few Quakers in an area to justify reading the newspapers that were available. Thus, based upon the data found in the counties surveyed, the author believes that it is reasonable to conclude that Quakers in the remaining counties also contributed to the Indiana Sanitary Commission. In a letter from Cecil Charles, a Quaker who lived in Richmond, to the author dated 6 April 1982, he wrote that many Quakers contributed to the Indiana Sanitary Commission. In 1863, for example, this organization provided a steamboat to be loaded at Lawrenceburg and Madison with supplies for the soldiers after the surrender of Vicksburg. Among the items were barrels of apples, salt pork, flour, and even four barrels of whiskey (for medicinal use). Writing in regard to his Quaker ancestors who lived in Randolph County at the time of the war, he wrote, "I cannot believe that Thomas Marshall [whose three sons were in the war], John Hunnicutt and many other Quakers failed to contribute."

10. *Richmond Jeffersonian*, 29 May 1862; *Richmond Palladium*, 12 April, 22 February 1862; 6 October 1864; *Howard Tribune*, 12 November 1861; *Parke County Republican*, 7 September 1864.

11. *New Castle Courier*, 25 February 1864; *Indianapolis Daily Journal*, 15 March 1862.

12. Isaac Barker to Josephine Barker, 14 March 1865, Isaac Barker Papers, Indiana Historical Society; John E. Morgan to his sister Abbie, 17 December 1862, John Edward Morgan Collection, ibid.; Alonzo Marshall to his parents, 20, 21 October 1862; 8 April 1863, Marshall Correspondence, ibid.; Swain Marshall to his parents, 22 April 1863, ibid.

13. Alonzo Marshall to Elvira Marshall, 24 May 1864, Marshall Correspondence.

14. Swain Marshall to his parents, undated letter that was in the possession of the late Cecil Charles in 1981; Cecil Charles to Jacquelyn Nelson, 6 April 1982, in the possession of the author.

15. Minutes of the Back Creek Monthly Meeting of Men Friends held at Back Creek, Grant County, Indiana, 6th month 15th 1865; Minutes of the Oak Ridge Monthly Meeting of Men Friends held at Oak Ridge, Grant County, Indiana, 9th month 12th 1865; Cecil Charles to Jacquelyn Nelson, 6 April 1982. Horseshoe Bend is in Randolph County, just north of the small town of Economy. "Uncle John" was Mr. Charles's great-uncle John Hunnicutt.

16. Minutes of the Back Creek Monthly Meeting of Men Friends, 9th month 14th 1865; 2nd month 15th 1866; Minutes of the Mississinewa Monthly Meeting of Men Friends held at Mississinewa, Grant County, Indiana, 3rd month 18th 1863; Minutes of the Oak Ridge Monthly Meeting of Men Friends, 9th month 12th 1865.

17. Terrell, *Report of the Adjutant General*, 1:65-68, 355; Randall and Donald, *The Civil War*, 328.

18. Minutes of the Back Creek Monthly Meeting of Men Friends, 7th month 13th and 9th month 14th 1865; Minutes of the Oak Ridge Monthly Meeting of Men Friends, 9th month 12th 1865; Minutes of the Poplar Ridge Monthly Meeting of Men Friends held at Poplar Ridge, Hamilton County, Indiana, 8th month 27th 1866; Minutes of the Springfield Monthly Meeting of Men Friends held at Springfield, Wayne County, Indiana, 2nd month 15th 1868; Minutes of the Dover Monthly Meeting of Men Friends held at Dover, Wayne County, Indiana, 4th month 25th, 1st month 24th, 5th month 23rd 1866; *New Castle Courier*, 2 March 1865. These two men gave sums of $25 and $50; they also had signed the Militia Enrollment of 1862 as "conscientiously opposed to bearing arms." The author also found the names of two other Henry County Quakers who served as enrolling officers but were not disciplined by their meetings. Just as a sizable number of Friends escaped disciplinary action for participating in military service, the author suspects that many more Friends participated in these and similar wartime activities than were recorded in the church records.

19. *Richmond Jeffersonian*, 28 August, 4 September 1862. The *Broad Axe of Freedom* editorial was, in part, quoted in the *Richmond Jeffersonian*, 4 September 1862.

20. Anna Starr to William Starr, 31 May 1863, William Starr Collection, Indiana Historical Society. Anna Starr refers to this Friend as "brother Clinton." The author is unsure if Clinton was Anna's or William's brother, for no last name was given.

21. *Richmond Palladium*, 14 November 1862; Coffin Family Papers, Lilly Library, Earlham College.

22. Circular from the Central Book and Tract Committee of the Indiana Yearly Meeting of Friends quoted in Minutes of the Spiceland Monthly Meeting of Men Friends held at Spiceland, Henry County, Indiana, 5th month 20th 1863; *Indianapolis Daily Journal*, 26 April 1861; First Quarterly

Report of the Chaplain of the Thirty-sixth Regiment, 10 January 1862, quoted in the *Richmond Jeffersonian*, 6 February 1862.

23. Minutes of the Milford Monthly Meeting of Men Friends held at Milford, Wayne County, Indiana, 1st month 28th 1865; Minutes of the Plainfield Monthly Meeting of Men Friends held at Plainfield, Hendricks County, Indiana, 6th month 29th 1864; Minutes of the Bridgeport Monthly Meeting of Men Friends held at Bridgeport, Marion County, Indiana, 7th month 30th 1863. In addition to the meetings cited above, the Book and Tract Committees of the following monthly meetings reported contributions of religious literature for the soldiers: New Garden, Dover, Whitewater, West Grove, and Springfield in Wayne County and Hopewell in Henry County. Although the committees of the remaining monthly meetings did not specifically state that they had performed similar service, it seems likely that they also participated in this activity.

24. Minutes of the Fairfield Monthly Meeting of Men Friends held at Fairfield, Hendricks County, Indiana, 1st month 8th 1863; Minutes of the White Lick Monthly Meeting of Men Friends held at White Lick, Morgan County, Indiana, 5th month 7th 1862.

25. Minutes of the Central Book and Tract Committee of the Indiana Yearly Meeting, 9th month 30th 1863. The United States Christian Commission, another wartime humanitarian agency, was a project of the Young Men's Christian Association and supplemented the work of the United States Sanitary Commission. It provided religious inspiration, sent soldiers' money home to their families, and offered various types of diversions to relieve camp boredom as well as distributing Bibles and other reading material. Randall and Donald, *The Civil War*, 489; Minutes of the Central Book and Tract Committee of the Indiana Yearly Meeting, 10th month 27th 1862.

26. Minutes of the Indiana Yearly Meeting of Friends, 1862, p. 55; Minutes of the Central Book and Tract Committee of the Indiana Yearly Meeting, 4th month 28th 1862; 6th month 15th 1863; 5th month 1st 1863; C[aroline] Hare, comp., *Life and Letters of Elizabeth L. Comstock* (Philadelphia: J. C. Winston, 1895).

27. Minutes of the Raysville Monthly Meeting of Men Friends held at Raysville, Henry County, Indiana, 2nd month 25th 1865 and 10th month 28th 1865; Minutes of the Spiceland Monthly Meeting of Women Friends held at Spiceland, Henry County, Indiana, 11th month 20th 1864; Minutes of the Milford Monthly Meeting of Men Friends, 9th month 26th 1863 to 7th month 22nd 1865; Minutes of the Bloomfield Monthly Meeting of Men Friends held at Bloomfield, Parke County, Indiana, 8th month 13th 1862.

28. Hirst, *Quakers in Peace and War*, 427; Geneva V. Noland, "Memories of Quaker Meeting," *Quaker Life* 9 (October 1982): 26. The records of the monthly meetings and those of the Indiana and the Western Yearly Meetings included no Quaker service of this type. The author inquired at the Indiana Commission on Public Records, State Archives Division, about names of volunteers who worked in hospitals. While the Archives had lists of names of patients in the army hospitals, those records did not include names of persons who performed voluntary services such as nursing. Rebecca A.

Shepherd et al., comps. and eds., *A Biographical Directory of the Indiana
General Assembly*, 2 vols. (Indianapolis: Indiana Historical Bureau, 1980–84),
1:324.

29. Terrell, *Report of the Adjutant General*, 1:356; *Howard Tribune*, 15 October
1861. Most of this information was found in Wayne County newspapers.
The *Indiana True Republican* and the *Richmond Palladium* donated space in their
newspapers to list contributors. The names of donors were then cross-
checked against Heiss' *Abstracts* to identify those who were members of the
Society of Friends. Unfortunately, not all publications that the author
reviewed were as thorough as the two Wayne County publications. In many
instances newspapers did not list contributors but merely mentioned that
money and goods had been donated. Since many Quakers have previously
been shown to have given to the Indiana Sanitary Commission, it seems only
logical to conclude, in the absence of lists of contributors in many of the
counties, that Quakers also aided the families of soldiers. After all, many of
these families were Quaker, too. *Indianapolis Daily Journal*, 2 July 1862.

30. Minutes of the Honey Creek Monthly Meeting of Women Friends held
at Honey Creek, Howard County, Indiana, 4th month 13th 1861; *Randolph
County Journal*, 16 May 1861; Minutes of the Walnut Ridge Monthly Meeting
of Men Friends held at Walnut Ridge, Rush County, Indiana, 1st month 21st
1865; Minutes of the West Union Monthly Meeting of Men Friends held in
Morgan County, Indiana, 5th month 18th 1865; Minutes of the Whitewater
Monthly Meeting of Men Friends held at Richmond, Wayne County,
Indiana, 4th month 2nd and 26th 1865.

31. This information can be found in all of the monthly meeting minutes
that the author reviewed for the years 1861-69. For a more complete
discussion of Quaker activities on behalf of the blacks see John William
Buys, "Quakers in Indiana in the Nineteenth Century" (Ph.D. diss.,
University of Florida, 1973); Minutes of the Wabash Monthly Meeting of
Men Friends held at Wabash, Wabash County, Indiana, 12th month 10th
1864; Minutes of the White River Monthly Meeting of Men Friends held at
White River, Randolph County, Indiana, 10th month 13th 1864.

32. Minutes of the Cherry Grove Monthly Meeting of Men Friends held at
Lynn, Randolph County, Indiana, 6th month 13th and 9th month 12th 1863;
Minutes of the Rush Creek Monthly Meeting of Men Friends held at Rush
Creek, Parke County, Indiana, 9th month 10th 1864; Minutes of the
Mississinewa Monthly Meeting of Men Friends, 4th month 13th 1864;
*Richmond Jeffersonian*, 24 March 1864; Levi Coffin, *Reminiscences of Levi Coffin*
(Cincinnati: Western Tract Society, 1876; reprint, New York: Arno Press and
New York Times, 1968), 620; Cyrus Green to Miriam W. Green, 20
November 1864, Miriam W. Green Papers, Indiana Historical Society.

33. Minutes of the Bridgeport Monthly Meeting of Men Friends, 12th
month 31st 1863; Minutes of the New Garden Monthly Meeting of Men
Friends held at New Garden, Wayne County, Indiana, 12th month 19th 1863;
*Parke County Republican*, 25 November 1863; *Broad Axe of Freedom*, 9 January
1864.

34. Coffin, *Reminiscences*, 625-26. Another similar organization was
formed with Cincinnati as its distribution point; it was called the

Contrabands Relief Commission. *New Castle Courier*, 2 April 1863. One Quaker, Daniel Hill, worked as an agent in both the Friends Freedmen's Aid Society and Western Freedmen's Aid Society in 1864. He hailed from Randolph County. Shepherd et al., *A Biographical Directory*, 1:184.

35. Coffin, *Reminiscences*, 626-46.

36. Ibid., 647-48. The Freedmen's Bill, passed in March 1865, created the Freedmen's Bureau, which provided food, shelter, and jobs for needy blacks. For a complete firsthand account of Coffin's activities on behalf of the freedmen see chapter nineteen of his *Reminiscences*, "Work Among Freedmen."

37. Byron Jones of the Whitewater Monthly Meeting lost his Quaker membership for administering oaths. Minutes of the Whitewater Monthly Meeting of Men Friends, 3rd month 25th 1863.

CHAPTER 6

1. W. H. H. Terrell, *Report of the Adjutant General of the State of Indiana*, 8 vols. (Indianapolis: State Printer, 1865-69), 1:41-42; George P. Sanger, ed., *The Statutes at Large, Treaties, and Proclamations of the United States of America* (Boston: Little, Brown & Co., 1863; reprint, Buffalo, N.Y.: Dennis & Co., 1961-64), 12:597-600 (hereafter cited as *U.S. Statutes at Large*).

2. U.S. Department of War, *The War of the Rebellion: A Compilation of the Official Records of the Union and Confederate Armies* (Washington, D.C.: U.S. Government Printing Office, 1900), series 3, 2:291-92. President Lincoln had previously called for 300,000 troops on 7 July 1862. Indiana's quota under that call was 21,250. The total number of soldiers required from the state of Indiana came to 42,500. "Message of the Governor of Indiana, to the General Assembly," 9 January 1863, Document No. 1, quoted in *Documents of the General Assembly of Indiana, at the Forty-second Regular Session* (Indianapolis: Joseph J. Bingham, State Printer, 1863), 1:4. Of the remaining drafted men, 1,441 volunteered in old three-year regiments or companies for twelve months' service, 396 were discharged for disability and other causes, and 424 failed to report and were classified as deserters. Terrell, *Report of the Adjutant General*, 1:44. The name of the Quaker draftee was John Butler from Grant County. See Appendix C for his military record. Enrollment records show that he did not sign the militia registration of 1862 as "conscientiously opposed to bearing arms."

3. *U.S. Statutes at Large*, 12:597-600. Although the term "conscientious objector" was not in use during the Civil War, the concept certainly was. For a discussion of the origin of this phrase see Edward Needles Wright, *Conscientious Objectors in the Civil War* (New York: A. S. Barnes, 1931), 1-2. Throughout the remaining pages, this expression will be used to refer to those persons who belonged to a religious denomination that opposed all wars. According to J. G. Randall and David Donald, *The Civil War and Reconstruction*, 2d ed. (Boston: D. C. Heath & Co., 1961), 318n., other sects besides the Society of Friends whose abhorrence to war was a recognized belief included Mennonites, Dunkers, Shakers, Schwenkfelders, Christadelphians, Rogerenes, and those of the Amana following. In Indiana, in the

counties designated for this study, the only group besides Friends who signed the enrollment of 1862 as "conscientiously opposed to bearing arms" were Dunkers.

The secretary of war directed in September 1862 that every minister who had pastoral charge of a church or congregation was exempt from military service by draft. General Order No. 5, State of Indiana, General Commissioner's Office, quoted in the *Indianapolis Daily Journal*, 5 September 1862. The militia enrollment for the counties in which Quakers resided shows that 2,486 male members of the Society of Friends designated themselves as opposed to war.

4. Indiana Constitution (1851), Article XII, Section 6; *Official Records*, series 3, 2:587-90; "Conscientious Exempts," General Commissioner's Office, Indianapolis, Indiana, 10 October 1862 (unidentified photocopy, Lilly Library, Earlham College, Richmond, Indiana). In each township the names of the conscientious objectors were placed in a separate ballot box from the rest of the militia; 40 percent of their names were then drawn. Of the 3,169 men of this class in the state of Indiana, approximately 1,250 were assessed the exemption fee. Terrell, *Report of the Adjutant General*, 1:44; General Order No. 3, State of Indiana, General Commissioner's Office, quoted in the *Indiana True Republican*, 2 October 1862.

5. *New Castle Courier*, 16 October 1862.

6. *Richmond Jeffersonian*, 9 October 1862.

7. *Indianapolis Daily Journal*, 30 October 1862; *Indiana True Republican*, 30 October 1862.

8. *Richmond Jeffersonian*, 9 October 1862. There is some evidence, however sparse, that a few of the Quaker soldiers disagreed with the views of the conscientious men on the draft of those opposed to fighting. The *New Castle Courier* of 16 October 1862 reported that a Quaker soldier had written to the newspaper on the subject of the operation of the draft on members of the Society of Friends. The letter, however, was not published. The editor wrote: "We think our young friend is rather too severe on those Friends who have claimed an exemption on the ground of conscience, and that no good would be accomplished by the publication of his article."

9. Charles F. Coffin to Governor Oliver P. Morton, n.d., Coffin Family Papers, assembled by Percival Brooks Coffin, 1917, Lilly Library, Earlham College.

10. *Indianapolis Daily Journal*, 21 October 1862.

11. Ibid.

12. Ibid., 25 October 1862. In the light of current research findings, hindsight confers to the historian the luxury of seeing the absurdity of this argument which, at the time it was written, could have been the prevailing view among the general non-Quaker population.

13. "Message of the Governor of Indiana," 9 January 1863, pp. 4-5; Terrell, *Report of the Adjutant General*, 1:44-45; *Wabash Plain Dealer*, 12 December 1862; *Indiana True Republican*, 27 November 1862; *Indianapolis Daily Journal*, 10 January 1863; Charles F. Coffin to Governor Morton, 17 October 1862, Coffin Family Papers; Charles F. Coffin to J. P. Siddall, 17 October 1862, ibid.

14. "Message of the Governor of Indiana," 9 January 1863, p. 5; Terrell, *Report of the Adjutant General*, 1:45. Terrell reported the amount in excess of $20,000. At least one group of non-Quaker citizens in Indiana, however, did not approve of Friends' efforts to have the exemption fee rescinded. Several conscientious Friends in Wayne County received threats and suffered harassment from persons who opposed their antiwar and antidraft stance. Quakers reported that people were trespassing on their property, shooting rifles, annoying their families, and destroying their property. Twenty-one Friends placed a notice in the *Richmond Jeffersonian* that a "stop shall be put to this kind of business, and we now give fair notice, and warning to that effect." Does this statement suggest that pacifist Quakers might have used violence to protect their families and property? *Richmond Jeffersonian*, 6, 13 November 1862. Although cases of private harassment of Quakers for their antiwar testimony may have occurred in other Quaker communities, the reading of newspapers, letters, diaries, and other sources failed to uncover any empirical evidence to support such a statement.

15. For a complete discussion of the passage of this law see Wright, *Conscientious Objectors*, 58-64 and *U.S. Statutes at Large*, 12:731, 733.

16. Minutes of the Meeting for Sufferings of Western Yearly Meeting, 7th month 21st 1863, quoted in Daisy Newman, *A Procession of Friends: Quakers in America* (Garden City, N.Y.: Doubleday, 1972), 113; Rufus M. Jones, *The Later Periods of Quakerism*, 2 vols. (London: Macmillan & Co., 1921), 2:730. The Western Yearly Meeting also joined the New England Yearly Meeting in appointing committees to appear before federal authorities to plead the Friends' case. Communication from the Meeting for the Sufferings of the Western Yearly Meeting, quoted in Minutes of the Plainfield Monthly Meeting of Men Friends held at Plainfield, Hendricks County, Indiana, 7th month 29th 1863; Wright, *Conscientious Objectors*, 65, 70.

17. Wright, *Conscientious Objectors*, 65-69.

18. Ibid., 71; *Official Records*, series 3, 3:606.

19. One historian said that Abraham Lincoln also had Quaker ancestry. Lincoln and Edwin Stanton were called the "Quaker War Cabinet." Margaret E. Hirst, *The Quakers in Peace and War: An Account of Their Peace Principles and Practice* (London: Swarthmore Press, 1923), 428; Margaret H. Bacon, *The Quiet Rebels: The Story of the Quakers in America* (New York: Basic Books, 1969), 116; Minutes of the Meeting for Sufferings of the Baltimore Yearly Meeting, 11th month 21st 1863, quoted in Minutes of the Blue River Monthly Meeting of Men Friends held at Blue River, Washington County, Indiana, 1st month 9th 1864; Minutes of the Baltimore Conference, 12th month 8th 1863, quoted in Minutes of the Blue River Monthly Meeting of Men Friends, 1st month 9th 1864; *Official Records*, series 3, 3:1173; Wright, *Conscientious Objectors*, 75.

20. Terrell, *Report of the Adjutant General*, 1:47-48. Friends in other states were not as fortunate as those in Indiana. According to Randall and Donald, *The Civil War*, 319, a "goodly number [of Quakers in other states] did military service under protest."

21. *U.S. Statutes at Large*, 13:9. For a full discussion of the passage of this law see Wright, *Conscientious Objectors*, 79-83. Commutation was discontin-

ued for all draftees except those who expressed conscientious scruples against war. Substitution, however, was retained for all draftees. Quakers who rejected the above options could still avoid military service in this manner. Randall and Donald, *The Civil War*, 314n.

22. *The Friend* (Philadelphia), 37, no. 27, p. 215, quoted in Wright, *Conscientious Objectors*, 84.

23. Minutes of the Meeting for Sufferings of the Indiana Yearly Meeting, 9th month 27th 1864, quoted in Wright, *Conscientious Objectors*, 84; Minutes of Advice from the Western Yearly Meeting, quoted in Minutes of the Plainfield Monthly Meeting of Men Friends, 9th month 28th 1864. The Ohio and the New York Yearly meetings made similar provisions for their members. Wright, *Conscientious Objectors*, 84.

24. Meetings are Spiceland in Henry County; New Salem in Howard County; Fairfield, Mill Creek, and Plainfield in Hendricks County; Bridgeport in Marion County; Springfield and West Grove in Wayne County; Rush Creek, Bloomfield, and Rocky Run in Parke County; and White Lick in Morgan County. More than eighty-seven Quakers were actually drafted. Meetings at Spiceland, New Salem, Springfield, West Grove, and White Lick, although noting that men were drafted, failed to record the number. Minutes of the Bridgeport Monthly Meeting of Men Friends, 11th month 3rd and 12th month 1st 1864; Minutes of the Rush Creek Monthly Meeting of Men Friends, 12th month 10th 1864 and 2nd month 11th 1865; Minutes of the Plainfield Monthly Meeting of Men Friends, 1st month 4th 1865. The remaining uncollected money was to be paid by Friends whom the meeting classified as "doubtful."

25. The meetings were Fall Creek (Hicksite) in Madison County; Milford in Wayne County; Poplar Ridge in Hamilton County; Oak Ridge, Back Creek, and Mississinewa in Grant County; Walnut Ridge in Rush County; and Plainfield in Hendricks County. The Quaker from Plainfield who supplied a substitute also produced an offering for serving in the army. The revelation that a large number of Quakers were not disciplined for military service was previously discussed in chapter 1. It seems possible, therefore, that more Quakers may have hired substitutes than were reported to the meetings. Names of men who hired substitutes are on file in the Indiana Commission on Public Records, State Archives Division. No information is given, however, about the residences of these men. This lack of information rendered it virtually impossible to identify those who were members of the Society of Friends. As reported in chapter 2, there also were six Quakers who were hired as substitutes. Five of these men enrolled in 1864 (one enrolled in 1862) prior to the actual draft of December of the same year; two produced acknowledgments for military service and one died in the war. The author was unable to determine, however, whether or not these men were hired by Quakers or non-Quakers. Minutes of the Back Creek Monthly Meeting of Men Friends, 12th month 14th 1865; Minutes of the Springfield Monthly Meeting of Men Friends, 2nd month 15th 1868. These drafted Quakers were from Back Creek and Mississinewa meetings in Grant County; New Garden, Springfield, and West Grove meetings in Wayne County; Wabash Meeting in Wabash County; Blue River and Blue River

(Hicksite) meetings in Washington County; Duck Creek Meeting in Henry County; Walnut Ridge Meeting in Rush County; Mill Creek Meeting in Hendricks County; and Driftwood Meeting in Jackson County.

26. Cyrus Pringle, *The Record of a Quaker Conscience: Cyrus Pringle's Diary* (New York: Macmillan Co., 1918), 64-77; Wright, *Conscientious Objectors,* 165; Lillian Schlissel, ed., *Conscience in America: A Documentary History of Conscientious Objection in America, 1757-1967* (New York: E. P. Dutton & Co., 1968), 102-11; Charles M. Woodman, *Quakers Find a Way: Their Discoveries in Practical Living* (Indianapolis: Bobbs-Merrill Co., 1950), 245; Bacon, *Quiet Rebels,* 117; Newman, *A Procession of Friends,* 113.

27. Wright, *Conscientious Objectors,* 126, 135; Peter Brock, *Pacifism in the United States from the Colonial Era to the First World War* (Princeton, N.J.: Princeton University Press, 1968), 743-44.

28. Minutes of the Raysville Monthly Meeting of Men Friends held at Raysville, Henry County, Indiana, 4th month 28th 1866. The author suspects that Bell received his military punishment, however, at the hands of the Confederate military authorities. On 24 March 1866, the Back Creek Monthly Meeting of Randolph County, North Carolina, requested that Raysville counsel Bell for the above offense. Wright's book, which covers both Union and Confederate states, does not include any references to Quaker monthly meeting minutes of Indiana. He noted records of Meetings for Sufferings of both the yearly meetings in Indiana (as well as other states), however. Brock, *Pacifism,* 764; Minutes of the Meeting for Sufferings of Indiana Yearly Meeting, 10th month 1st 1864, quoted in Wright, *Conscientious Objectors,* 186-87. Many of these Quakers actually lived in Ohio but belonged to quarterly meetings that formed part of the Indiana Yearly Meeting. It is impossible to determine, therefore, how many of these persons actually suffered at the hands of Indiana authorities.

29. Wright, *Conscientious Objectors,* 187; Minutes of the Whitewater Monthly Meeting of Men Friends held at Richmond, Wayne County, Indiana, 8th month 23rd 1865; Minutes of the Cherry Grove Monthly Meeting of Men Friends held at Lynn, Randolph County, Indiana, 7th month 8th and 8th month 12th 1865. The minutes do not say why or for what purpose the money was taken.

30. Brock, *Pacifism,* 743.

## CONCLUSION

1. Henry Steele Commager, ed., *The Blue and the Gray,* 2 vols. (Indianapolis: Bobbs-Merrill Co., 1950), 1:xv.

## APPENDIX A

1. Minutes of the Milford Monthly Meeting of Men Friends held at Milford, Wayne County, Indiana, 6th month 24th 1865.

## APPENDIX C

1. These cards also include the soldiers' height and hair and eye color.

# Selected Bibliography

## Manuscripts

Barker, Isaac. Papers. Indiana Historical Society. Indianapolis, Indiana.

Civil War Collections. Indiana Historical Society. Indianapolis, Indiana.

Coffin Family Papers. Earlham College. Richmond, Indiana.

Earlham College Students, Letters Written by and about, 1861-65. Earlham College. Richmond, Indiana.

Elliott, William S. Diary. Indiana Historical Society. Indianapolis, Indiana.

Green, Miriam W. Papers. Indiana Historical Society. Indianapolis, Indiana.

Marshall Correspondence. Indiana Historical Society. Indianapolis, Indiana.

Meredith, Solomon. Papers. Indiana Historical Society. Indianapolis, Indiana.

Moore, Joseph. Papers. Earlham College. Richmond, Indiana.

Spray, Sarah. Diary. Indiana Historical Society. Indianapolis, Indiana.

Starr, William. Collection. Indiana Historical Society. Indianapolis, Indiana.

Unthank, Susan. Collection. Indiana State Library. Indianapolis, Indiana.
White, Martha Talbert. Diary. Indiana Historical Society. Indianapolis, Indiana.


## Minutes of Societies

*Yearly Meetings*

Minutes of the Central Book and Tract Committee of the
Indiana Yearly Meeting, 1861-65.
Minutes of the Indiana Yearly Meeting of Anti-Slavery
Friends. Newport, Indiana. 1850-57.
Minutes of the Indiana Yearly Meeting of Friends. Richmond,
Indiana. 1860-65.
Minutes of the Western Yearly Meeting of Friends. Plainfield,
Indiana. 1861-65.


*Monthly Meetings*

Back Creek Monthly Meeting of the Society of Friends. Grant
County, Indiana. 1861-69.
Beech Grove Monthly Meeting of the Society of Friends.
Marion County, Indiana. 1863-69.
Bloomfield Monthly Meeting of the Society of Friends. Parke
County, Indiana. 1861-69.
Blue River Monthly Meeting of the Society of Friends. Wash-
ington County, Indiana. 1861-69.
Blue River (Hicksite) Monthly Meeting of the Society of
Friends. Washington County, Indiana. 1861-69.
Bridgeport Monthly Meeting of the Society of Friends. Mar-
ion County, Indiana. 1861-69.
Cherry Grove Monthly Meeting of the Society of Friends.
Randolph County, Indiana. 1861-69.

Chester Monthly Meeting of the Society of Friends. Wayne County, Indiana. 1861–69.

Dover Monthly Meeting of the Society of Friends. Wayne County, Indiana. 1861–69.

Driftwood–Sand Creek Monthly Meeting of the Society of Friends. Bartholomew and Jackson Counties, Indiana. 1861–69.

Duck Creek Monthly Meeting of the Society of Friends. Henry County, Indiana. 1861–69.

Fairfield Monthly Meeting of the Society of Friends. Hendricks County, Indiana. 1861–69.

Fall Creek (Hicksite) Monthly Meeting of the Society of Friends. Madison County, Indiana. 1861–69.

Greenfield Monthly Meeting of the Society of Friends. Tippecanoe County, Indiana. 1861–69.

Greenwood Monthly Meeting of the Society of Friends. Hamilton County, Indiana. 1861–69.

Honey Creek Monthly Meeting of the Society of Friends. Howard County, Indiana. 1861–69.

Hopewell Monthly Meeting of the Society of Friends. Henry County, Indiana. 1861–69.

Lick Creek Monthly Meeting of the Society of Friends. Orange County, Indiana. 1861–69.

Milford Monthly Meeting of the Society of Friends. Wayne County, Indiana. 1861–69.

Milford (Hicksite) Monthly Meeting of the Society of Friends. Wayne County, Indiana. 1861–69.

Mill Creek Monthly Meeting of the Society of Friends. Hendricks County, Indiana. 1861–69.

Mississinewa Monthly Meeting of the Society of Friends. Grant County, Indiana. 1861–69.

New Garden Monthly Meeting of the Society of Friends. Wayne County, Indiana. 1861–69.

New Salem Monthly Meeting of the Society of Friends. Howard County, Indiana. 1861–69.

Pipe Creek Monthly Meeting of the Society of Friends. Miami County, Indiana. 1861-69.

Plainfield Monthly Meeting of the Society of Friends. Hendricks County, Indiana. 1861-69.

Pleasant Hill Monthly Meeting of the Society of Friends. Howard County, Indiana. 1861-69.

Poplar Ridge Monthly Meeting of the Society of Friends. Hamilton County, Indiana. 1866-69.

Raysville Monthly Meeting of the Society of Friends. Henry County, Indiana. 1861-69.

Rocky Run Monthly Meeting of the Society of Friends. Parke County, Indiana. 1864-69.

Rush Creek Monthly Meeting of the Society of Friends. Parke County, Indiana. 1861-69.

Silver Creek-Salem Monthly Meeting of the Society of Friends. Union County, Indiana. 1861-69.

Sparrow Creek Monthly Meeting of the Society of Friends. Randolph County, Indiana. 1861-69.

Spiceland Monthly Meeting of the Society of Friends. Henry County, Indiana. 1861-69.

Springfield Monthly Meeting of the Society of Friends. Wayne County, Indiana. 1861-69.

Wabash Monthly Meeting of the Society of Friends. Wabash County, Indiana. 1861-69.

Walnut Ridge Monthly Meeting of the Society of Friends. Rush County, Indiana. 1861-69.

Westfield Monthly Meeting of the Society of Friends. Hamilton County, Indiana. 1861-69.

West Grove Monthly Meeting of the Society of Friends. Wayne County, Indiana. 1861-69.

West Union Monthly Meeting of the Society of Friends. Morgan County, Indiana. 1861-69.

White Lick Monthly Meeting of the Society of Friends. Morgan County, Indiana. 1861-69.

White River Monthly Meeting of the Society of Friends. Randolph County, Indiana. 1861-69.

Whitewater Monthly Meeting of the Society of Friends. Wayne County, Indiana. 1861-69.

Whitewater (Hicksite) Monthly Meeting of the Society of Friends. Wayne County, Indiana. 1861-69.

Cemetery Records

Adams, Edna Hall, comp. "Cemeteries of Sand Creek Township." Columbus Public Library. Columbus, Indiana.

Amos, Anne E. P., comp. "Rush County Indiana Records, Early Cemetery Records Prior to 1886." Rushville Public Library. Rushville, Indiana, 1974.

"Burial of Soldiers, Sailors, and Marines, Under an Act Approved March 6, 1889." Randolph County Recorder's Office. Winchester, Indiana.

"Cemeteries in Union County, Indiana." Genealogy Division, Indiana State Library. Indianapolis, Indiana.

"Cemeteries of Noble Township, Wabash County, Indiana." Wabash Carnegie Public Library. Wabash, Indiana, 1979.

"Cemetery Records of Hamilton County, Indiana." 4 vols. Noblesville Public Library. Noblesville, Indiana, 1980-81.

Cummings, Ethel Shield, comp. *Historical and Genealogical Records Pertaining to Jackson County, Indiana*, vol. 1. Published by the Daughters of the American Revolution, 1952.

Gibbs, ___. "Hancock County Cemeteries, Military Service Men Buried in Hancock County." Greenfield Public Library. Greenfield, Indiana, 1972.

Grand Army of the Republic. "Burial Record Book Giving Names and Locations of Graves of Civil War Veterans." Boone County Recorder's Office. Lebanon, Indiana.

Hamm, Thomas D., ed. *Blue River Township Henry County, Indiana Cemetery Inscriptions.* New Castle: Henry County Historical Society, Inc., 1973.

—, *Early Cemetery Records, Liberty Township Henry County, Indiana.* New Castle: Henry County Historical Society, Inc., 1973.

Harvey, Anna, comp. "Four Waltz Township Cemeteries Not Included in Mississinewa Memorial Cemetery." Wabash Carnegie Public Library. Wabash, Indiana, 1979.

"Hendricks County Cemetery Inscriptions." Danville Public Library. Danville, Indiana.

"Indiana Cemeteries." Winchester Public Library. Winchester, Indiana.

Indiana Junior Historical Society, Rushville High School, comp. "Rush County, Indiana Cemetery Records." Rushville Public Library. Rushville, Indiana, 1974.

Mayhill, R. Thomas, comp. *Cemetery Records Henry County, Indiana.* Knightstown: Eastern Indiana Publishing Co., 1968.

Montrose, Beverly, comp. "Hancock County Cemeteries, Blue River Township." Greenfield Public Library. Greenfield, Indiana, 1965.

Morin, H. L. "Campbell Township Cemeteries." North Vernon Public Library. North Vernon, Indiana, 1969.

"Quaker Cemetery Records, Vigo County, Indiana." Genealogy Division, Indiana State Library. Indianapolis, Indiana.

Ratcliff, Richard, ed. *Cemetery Records Spiceland Township Henry County, Indiana 1824-1974.* New Castle: Henry County Historical Society, Inc., 1974.

Russ, Jennie A., comp. "Quakerdom Cemetery." Jackson Township, Porter County. Genealogy Division, Indiana State Library. Indianapolis, Indiana, 1956.

Shoemaker, Irene, comp. "Madison County, Indiana Cemetery Records." 2 vols. Anderson Public Library. Anderson, Indiana, 1957-59.

Shuck, Opal, and Horstman, Helen, comps. "Vernon Township Cemeteries." North Vernon Public Library. North Vernon, Indiana, 1973.

"Veterans Graves Registration." State Archives Division, Commission on Public Records, Indiana State Library. Indianapolis, Indiana.

Woodward, Ron, comp. "Fourteen Cemeteries of Lagro Township Wabash County, Indiana." Wabash Carnegie Public Library. Wabash, Indiana, 1975.

Yount, Beverly, comp. *Tombstone Inscriptions in Wayne County Indiana.* 4 vols. Fort Wayne: Fort Wayne Public Library, 1968-70.

## Newspapers

*The American Eagle* (Paoli), 1861-65.
*Broad Axe of Freedom* (Richmond), 1861-65.
*Crawfordsville Weekly Review*, 1861-65.
*Hancock Democrat* (Greenfield), 1861-65.
*Howard Tribune* (Kokomo), 1861-65.
*Indianapolis Daily Journal*, 1861-65.
*Indiana True Republican* (Centerville), 1861-65.
*New Castle Courier*, 1861-65.
*Parke County Republican* (Rockville), 1861-65.
*Randolph County Journal* (Winchester), 1861-63.
*Richmond Jeffersonian*, 1861-65.
*Richmond Palladium*, 1861-65.
*Rushville Weekly Republican*, 1861-65.
*Wabash Plain Dealer* (Wabash), 1861-65.
*Weekly Intelligencer* (Wabash), 1861-65.

## Other Sources

Bacon, Margaret H. *The Quiet Rebels: The Story of the Quakers in America.* New York: Basic Books, 1969.

Barnhart, John D. *Valley of Democracy: The Frontier Versus the Plantation in the Ohio Valley, 1775-1818*. Lincoln: University of Nebraska Press, 1970.

Bash, Frank Sumner, ed. *History of Huntington County, Indiana*. 2 vols. Chicago: Lewis Publishing Co., 1914.

Binford, J. H. *History of Hancock County, Indiana*. Greenfield, Indiana: King & Binford, Publishers, 1882.

Blanchard, Charles, ed. *Counties of Morgan, Monroe, and Brown, Indiana, Historical and Biographical*. Chicago: F. A. Battey & Co., 1884.

Bodurtha, Arthur L., ed. *History of Miami County, Indiana*. 2 vols. Chicago: Lewis Publishing Co., 1914.

Boley, Edwin J. *The First Documented History of Jackson County, Indiana 1816-1976*. Seymour, Indiana: n.p., 1980.

Bond, James O. "He Carried Three Packs: A Biography of Elisha Mills." Typescript. Noblesville Public Library. Noblesville, Indiana.

Boorstin, Daniel J. *The Americans: The Colonial Experience*. New York: Random House, 1958.

Bowden, James. *The History of the Society of Friends in America*. London: Charles Gilpin, 1850. Reprint. New York: Arno Press, 1972.

"Brief History of Carthage Friends Meeting." Typescript. Rushville Public Library. Rushville, Indiana, 1939.

Brinton, Howard. *Friends for 300 Years: The History and Beliefs of the Society of Friends since George Fox Started the Quaker Movement*. New York: Harper & Brothers, 1952.

Brock, Peter. "Colonel Washington and the Quaker Conscientious Objector." *Quaker History, The Bulletin of Friends Historical Association* 53 (Spring 1964): 12-26.

Brock, Peter. *Pacifism in the United States from the Colonial Era to the First World War*. Princeton: Princeton University Press, 1968.

Burgess, Joe H. *Hamilton County and the Civil War.* Noblesville, Indiana: n.p., 1967.

Butler, Lorine Letcher. *John Morgan and His Men.* Philadelphia: Dorrance & Co., 1960.

Buys, John William. "Quakers in Indiana in the Nineteenth Century." Ph.D. diss., University of Florida, 1973.

Ceder, Robert W. "The Raising and Equipping of Armies in Indiana 1860-1865." Ed.D. diss., Ball State University, 1968.

Clarkson, Thomas. *A Portraiture of Quakerism.* Indianapolis: Merrill & Field, 1870.

Coffin, Levi. *Reminiscences of Levi Coffin.* Cincinnati: Western Tract Society, 1867. Reprint. New York: Arno Press and New York Times, 1968.

Commager, Henry Steele, ed. *The Blue and the Gray*, vol. 1. Indianapolis: The Bobbs-Merrill Co., 1950.

Crist, L. M. *History of Boone County Indiana.* 2 vols. Indianapolis: A. W. Bowen & Co., 1914.

Davis, Russell W. *Militia Enrollments and Volunteer Lists of Able-bodied Male Citizens Aged between 18 and 45 Years Who Were Resident on August 1, 1861 in Madison County, Indiana.* Anderson, Indiana: n.p., 1970.

*Documents of the General Assembly of Indiana at the Forty-second Regular Session*, vol. 1. Indianapolis: Joseph J. Bingham, State Printer, 1863.

Drake, Thomas E. *Quakers and Slavery in America.* New Haven: Yale University Press, 1950.

Dunham, Chester Forrester. *The Attitude of the Northern Clergy Toward the South, 1860-1865.* Toledo, Ohio: Gray Co., 1942.

Elliott, Erroll T. *Quakers on the American Frontier: A History of the Westward Migration, Settlements and Developments of Friends on the American Continent.* Richmond, Indiana: Friends United Press, 1969.

Fields, Ludovic and Clayton. "History of Westfield Monthly
    Meeting of Friends." Noblesville Public Library. No-
    blesville, Indiana.
Freeman, J. B. "History of New Salem Church." Typescript.
    New Salem Monthly Meeting of the Society of Friends.
    Published in a Kokomo newspaper, 1932.
Gary, A. L., and Thomas, E. B., eds. *Centennial History of
    Rush County, Indiana*. 2 vols. Indianapolis: Historical
    Publishing Co., 1921.
*General Orders*. State of Indiana, Adjutant General's Office.
    Indianapolis, Indiana, 1862. Unidentified photocopy,
    Lilly Library, Earlham College.
Grob, Gerald N., and Billias, George Athan, eds. *Interpreta-
    tions of American History, Patterns and Perspectives*. 3d ed.
    New York: The Free Press, 1978.
Hazzard, George. *Hazzard's History of Henry County Indiana
    1822-1906*. 2 vols. New Castle, Indiana: n.p., 1906.
Heiss, Willard. *A List of All the Friends Meetings that Exist or
    Ever Have Existed in Indiana 1807-1955*. Published by the
    author, 1959.
Heiss, Willard, ed. *Abstracts of the Records of the Society of Friends
    in Indiana*. 7 vols. Indianapolis: Indiana Historical Soci-
    ety, 1962-77.
Helm, T. B. *History of Wabash County, Indiana*. Chicago: John
    Morris, 1884.
Hirst, Margaret E. *The Quakers in Peace and War: An Account
    of Their Peace Principles and Practice*. London: Swarthmore
    Press, 1923.
*History of Grant County, Indiana, from the Earliest Time to the
    Present*. Chicago: Brant & Fuller, 1816. Reprint. Evans-
    ville: Unigraphic, Inc., 1974.
*History of Hendricks County, Indiana*. Chicago: Interstate Pub-
    lishing Co., 1885. Reprint. Evansville: Unigraphic, Inc.,
    1973.

*History of Montgomery County Indiana with Personal Sketches of Representative Citizens.* 2 vols. Indianapolis: A. W. Bowen & Co., n.d.

Holland, Cecil Fletcher. *Morgan and His Raiders: A Biography of the Confederate General.* New York: Macmillan Co., 1942.

Horney, Ethyl Clark, and Moore, George W. "The Hinkle Creek Friends." Typescript. Noblesville Public Library. Noblesville, Indiana, 1966.

Indiana Constitution (1851). Article XII, Section 6.

Jacob, Caroline N. *Builders of the Quaker Road, 1652-1952.* Chicago: H. Regnery Co., 1953.

Jay, Milton T., ed. *History of Jay County, Indiana.* 2 vols. Indianapolis: Historical Publishing Co., 1922.

*Jericho Friend's Meeting and Its Community, Randolph County, Indiana, 1818-1958.* Ann Arbor: Edwards Brothers, 1958.

Jones, Louis Thomas. *The Quakers of Iowa.* Iowa City: State Historical of Iowa, 1914.

Jones, Rufus M. *The Faith and Practice of the Quakers.* London: Methuen and Co., 1927. Reprint. Book and Publishing Committee, Philadelphia Yearly Meeting of the Religious Society of Friends, 1958.

——, *The Later Periods of Quakerism.* London: Macmillan Co., 1921.

——, *The Quakers in the American Colonies.* 2 vols. New York: Russell & Russell, 1962.

Knollenberg, Bernhard. *Pioneer Sketches of the Upper Whitewater Valley: Quaker Stronghold of the West.* Indianapolis: Indiana Historical Society, 1945.

Leedom, Phyllis Hart. *Madison County, Indiana Civil War Soldiers.* Anderson, Indiana: n.p., 1981.

Montgomery, Pauline. *Indiana Coverlet Weavers and Their Coverlets.* Indianapolis: Hoosier Heritage Press, 1974.

Netterville, James J. *Centennial History of Madison County Indiana: An Account of One Hundred Years of Progress 1823–1923.* 2 vols. Anderson, Indiana: Historian's Association, 1925.

Newman, Daisy. *A Procession of Friends: Quakers in America.* Garden City, New York: Doubleday, 1972.

Nickalls, John L., ed. *The Journal of George Fox.* Cambridge: University Press, 1952.

Noland, Geneva V. "Memories of a Quaker Meeting." *Quaker Life* 9 (October 1982): 26–28.

Pickard, Samuel T. *The Life and Letters of John Greenleaf Whittier.* 2 vols. Cambridge: Riverside Press, 1894.

Power, J. C., ed. *Directory and Soldiers' Register of Wayne County, Indiana.* Richmond, Indiana: W. H. Lanthurn & Co., 1865.

Pringle, Cyrus. *The Record of a Quaker Conscience: Cyrus Pringle's Diary.* New York: Macmillan Co., 1918.

Radbill, Kenneth Alan. "Socioeconomic Backgrounds of Nonpacifist Quakers during the American Revolution." Ph.D. diss., University of Arizona, 1971.

Randall, J. G., and Donald, David. *The Civil War and Reconstruction.* 2d ed. Boston: D. C. Heath & Co., 1961.

Ratcliff, Richard P. *Our Special Heritage: Sesquicentennial History of Indiana Yearly Meeting of Friends 1821-1971.* New Castle: Community Printing Co., 1970.

—, *The Quakers of Spiceland, Henry County, Indiana: A History of Spiceland Friends Meeting 1828-1968.* New Castle: Community Printing Co., 1968.

Russell, Elbert. *The History of Quakerism.* New York: Macmillan Co., 1942.

Sanger, George P., ed. *The Statutes at Large, Treaties, and Proclamations, of the United States of America,* vols. 12-13. Boston, Mass.: Little, Brown & Co., 1863. Reprint. Buffalo, N.Y.: Dennis & Co., Inc., 1961-64.

Schlissel, Lillian, ed. *Conscience in America: A Documentary History of Conscientious Objection in America, 1757-1967.* New York: E. P. Dutton & Co., 1968.

Shepherd, Rebecca A., et al., comp. *A Biographical Directory of the Indiana General Assembly, 1816-1819.* 2 vols. Indianapolis: Indiana Historical Bureau, 1980-84.

Shirts, Augustus Finch. *A History of the Formation, Settlement and Development of Hamilton County, Indiana, from the Year 1818 to the Close of the Civil War.* N.p., 1901.

Smith, John L., and Driver, Lee L. *Past and Present of Randolph County Indiana.* Indianapolis: A. W. Bowen & Co., 1914.

Stubbs, Roger A. and Rena M. "Some Grave People in America, 1673-1973." Typescript. Morrisson-Reeves Library. Richmond, Indiana.

Sulgrove, Berry Robinson. *History of Indianapolis and Marion County, Indiana.* Philadelphia: L. H. Everts & Co., 1884.

Terrell, W. H. H. *Report of the Adjutant General of the State of Indiana.* 8 vols. Indianapolis: State Printer, 1865-69. *Statistics and Documents* is a separately paginated part of *Report of the Adjutant General.*

Thornbrough, Emma Lou. *Indiana in the Civil War Era 1850-1880.* Indianapolis: Indiana Historical Bureau and Indiana Historical Society, 1965.

Thornburg, Opal. *Whitewater, Indiana's First Monthly Meeting 1809-1959.* Richmond, Indiana: n.p., 1959.

U.S. Department of Interior. *Population of the United States in 1860; Compiled from the Original Returns of the Eighth Census.* Washington, D.C.: U.S. Government Printing Office, 1864.

U.S. Department of Interior. *Statistics of the United States in 1860; Compiled from the Original Returns and Being the Final Exhibit of the Eighth Census.* Washington, D.C.: U.S. Government Printing Office, 1866.

U.S. Department of War. *The War of the Rebellion: A Compilation of the Official Records of the Union and Confederate Armies*, 3d ser., vols. 2-4. Washington, D.C.: U.S. Government Printing Office, 1900.

Weeks, Stephen B. *Southern Quakers and Slavery: A Study in Institutional History*. Baltimore: The Johns Hopkins Press, 1896.

Wildes, Harry Emerson. *Voice of the Lord: A Biography of George Fox*. Philadelphia: University of Pennsylvania, 1965.

Wiley, Bell Irvin. *The Life of Billy Yank, the Common Soldier of the Union*. Indianapolis: Bobbs-Merrill Co., 1951.

Wilson, Edward R. *Uphill for Peace: Quaker Impact on Congress*. Richmond, Indiana: Friends United Press, 1975.

Woodman, Charles M. *Quakers Find a Way: Their Discoveries in Practical Living*. Indianapolis: Bobbs-Merrill Co., Inc., 1950.

Wright, Edward Needles. *Conscientious Objectors in the Civil War*. New York: A. S. Barnes, 1931.

# Index

This index covers the contents of the introduction and chapters but not the preface and appendixes.

Adams, Samuel C., 74
Age range, of Quaker servicemen, 34
Alcohol. *See* Drinking
Antislavery: Quaker involvement in movement, 4-6; as enlistment motivation, 38-39
Anti-Slavery Society: on boycott of slave-made goods, 5
Apology (Offering): by war veterans, 18-19, 31, 40, 91, 97-98
Arms procurement, 60

Back Creek Monthly Meeting of Men (Grant County), 17-18
Bacon, Margaret H., *The Quiet Rebels*, 15, 92
Baltimore Yearly Meeting: on commutation payments, 87-88
Barker, Isaac, 50, 52
Battle accounts, 48, 53, 56
Beale, Howard K., xiv
Beard, Elkanah, 74
Bell, William F., 92
Bible: on opposition to military force, 10-11; distribution to military personnel, 68-71; distribution to former slaves, 73
Blacks, 6; Quaker soldiers' opinions about, 38-39; Quaker aid to former slaves, 73-76. *See also* Slavery

Blankets: procurement for army, 60-61, 62
Bloomingdale Aid Society, 63
Bloomingdale Friends Quarterly Meeting (Parke County), 75
Bond, James O., 38
Book and Tract Committee (Milford Monthly Meeting), 69
Boorstin, Daniel J., 9-10, 26-27
Boston, Lide, 71-72
Bounties: as enlistment incentive, 35, 37, 42, 66-67; raising funds for, 66-67, 96
Bridgeport Monthly Meeting (Marion County), 90-91
*Broad Axe of Freedom* (newspaper), 67
Brock, Peter, 16, 94; *Pacifism in the United States*, 92
Buckingham, Gen. Catharinus P., 81, 85
Buys, John William, 27

Camp life, 45-46, 51, 55
Carpenter, Walter, 35, 75
Carthage Friends (Rush County), 16, 26
Central Book and Tract Committee (Indiana Yearly Meeting), 69-71, 73
Clothing: for Indiana volunteers, 61, 62; for Southern white refugees, 73; for former black slaves, 73, 74

Coffin, Charles F., 60, 68; on com-
    mutation payments, 83, 85, 97
Coffin, Levi, 38, 74, 75-76
Coffin, Rhoda (Mrs. Charles F.),
    60-61, 68
Commager, Henry Steele, 97
Committee on the Concerns of the
    People of Color (Indiana Yearly
    Meeting), 73
Commutation payments, 81-91, 94,
    97
Companies, military: Quakers serv-
    ing in, 22-24
Comstock, Elizabeth, 70
Conscience, freedom of, 90
Conscientious objectors, 21-22, 67,
    80, 81, 83-84, 86
*Conscientious Objectors in the Civil War*
    (Wright), xiv, 92
Conscription, 42, 80; and enlistment
    bounty monies, 66-67; as Quaker
    issue, 95-96
Conscription law: national (1863),
    86-88, 93
Constitution, Indiana (1851): on
    militia duty, 81, 83-84
Crittenden, Thomas T., 22

Daughters of Temperance, 65
*Discipline* (code of behavior), 6-7;
    antiwar stance, 11; on military
    service, 18
Discipline: church, 6-8, 25, 26
Disownment: of military enlistees,
    18, 20, 25-26, 54, 98
Donations: war effort, 60-64
Draft. *See* Conscription
Drake, Thomas E., 22, 26
Drill, military, 46, 55-56
Drinking, among soldiers, 51-52, 53
Dunham, Chester, 15

89th Regiment, Indiana, 23, tables
    24, 25
Elliott, Franklin, 19, 31-32
Elliott, William S., 38, 52
Enlistment, military: of Quakers,
    15-18, 21, 23, 96; disownment for,

18, 20, 25-26, 54, 98; patriotism as
    justification, 29-32, 42; recruit-
    ment methods, 34-35; bounty
    payment for, 35, 37, 42, 66-67;
    incentives for, 35-39; reasons for,
    42-43; and conscription, 79-80,
    93. *See also* Reenlistment, military

Fairfield Monthly Meeting (Hen-
    dricks County), 69-70
Federal Militia Act (1862), 79-80, 85,
    93
Foraging, 52, 58
Fox, George, 1, 6, 9
Freedmen, care of, as alternate to
    military service, 89
Freedmen's committees, Quaker, 73
Free Produce Movement, 5
*Friend, The* (periodical), 89
Fund solicitations: for Indiana Sani-
    tary Commission, 62-63; for
    bounty payments, 66-67

Grant, Gen. Ulysses S., 75
Grant County: Quaker enlistments,
    18, 21; Quaker horse sales, 65
Green, Miriam, 53-54
Griffin, John W., 38

Hadley, Job, 74
Hannaman, Dr. William, 62
Harassment: of conscientious objec-
    tors, 92-93, 94
Haughton, William, 71
Heiss, Willard, 17, 26; *Records of the
    Abstracts of the Society of Friends in
    Indiana*, xv-xvi
Henry County: Quaker enlistments,
    18
Hirst, Margaret E., 15, 59, 71
"History of New Salem Church"
    (Howard County), 16-17
Hobbs, Barnabas C., 71, 75, 83-85,
    97
Hopewell Monthly Meeting (Henry
    County), 18
Horses: military use, 11, 65-66, 77

Hospital duty: as alternate to military service, 89
*Howard Tribune* (Kokomo), 23

Indiana Bible Association, 73
Indiana Freedmen's Aid Commission, 74-75
Indiana Sanitary Commission, 62-63, 65, 70
*Indiana True Republican* (newspaper), 82
Indiana Union Refugee Relief Association, 72-73
Indiana Yearly Meeting, 3, 90; views on antislavery activities, 4-5; on involvement in the Civil War, 13-15
Indiana Yearly Meeting of Anti-Slavery Friends, 5
Inner Light: as Quaker concept, 1, 8, 42; as antiwar concept, 11, 27

Jay County: Quaker enlistments, 21
Jericho Friends Meeting (Randolph County), 16, 26
Johnson, Caleb, 67
Jones, Rufus, 15
*Journal* (Fox), 9
Julian, George W., 17

King, Lavinus, 35
Kinley, Capt. Isaac, 23

Ladies Union Aid Association, 63
Language: foul, 53
Lemon, O. V., 68, 71
Letters from home, 47-48, 56
"Liberty Halls," 5
Life: human, value of, 48, 49-50, 53
*Life of Billy Yank: The Common Soldier of the Union, The* (Wiley), 42
Lincoln, Abraham, 76, 80, 91
Literature: religious, 68-71
Lozier, John H., 64

Macy, John, 47-48
Madison County: Quaker enlistments, 21
Marksmanship pride, 57

Marshall, Alonzo, 32-33, 39, 64
Marshall, Elvira, 65
Marshall, Swain, 39, 41, 46, 49, 52, 64; advice to brother, 32-33; reenlistment, 33-34; appeal for letters, 47, 65; at Vicksburg, 50, 53; on attending religious services, 50-51; on temperance, 51-52
"Memories of a Quaker Meeting" (Noland), 71
Meredith, Gen. Solomon, 30
Military life, 45-58
Military service: Quaker, 9-28
Militia Enrollment of 1862, p. 67
Ministers: and conscription laws, 80, 86
Moral conduct concerns, 51, 57-58
Moreau, Capt. William C., 22
Morgan, John E., 39-40, 50
Morgan's raid, 36-37, 96
Morton, Gov. Oliver P., 36-37, 72; and military equipment, 60, 61-62; and state draft registration, 80-81, 97

*New Castle Courier* (newspaper), 64, 81
Newman, Daisy, *A Procession of Friends*, 92
Nicholson, Timothy, 3-4
Noland, Geneva V., "Memories of a Quaker Meeting," 71
Noncombat positions: filled by Quakers, 36, 89

Offering. *See* Apology
101st Regiment, Indiana, 23, tables 24, 25
147th Regiment, Indiana, 23, tables 24, 25
Orange County: Quaker enlistments, 21
Overman, Anderson, 66
Owen, Robert Dale, 60

Pacifism, 9-14, 38
*Pacifism in the United States* (Brock), 92

Parker, Robert, 20
Patriotism: as enlistment justifica-
tion, 29-32, 42, 95
Patterson, Eli, 36
Peace testimony: compliance and
noncompliance, 11-13, 17, 27, 40,
95, 97
Perry, Oran, 60
Plainfield Monthly Meeting (Hen-
dricks County), 69, 91
Pringle, Cyrus, 91-92
Prisoners: Confederate, Quaker aid
to, 64, 68, 71
*Procession of Friends, A* (Newman), 92
Property destruction, indifference by
soldiers, 48, 49, 52, 53

Quarterly meeting, 7
Queries: annual, 7
*Quiet Rebels, The* (Bacon), 15, 92

Rank, military, acceptance by Quak-
ers, 40, 41
Raysville Monthly Meeting (Henry
County), 18, 20
*Record of a Quaker Conscience, The*
(Pringle), 91
*Records of the Abstracts of the Society of
Friends in Indiana* (Heiss), xv-xvi
Reeder, Martin A., 72
Reenlistment: military, 33-34, 39-40,
41, 46-47
Refugees: white Southern, 72-73, 96
Regiments: Indiana, Quakers serving
in, 22-25
Religious beliefs: during war, 50-51
Revolutionary War: Quaker position
during, 12-13
Richmond (Indiana): as Quaker cen-
ter, 3-4
*Richmond Jeffersonian* (newspaper), 67,
82
Richmond Sanitary Committee, 63
Roberts, John, 63
Rogers, Mary H., 71
Rush Creek Meeting (Parke
County), 91
Russell, Elbert, 16, 27

Sick: military, 71
Siddall, John P., 81, 83, 85
6th Regiment, Indiana, 22
66th Regiment, Indiana, 23, tables
24, 25
Skirmish recounts, 48, 56
Slavery, 2, 4-5; as Quaker military
duty issue, 16, 28, 38-39, 41, 42
Smith, Sarah, 71
Stanton, Edwin M., 87-88
Starr, Anna, 32
Substitutes: draft, 37, 91

Tax collector: federal, view of
Quakers as, 67-68
Taxes: war, 11, 13
Temperance: among Quaker soldiers, 51-52
36th Regiment, Indiana, 22-23,
tables 24, 25
Thornbrough, Emma Lou, 15
Tracts: religious, 68-71
12th Regiment, Indiana, 23,
tables 24, 25

Union Literary Institute, 6
United States Christian Commission, 70
United States Sanitary Commission,
62

War Department, United States: on
commutation payments, 87-88
Wayne County antislavery move-
ment, 4, 5
Weeks, Stephen, 15
Western Freedmen's Aid Commis-
sion, 75-76
Western Yearly Meeting of Indiana,
3, 90; on involvement in the Civil
War, 13, 15; on commutation pay-
ments, 86
West Union Monthly Meeting
(Morgan County), 73
White, Martha Talbert, 48
White Lick Monthly Meeting
(Morgan County), 70

Whitewater Monthly Meeting
(Wayne County), 2, 73
White's Indiana Manual Labor Institute, 6
Whittier, John Greenleaf, 59
Wiggins, Stephen R., 63
Wiles, Capt. William Davis, 23
Wiley, Bell Irvin, 42-43, 55-58; *The Life of Billy Yank: The Common Soldier of the Union*, 42

Wooton, Daniel, 30, 33, 41, 51; reenlistment, 34, 46-47; insensitivity toward warfare, 48-49; character metamorphosis, 53-55
Wooton, James, 33
Wounded: military, 71
Wright, Edward N.: *Conscientious Objectors in the Civil War*, xiv, 92
Wright, Isaac, 72